Family Circle®

Healthy
Home-Style
Cooking

Meredith® Consumer Marketing
Des Moines, Iowa

Family Circle® Healthy Home-Style Cooking

Meredith® Corporation Consumer Marketing
Vice President, Consumer Marketing: Janet Donnelly
Consumer Marketing Product Director: Steve Swanson
Consumer Marketing Product Manager: Wendy Merical
Business Director: Ron Clingman
Senior Production Manager: Al Rodruck

Waterbury Publications, Inc.
Editorial Director: Lisa Kingsley
Associate Editor: Tricia Bergman
Creative Director: Ken Carlson
Associate Design Director: Doug Samuelson
Production Assistant: Mindy Samuelson
Contributing Copy Editors: Terri Fredrickson, Peg Smith
Contributing Indexer: Elizabeth T. Parson

***Family Circle®* Magazine**
Editor in Chief: Linda Fears
Creative Director: Karmen Lizzul
Food Director: Regina Ragone, M.S., R.D.
Senior Food Editor: Julie Miltenberger
Associate Food Editor: Michael Tyrrell

Meredith Publishing Group
President: Tom Harty
Vice President, Manufacturing: Bruce Heston

Meredith Corporation
President and Chief Executive Officer: Stephen M. Lacy

In Memoriam: E.T. Meredith III (1933–2003)

Pictured on the front cover:
Black Tie Cake
(recipe page 285)
Photography by Kritsada Panichgul

First Edition.
Printed in the United States of America.
ISSN: 1942-7468
ISBN: 978-0-696-30094-3

All of us at Meredith® Consumer Marketing are dedicated to providing you with information and ideas to enhance your home. We welcome your comments and suggestions. Write to us at: Meredith Consumer Marketing, 1716 Locust St., Des Moines, IA 50309-3023.

Do you swoon at the sight of cheesy scalloped potatoes? Or fresh-from-the-fryer french fries? How about bread pudding with caramel sauce?

We all do. It's the kind of hearty, satisfying, universally loved fare that Mom or Grandma makes—the kind that just tastes like home—with no regard to what it does to our waistlines. It's good-mood food.

Home-style cooking is synonymous with comfort and happiness, but not necessarily with healthfulness. Traditional recipes are made with ingredients that pack in unwanted calories and fat grams. But they don't have to be made that way.

Healthy Home-Style Cooking serves up more than 300 recipes for favorite family classics revamped for the way you want to eat now—lower in calories and fat, but still packed with flavor.

Although these recipes are updated for today, they're made the old-fashioned way. They start with fresh foods that naturally abound with good-for-you-ingredients but simply call for less fat than the traditional version—or they substitute a more healthful fat. They also take advantage of cooking methods and techniques that don't require large amounts of unhealthy fats and sugar.

Whether you're looking for a 30-minute weeknight dinner or want to spend a leisurely Saturday cooking or baking with friends, *Healthy Home-Style Cooking* offers a buffet of choices.

As an added help, suggested menus are scattered throughout the book to make meal planning easier and more fun. You can enjoy your favorite foods and your good health too.

Because meal planning for a busy family can be challenging, look for these helpful icons throughout the book:

 30 minutes or less: Any recipe that can be made from start to finish in 30 minutes or less.

 Kid-friendly: This symbol denotes recipes approved by kids.

105

123

40

293

Contents

Shrimp-and-Bacon-Stuffed Baby Potatoes, page 23

Smart Snacks & Starters

Spicy Black Bean Crab Cakes

MAKES 8 servings **PREP** 25 minutes **COOK** 6 minutes

- ½ cup refrigerated or frozen egg product, thawed, or 2 eggs, lightly beaten
- ⅓ cup light sour cream
- ½ cup whole wheat panko (Japanese-style bread crumbs)
- 1 clove garlic, minced
- ¾ cup canned no-salt-added black beans, rinsed and drained
- 1 6- to 6.5-ounce can crabmeat, drained and flaked
- 1 fresh jalapeño, seeded and finely chopped*
- ¼ cup frozen whole kernel corn, thawed
- ¼ cup seeded and finely chopped tomato
- 1 tablespoon canola oil
- 1 recipe Lime-Onion Cream
   Cilantro leaves (optional)

① In a large bowl combine egg and sour cream. Stir in panko and garlic. Mash ½ cup of the black beans and leave ¼ cup whole. Add mashed and whole beans to panko mixture along with crab, jalapeño pepper, corn, and tomato. Mix well. Shape mixture into eight ¾-inch-thick patties.

② In a very large nonstick skillet heat oil over medium heat. Add crab cakes; cook for 6 to 8 minutes or until golden brown and heated through, turning once. If crab cakes brown too quickly, reduce heat to medium-low.

③ Serve crab cakes immediately with Lime-Onion Cream. If desired, garnish with cilantro leaves.

Lime-Onion Cream: In a small bowl stir together ⅓ cup light sour cream, 2 tablespoons bottled chunky salsa, 1 tablespoon thinly sliced green onion, 1 teaspoon fat-free milk, and ½ teaspoon finely shredded lime peel.

*Tip: Because hot chile peppers, such as jalapeños, contain volatile oils that can burn your skin and eyes, avoid direct contact with them as much as possible. When working with chile peppers, wear plastic or rubber gloves. If your bare hands do touch the chile peppers, wash your hands and nails well with soap and water.

PER SERVING 107 calories; 4 g total fat (1 g sat. fat); 27 mg cholesterol; 138 mg sodium; 9 g carbohydrate; 2 g fiber; 9 g protein

Sweet Potato Wontons

MAKES 24 servings **PREP** 25 minutes **BAKE** 10 minutes **OVEN** at 350°F

- 24 wonton wrappers
   Nonstick cooking spray
- 3 tablespoons mango chutney
- 2 tablespoons canola oil
- ⅓ cup finely chopped onion
- 2 teaspoons curry powder
- 1 teaspoon minced fresh ginger
- 1 clove garlic, minced
- 1 tablespoon flour
- 1½ cups chopped cooked sweet potato*
- ⅓ cup half-and-half or light cream

① Preheat oven to 350°F. Lightly coat wonton wrappers with cooking spray. Press wrappers, sprayed sides down, into twenty-four 1¾-inch muffin cups, pleating as necessary. Bake about 10 minutes or until golden brown.

② Meanwhile, cut up any large pieces of fruit in the chutney; set aside. In a large heavy skillet heat the canola oil over medium heat. Add onion, curry powder, ginger, and garlic; cook until onion is tender. Stir in flour. Stir in cooked sweet potato, half-and-half, and chutney. Cook and stir until thickened. Cook and stir for 1 minute more.

③ Spoon sweet potato mixture into wonton shells. Serve immediately.

*Tip: For cooked sweet potato, peel one 10- to 12-ounce sweet potato and cut into thirds. In a small covered saucepan cook potato in lightly salted boiling water about 20 minutes or just until tender. Drain and chop.

PER SERVING 61 calories; 2 g total fat (0 g sat. fat); 2 mg cholesterol; 69 mg sodium; 10 g carbohydrate; 1 g fiber; 1 g protein

Spring Rolls with Cilantro Dipping Sauce

Spring Rolls with Cilantro Dipping Sauce

MAKES 12 rolls **PREP** 45 minutes **CHILL** up to 6 hours

12	medium fresh or frozen shrimp in shells
1	ounce dried rice vermicelli noodles
1	tablespoon sesame oil
2	cloves garlic, minced
1	teaspoon sesame seeds
¼	teaspoon crushed red pepper
1	cup finely shredded napa cabbage
1	medium carrot, coarsely shredded
2	green onions, chopped
¼	cup fresh cilantro leaves
¼	cup fresh mint leaves
2	tablespoons chopped dry-roasted cashews
1	tablespoon rice vinegar
1	teaspoon packed brown sugar
1	teaspoon reduced-sodium soy sauce
1	teaspoon grated fresh ginger
12	8½-inch round rice papers
	Fresh cilantro leaves, fresh chives, and/or crushed red pepper (optional)
1	recipe Cilantro Dipping Sauce or sweet Asian chili sauce

① Thaw shrimp, if frozen. Peel and devein shrimp. Rinse shrimp; pat dry with paper towels. Set aside. In a medium saucepan cook the vermicelli in lightly salted boiling water for 2 to 3 minutes or just until tender; drain. Rinse under cold water; drain well. Use kitchen shears to snip the noodles into small pieces; set aside.

② In a large skillet heat sesame oil over medium heat. Cook shrimp, garlic, sesame seeds, and the ¼ teaspoon crushed red pepper in hot oil about 3 minutes or until shrimp are opaque, stirring occasionally. Remove from skillet. When cool enough to handle, halve shrimp lengthwise; set aside.

③ For filling, in a large bowl combine cooked vermicelli, cabbage, carrot, green onions, the ¼ cup cilantro, the mint, and cashews. In a small bowl combine rice vinegar, brown sugar, soy sauce, and ginger. Add to cabbage mixture; toss to coat.

④ Fill a very large skillet about half full with water. Bring just to simmering then remove from heat. Place one rice paper in the skillet at a time, pushing it down gently to cover with water. Allow to soften about 10 seconds. Using tongs, gently lift the paper from the water and place it on a dinner plate (make sure it is lying flat on the plate so the rice paper doesn't stick to itself). Pull gently and carefully on the edges of the paper to straighten while it is still warm.

⑤ Spoon a scant ¼ cup of the filling across the lower third of each softened rice paper. Arrange two shrimp halves on the filling. Fold bottom of rice paper over filling; fold in the sides of the rice paper. Tightly roll up. If desired, place additional cilantro leaves, chives, and/or crushed red pepper on the rice paper before the last turn. Place, seam sides down, on a large plate.

⑥ Cover and chill up to 6 hours. Serve with Cilantro Dipping Sauce.

Cilantro Dipping Sauce: In a blender combine ½ cup fresh cilantro leaves, ¼ cup lime juice, 2 tablespoons water, 2 teaspoons granulated sugar, 1 teaspoon finely chopped fresh jalapeño (see tip, page 8), and ⅛ teaspoon salt. Cover and blend until nearly smooth.

PER ROLL 90 calories; 2 g total fat (0 g sat. fat); 11 mg cholesterol; 66 mg sodium; 15 g carbohydrate; 1 g fiber; 3 g protein

Chicken-and-Raisin-Stuffed Mushrooms

MAKES 15 servings **PREP** 30 minutes **BAKE** 13 minutes
OVEN at 425°F

- 15 large fresh mushrooms (2½ to 3 inches in diameter)
- 3 tablespoons butter
- ¼ cup thinly sliced green onions (2)
- 1 clove garlic, minced
- ¾ cup finely chopped cooked chicken or turkey (about 4 ounces)
- 2 tablespoons fine dry bread crumbs
- 2 tablespoons grated Parmesan cheese
- 2 tablespoons finely chopped smoke-flavor almonds
- 2 tablespoons chopped golden raisins
- 1 tablespoon snipped fresh parsley
  Olive oil

① Preheat oven to 425°F. Remove and discard stems from mushrooms. Set mushroom caps aside.

② For filling, in a small saucepan melt butter over medium heat. Add green onions and garlic; cook and stir about 2 minutes or until tender. Remove from heat. Stir in chicken, bread crumbs, cheese, almonds, raisins, and parsley. Set filling aside.

③ Place mushrooms, stemmed sides down, in a 15 x 10 x 1-inch baking pan. Bake for 5 minutes. Turn mushrooms stemmed sides up. Brush mushrooms with oil. Divide filling among mushrooms. Bake for 8 to 10 minutes more or until heated through.

PER SERVING 60 calories; 4 g total fat (2 g sat. fat); 13 mg cholesterol; 65 mg sodium; 3 g carbohydrate; 0 g fiber; 3 g protein

Polenta-Stuffed Mushrooms

MAKES 12 servings **PREP** 30 minutes
COOK 15 minutes **BAKE** 13 minutes **OVEN** at 425°F

- 1 cup fat-free milk
- ⅓ cup reduced-sodium chicken broth
- 1 clove garlic, minced
- ⅓ cup polenta (coarse cornmeal)
- ¼ cup finely shredded Parmesan cheese (1 ounce)
- 2 tablespoons snipped fresh chives
- 2 tablespoons snipped fresh basil
- 2 teaspoons snipped fresh oregano
- 24 1½- to 2-inch diameter cremini mushrooms (about 1 pound)
  Chopped bottled roasted red peppers

① In a small saucepan combine milk, broth, and garlic. Bring to boiling. Gradually stir in polenta. Cook and stir over medium heat until simmering. Continue to simmer, uncovered, for 15 to 20 minutes or until thickened and creamy, stirring frequently.

② Remove from heat. Stir in Parmesan cheese, chives, basil, and oregano. Remove from heat and cool about 10 minutes.

③ Meanwhile, preheat oven to 425°F. Clean mushrooms with a damp paper towel. Remove and discard mushroom stems. Place mushroom caps, stem sides down, in a 15 x 10 x 1-inch baking pan. Bake for 5 minutes.

④ Carefully turn mushrooms stem sides up. Spoon polenta mixture into a large resealable plastic bag. Cut one corner off the bag so there is about a ½-inch hole in the corner. Pipe about 1 tablespoon filling into each mushroom cap. Bake for 8 to 10 minutes or until heated through. Garnish tops of stuffed mushrooms with roasted red peppers. Serve warm.

PER SERVING 40 calories; 1 g total fat (0 g sat. fat); 2 mg cholesterol; 55 mg sodium; 6 g carbohydrate; 0 g fiber; 3 g protein

Mushroom caps make one-bite bowlfuls of savory filling.

Polenta-Stuffed Mushrooms

Goat Cheese and Tomato Bites

menu

Tuscan Cheesecake Bites

Spicy Peanut-Sauced Kabobs

Goat Cheese and Tomato Bites [below]

Pear-Mint Green Tea

Goat Cheese and Tomato Bites 30

MAKES 12 servings **START TO FINISH** 15 minutes

- 4 roma tomatoes or 4 small firm but ripe Fuyu persimmons
- 4 ounces goat cheese (chèvre), cut into 12 slices
- 2 tablespoons honey
- 2 tablespoons coarsely chopped walnuts, toasted*
- ¼ to ½ teaspoon freshly ground black pepper

① Trim ends off tomatoes; discard ends. Cut tomatoes in 3 slices each. Place slices on a serving platter. Top each with a slice of goat cheese. Drizzle with honey and sprinkle with walnuts and pepper.

PER SERVING 58 calories; 4 g total fat (2 g sat. fat); 7 mg cholesterol; 50 mg sodium; 4 g carbohydrate; 0 g fiber; 2 g protein

*Tip: Toast nuts, seeds, or coconut in a single layer in a shallow baking pan. Bake in a 350°F oven for 5 to 10 minutes or until golden brown. Check the pieces frequently to make sure they aren't getting too brown. If they start to burn, they go quickly and generally can't be salvaged. Stir once or twice.

Crostini with Lemon-Tarragon Cream and Lox

MAKES 12 servings **START TO FINISH** 30 minutes

- ½ cup plain low-fat yogurt
- ¼ cup tub-style light cream cheese, softened
- 1 tablespoon snipped fresh chives
- 1 teaspoon finely shredded lemon peel
- 1 teaspoon snipped fresh tarragon
- 1 8-ounce loaf baguette-style French bread, cut into 24 slices (¼- to ½-inch thick) and toasted
- 1 3-ounce package thinly sliced smoked salmon (lox-style), cut into thin strips
- ½ teaspoon freshly ground black pepper

Thin slivers seeded cucumber, thin slivers radish, and/or fresh chives (optional)

① In a small bowl whisk together yogurt and cream cheese until smooth. Stir in snipped chives, lemon peel, and tarragon.

② Spread cream cheese mixture evenly on toasted baguette slices. Top with salmon, folding as needed. Sprinkle with pepper. If desired, garnish with cucumber, radish, and/or additional chives. Serve at once or cover and chill up to 1 hour.

PER SERVING 80 calories; 2 g total fat (1 g sat. fat); 5 mg cholesterol; 297 mg sodium; 12 g carbohydrate; 1 g fiber; 5 g protein

Crostini with Lemon-Tarragon Cream and Lox

Pumpkin Pesto ③⓪

MAKES 14 servings **START TO FINISH** 15 minutes

- 1 cup packed fresh basil leaves
- 1 cup packed fresh parsley leaves
- 1 cup canned pumpkin
- ⅓ cup chopped toasted walnuts (see tip, page 15)
- ¼ cup finely shredded Parmesan cheese (1 ounce)
- 2 tablespoons honey
- 3 cloves garlic, minced
- 1 teaspoon lemon juice
- ¼ teaspoon salt
- ¼ teaspoon black pepper
- 2 tablespoons olive oil
  Finely shredded Parmesan cheese (optional)
  Toasted baguette slices, assorted crackers, and/or pita wedges

① In a food processor combine basil, parsley, pumpkin, walnuts, ¼ cup cheese, honey, garlic, lemon juice, salt, and pepper. Cover and process with several on/off pulses until mixture is coarsely chopped. With food processor running, add oil in a thin, steady stream. (When necessary, stop processor and scrape down sides of bowl.)

② Transfer pesto to a serving bowl. If desired, garnish with additional cheese. Serve with toasted baguette slices, crackers, and/or pita wedges.

PER 2-TABLESPOON SERVING 60 calories; 4 g total fat (1 g sat. fat); 1 mg cholesterol; 70 mg sodium; 5 g carbohydrate; 1 g fiber; 1 g protein

Pumpkin Pesto

Bruschetta with Tomato and Arugula

MAKES 24 slices **PREP** 25 minutes **STAND** 1 hour
BAKE 5 minutes **OVEN** at 425°F

- 2 medium tomatoes, seeded and chopped (1½ cups)
- ½ cup chopped arugula leaves
- 1 small onion, finely chopped
- ¼ cup snipped fresh basil
- 1 clove garlic, minced
- 1 tablespoon olive oil
- 1 tablespoon balsamic vinegar
- ¼ teaspoon salt
- ¼ teaspoon black pepper
- 1 8-ounce loaf baguette-style French bread
- 2 to 3 tablespoons olive oil

① In a medium bowl stir together tomatoes, arugula, onion, basil, garlic, 1 tablespoon olive oil, balsamic vinegar, salt, and pepper. Let stand at room temperature for 1 hour.

② Preheat oven to 425°F. Slice bread diagonally into about twenty-four ½-inch thick slices. Lightly brush both sides with the 2 to 3 tablespoons olive oil. Place on a baking sheet. Bake for 5 to 7 minutes or until crisp and light brown, turning once. Cool on a wire rack.

③ To serve, top toasted bread slices with tomato mixture. Serve immediately.

PER SLICE 47 calories; 2 g total fat (0 g sat. fat); 0 mg cholesterol; 87 mg sodium; 6 g carbohydrate; 0 g fiber; 1 g protein

Although the tomato seeds won't affect the taste of the bruschetta topping, it will look prettier without them. The best way to seed a tomato is to cut it in half horizontally, then use a small spoon to scoop out the seeds.

Bruschetta with Tomato and Arugula

Caponata

Caponata 🕐

MAKES 6 servings **PREP** 10 minutes **BAKE** 20 minutes
STAND 10 minutes **OVEN** at 450°F /400°F

1	medium eggplant, halved lengthwise
1	medium red sweet pepper, halved and seeded
1	medium red onion, cut in wedges
2	cloves garlic
	Olive oil nonstick cooking spray
2	medium roma tomatoes, chopped
2	tablespoons red wine vinegar
2	teaspoons capers, drained
1	teaspoon honey
½	teaspoon Italian seasoning, crushed
1	recipe Pita Crisps

① Preheat oven to 450°F. Line a baking sheet with foil. Place the eggplant, cut sides up, on the baking sheet. Place sweet pepper halves, cut sides down, on baking sheet. Place onion wedges and garlic on baking sheet. Lightly coat vegetables with olive oil cooking spray. Bake, uncovered, for 20 minutes or until vegetables are tender and sweet pepper skin is lightly charred. Place vegetables in a bowl, cover, and let stand for 10 minutes.

② Remove and discard skins from eggplant and sweet pepper. Chop vegetables, or place vegetables in a food processor and pulse with several on/off turns until chopped.

③ In a large bowl place chopped vegetables. Stir in tomatoes, vinegar, capers, honey, and Italian seasoning. Serve with Pita Crisps.

Pita Crisps: Cut 3 whole wheat pita bread rounds in half horizontally. Cut each half into 6 wedges. Place wedges on a baking sheet. Lightly coat with nonstick cooking spray. Bake for 6 minutes at 400°F or until crisp.

PER SERVING 132 calories; 1 g total fat (0 g sat. fat); 0 mg cholesterol; 204 mg sodium; 28 g carbohydrate; 7 g fiber; 5 g protein

Caprese Bruschetta 🕐

MAKES 4 servings **START TO FINISH** 20 minutes

2	medium tomatoes, seeded and chopped
⅓	cup reduced-fat mozzarella cheese, coarsely chopped
¼	cup finely chopped red onion
2	tablespoons shredded fresh basil
2	teaspoons olive oil
1	teaspoon balsamic vinegar
¼	teaspoon black pepper
12	slices whole grain baguette, toasted

① In a medium bowl combine tomatoes, mozzarella cheese, red onion, basil, oil, balsamic vinegar, and pepper. Serve immediately or cover and chill up to 24 hours. Serve on toasted baguette slices.

PER SERVING 163 calories; 5 g total fat (1 g sat. fat); 5 mg cholesterol; 189 mg sodium; 22 g carbohydrate; 6 g fiber; 8 g protein

Caprese Bruschetta

Edamame Falafel with Lemon Aïoli

MAKES 4 servings **PREP** 25 minutes **COOK** 4 minutes

- 2 cups frozen sweet shelled soybeans (edamame)
- ¼ cup chopped green sweet pepper
- 2 tablespoons whole wheat flour
- 2 tablespoons snipped fresh parsley
- 1 egg white
- 2 cloves garlic, sliced
- 1 teaspoon finely shredded lemon peel
- ⅛ teaspoon salt
- ⅛ teaspoon black pepper
  Nonstick cooking spray
- 1 recipe Lemon Aïoli
  Black pepper (optional)
  Fresh parsley sprigs (optional)

① In a small saucepan cook edamame according to package directions. Drain and transfer to a food processor. Add sweet pepper, flour, parsley, egg white, garlic, lemon peel, salt, and black pepper. Cover and process until very finely chopped and mixture holds together.

② Shape mixture into twelve small patties. Coat an unheated large nonstick skillet with cooking spray. Heat skillet over medium-high heat. Add falafel patties to hot skillet. Cook for 4 to 5 minutes, turning halfway through or until evenly browned and heated through. Serve warm falafel patties with Lemon Aïoli. If desired sprinkle aïoli with black pepper and garnish with parsley sprigs.

Lemon Aïoli: In a small bowl combine ¼ cup fat-free or light mayonnaise, 1 teaspoon finely shredded lemon peel, and 1 tablespoon lemon juice.

PER SERVING 154 calories; 6 g total fat (1 g sat. fat); 2 mg cholesterol; 218 mg sodium; 15 g carbohydrate; 5 g fiber; 12 g protein

Pizza Meatballs ✪

MAKES 12 servings **PREP** 25 minutes **BAKE** 20 minutes **OVEN** at 350°F

  Nonstick cooking spray
- 1 cup fresh cremini or button mushrooms, finely chopped
- ½ cup finely chopped green sweet pepper
- ½ cup finely chopped onion
- 2 cloves garlic, minced
- ¾ cup soft whole wheat bread crumbs (about 1 slice)
- 1 egg white, lightly beaten
- 1½ teaspoons dried Italian seasoning, crushed
- ⅛ teaspoon black pepper
- 8 ounces uncooked bulk turkey sausage
- 8 ounces ground turkey breast
- 1 cup shredded reduced-fat Italian blend cheeses (4 ounces)
- 1½ cups purchased low-sodium pasta sauce

① Preheat oven to 350°F. Coat a large nonstick skillet with cooking spray; heat skillet over medium heat. Add mushrooms, green pepper, and onion. Cook for 5 to 8 minutes or until vegetables are tender, stirring frequently. Stir in garlic and set aside.

② In a large bowl combine bread crumbs, egg white, Italian seasoning, and black pepper. Stir in mushroom mixture. Add turkey sausage, turkey breast, and cheese. Mix well.

③ Line a 15 x 10 x 1-inch baking pan with foil. Spray foil with cooking spray; set aside. Using wet hands, shape meat mixture into twenty-four 1½-inch diameter meatballs; place meatballs in prepared pan. Bake about 20 minutes or until done (160°F).

④ Meanwhile, in a small saucepan heat pasta sauce over medium heat, stirring occasionally. Serve with meatballs.

PER SERVING 122 calories; 4 g total fat (2 g sat. fat); 29 mg cholesterol; 225 mg sodium; 8 g carbohydrate; 1 g fiber; 12 g protein

Spicy Peanut-Sauced Kabobs

Spicy Peanut-Sauced Kabobs ✪ ㉚

MAKES 8 servings **START TO FINISH** 30 minutes

1	pound boneless beef sirloin steak or skinless, boneless chicken breast halves
¼	teaspoon black pepper
⅛	teaspoon cayenne pepper (optional)
¼	cup creamy peanut butter
3	tablespoons water
1	tablespoon reduced-sodium soy sauce
1	tablespoon thinly sliced green onion
¼	teaspoon ground ginger
⅛	teaspoon crushed red pepper
	Sliced green onion (optional)

① Trim fat from meat. If using beef, cut steak across the grain into thin strips. If using chicken, cut breast halves lengthwise into thin strips. Sprinkle strips with black pepper and, if desired, cayenne pepper. Thread strips, accordion-style, onto sixteen 6- to 8-inch skewers.*

② Place skewers on the unheated rack of a broiler pan. Broil 3 to 4 inches from heat until beef is slightly pink in the center or chicken is no longer pink, turning once halfway through broiling. Allow 4 to 6 minutes for beef or 9 to 10 minutes for chicken.

③ Meanwhile, in a small saucepan combine peanut butter, the water, soy sauce, green onion, and ginger. Heat over medium-low heat until peanut butter is melted and mixture is smooth, whisking constantly. Sprinkle with crushed red pepper and green onion, if desired. Serve warm peanut sauce with kabobs (if sauce separates before serving, stir well to combine).

***Tip:** If using wooden skewers, soak them in enough water to cover for at least 30 minutes before using.

PER SERVING 124 calories; 6 g total fat (2 g sat. fat); 24 mg cholesterol; 135 mg sodium; 2 g carbohydrate; 1 g fiber; 15 g protein

Shrimp-and-Bacon-Stuffed Baby Potatoes (photo page 6)

MAKES 14 servings **PREP** 35 minutes **BAKE** 42 minutes **OVEN** at 425°F

14	tiny new potatoes (about 1¼ pounds)
2	tablespoons Dijon mustard
1	teaspoon olive oil
1	teaspoon Old Bay Seasoning (seafood seasoning)
1	7- to 8-ounce package frozen peeled cooked shrimp, thawed, drained, and chopped
½	of an 8-ounce package reduced-fat cream cheese (Neufchâtel), softened
¾	cup shredded reduced-fat mozzarella cheese (3 ounces)
4	slices bacon, crisp-cooked, drained, and crumbled
¼	cup snipped fresh chives (optional)

① Preheat oven to 425°F. Cut potatoes in half lengthwise. Using a melon baller or a very small spoon, scoop out potato flesh, leaving ¼-inch shells. Cut a thin slice from the bottom of each potato half so it stands upright. Place potatoes, cut sides up, in a 15 x 10 x 1-inch baking pan.

② In a small bowl combine mustard, oil, and ½ teaspoon of the Old Bay Seasoning. Brush insides of potato shells with mustard mixture. Bake about 30 minutes or until potatoes are tender.

③ Meanwhile, for filling, in a small bowl combine shrimp, cream cheese, mozzarella cheese, bacon, and the remaining Old Bay Seasoning. Spoon filling into potato shells, mounding slightly.

④ Bake for 12 to 15 minutes more or until filling is heated through and cheese is melted. Serve warm or at room temperature. If desired, garnish with chives.

PER SERVING 96 calories; 4 g total fat (2 g sat. fat); 40 mg cholesterol; 250 mg sodium; 7 g carbohydrate; 1 g fiber; 7 g protein

Turkey Vegetable "Sushi"

MAKES 8 servings **PREP** 20 minutes **CHILL** 1 hour

- 8 slices deli roasted turkey
- ½ of an 8-ounce package reduced-fat cream cheese, softened
- 2 teaspoons snipped fresh dill or ½ teaspoon dried dill
- 1 medium carrot, coarsely shredded
- ½ cup coarsely shredded zucchini
- ½ cup finely chopped red sweet pepper

① On each slice of turkey, spread cream cheese. Sprinkle with dill. Top with shredded and chopped vegetables. Tightly roll up turkey slices. Cover and chill 1 hour or until ready to serve. Cut rolls crosswise into 1-inch slices.

PER SERVING 51 calories; 3 g total fat (2 g sat. fat); 15 mg cholesterol; 154 mg sodium; 2 g carbohydrate; 0 g fiber; 3 g protein

Turkey Vegetable "Sushi"

Tuscan Cheesecake Bites ✪

MAKES 24 tarts **PREP** 25 minutes **BAKE** 12 minutes
STAND 10 minutes **OVEN** 350°F

- ⅓ cup panko (Japanese-style bread crumbs)
- ⅓ cup ground walnuts
- ½ teaspoon dried basil, crushed
- 2 tablespoons butter, melted
- 1 8-ounce package reduced-fat cream cheese (Neufchâtel), softened
- 1 4-ounce package crumbled feta cheese with basil and tomato
- 1 egg, beaten
- 2 tablespoons light sour cream
- 2 tablespoons chopped pitted ripe olives
- 2 tablespoons small fresh oregano leaves or snipped fresh basil

① Preheat oven to 350°F. Line twenty-four 1¾-inch muffin pans with small paper bake cups; set aside. In a small bowl combine panko, walnuts, and dried basil. Stir in melted butter. Spoon 1 slightly rounded teaspoon of the panko mixture into each paper cup. Press into bottoms using the rounded side of a measuring teaspoon; set aside.

② For filling, in a medium mixing bowl beat cream cheese with an electric mixer on medium speed until light and fluffy. Add feta cheese and egg; beat until combined. Stir in sour cream. Spoon about 1 tablespoon of the filling into each muffin cup.

③ Bake for 12 to 15 minutes or until filling is set. Cool in pan on a wire rack for 10 minutes. Carefully remove from muffin cups. To serve, top with olives and fresh oregano. Serve warm.

PER SERVING 64 calories; 6 g total fat (3 g sat. fat); 22 mg cholesterol; 103 mg sodium; 2 g carbohydrate; 0 g fiber; 3 g protein

These little savory cheesecakes are best served slightly warm. You can make both the crust and the filling ahead of time—just keep them separate until right before filling and baking. Line the bake cups with the crust mixture and set aside at room temperature. Make the filling, cover, and refrigerate until ready to use.

Tuscan Cheesecake Bites

Sweet Yogurt Fruit Dip

Sweet Yogurt Fruit Dip ⭐ 🕥

MAKES 6 servings **START TO FINISH** 15 minutes

1	6- to 7-ounce carton plain lowfat Greek yogurt
1	tablespoon maple syrup
¼	teaspoon ground cinnamon
⅛	teaspoon ground nutmeg
	Dash ground cloves
	Ground cinnamon (optional)
1	medium apple, cored and cut in wedges
1	medium pear, cored and cut in wedges
1	cup strawberries

① In a small bowl combine yogurt, maple syrup, ¼ teaspoon cinnamon, the nutmeg, and cloves. If desired, sprinkle dip with additional ground cinnamon. Serve fruit with dip.

PER SERVING 67 calories; 1 g total fat (0 g sat. fat); 1 mg cholesterol; 10 mg sodium; 14 g carbohydrate; 2 g fiber; 3 g protein

Cajun-Spiced Popcorn

MAKES 8 servings **START TO FINISH** 10 minutes

1	teaspoon paprika
½	teaspoon onion powder
½	teaspoon garlic powder
½	teaspoon black pepper
¼	teaspoon salt
¼	teaspoon dry mustard
⅛	to ¼ teaspoon cayenne pepper
⅛	teaspoon celery seeds
8	cups air-popped popcorn
2	tablespoons vegetable oil spread, melted

① In a small bowl combine paprika, onion powder, garlic powder, black pepper, salt, mustard, cayenne pepper, and celery seeds.

② Put popcorn in a large resealable plastic bag. Drizzle the melted vegetable oil spread over the popcorn, shaking occasionally to evenly coat. Sprinkle in about half the spice mixture. Seal bag and shake to coat. Open bag and sprinkle in the remaining spice mixture. Seal bag and shake to coat.

PER SERVING 55 calories; 3 g total fat (1 g sat. fat); 0 mg cholesterol; 92 mg sodium; 7 g carbohydrate; 1 g fiber; 1 g protein

Fiery Snack Mix

MAKES 20 servings **PREP** 5 minutes **BAKE** 18 minutes
COOL 10 minutes **OVEN** at 300°F

4	cups crisp mixed vegetable sticks
2	cups round toasted oat cereal
2	cups bite-size corn square cereal
1¾	cups pretzel sticks
½	cup whole almonds
1	teaspoon packed brown sugar
1	teaspoon paprika
½	teaspoon ground ancho or pasilla chili pepper or chili powder
½	teaspoon ground cumin
¼	teaspoon cayenne pepper
¼	teaspoon salt
	Olive oil nonstick cooking spray

① Preheat oven to 300°F. In a roasting pan combine vegetable sticks, cereals, pretzel sticks, and almonds. In a small bowl combine brown sugar, paprika, ancho chili pepper, cumin, cayenne pepper, and salt. Lightly coat cereal mixture with nonstick cooking spray; toss to coat evenly. Sprinkle cereal mixture with spice mixture; toss to coat.

② Bake 18 to 20 minutes or until toasted, stirring twice. Spread on a large sheet of foil to cool. Store in an airtight container up to 1 week.

PER SERVING 92 calories; 3 g total fat (0 g sat. fat); 0 mg cholesterol; 214 mg sodium; 13 g carbohydrate; 1 g fiber; 2 g protein

Fiery Snack Mix

Pear-Mint Green Tea ③⓪

MAKES 4 servings **PREP** 10 minutes **COOK** 5 minutes
STAND 5 minutes

- ½ cup lightly packed fresh mint leaves
- 2½ cups water
- 1 5.5- to 6-ounce can pear nectar (¾ cup)
- 4 green tea bags
- 3 wide strips fresh lemon peel*
  Fresh mint leaves and/or pear slices (optional)

① Place ½ cup mint leaves in a medium saucepan. Use the back of a spoon to lightly bruise the leaves. Add the water and pear nectar to the mint. Bring to boiling; reduce heat. Simmer, covered, for 5 minutes.

② Remove from heat and add tea bags and lemon peel. Cover and steep for 5 minutes. Remove and discard tea bags. Strain tea and discard lemon peel and mint leaves. If desired, garnish with additional mint leaves and/or pear slices.

*Tip: Use a sharp vegetable peeler to shave lemon peel strips. Make sure lemon strips contain no white pith, which will add bitterness. If white pith is showing, scrape it off with a sharp knife.

PER SERVING 31 calories; 0 g total fat; 0 mg cholesterol; 10 mg sodium; 8 g carbohydrate; 1 g fiber; 1 g protein

Pear-Mint Green Tea

Coconut Hot Chocolate ✪ ③⓪

MAKES 6 (about 5 ounces each) **START TO FINISH** 20 minutes

- ⅓ cup unsweetened cocoa powder
- ⅓ cup sugar
- 2½ cups water
- 1 13- to 14-ounce can unsweetened light coconut milk
- ⅓ cup coconut-flavor or light rum (optional)
  Frozen light whipped dessert topping, thawed (optional)
  Toasted coconut (optional)
  Cinnamon sticks (optional)

① In a medium saucepan whisk together cocoa powder and sugar. Gradually whisk in the water. Bring to boiling over medium heat, whisking to dissolve sugar. Reduce heat. Stir in coconut milk. Heat through but do not boil.

② If desired, stir in rum. Serve in warm mugs. If desired, add a small spoonful of whipped topping, a sprinkling of toasted coconut, and a cinnamon stick to each drink.

PER SERVING 91 calories; 4 g total fat (3 g sat. fat); 0 mg cholesterol; 20 mg sodium; 16 g carbohydrate; 1 g fiber; 1 g protein

Pomegranate-Orange Wine Spritzer

MAKES 12 (6 ounces each) **PREP** 15 minutes **CHILL** 2 hours

- 1 750-milliliter bottle sweet white wine (such as Gewurztraminer or Riesling), chilled
- 2 cups pomegranate juice, chilled
- 1 orange, halved and thinly sliced
- 2 12-ounce bottles sparkling water, chilled
  Orange peel twists (optional)

① In a large pitcher combine wine, pomegranate juice, and orange slices. Cover and chill for 2 to 6 hours.

② To serve, slowly pour sparkling water into wine mixture, stirring just until combined. Pour into martini glasses or other decorative glasses to serve. If desired, garnish with orange peel twists.

PER SERVING 78 calories; 0 g total fat; 0 mg cholesterol; 0 mg sodium; 8 g carbohydrate; 0 g fiber; 0 g protein

Coconut Hot Chocolate

Cinnamon Streusel Rolls, page 60

Better Breakfasts & Brunches

Wake-Me-Up Smoothies 🕒

MAKES 4 servings **START TO FINISH** 5 minutes

- 2   cups ice cubes
- 1   cup fat-free milk
- ¾   cup double-strength coffee
- 2   tablespoons sugar
- 1   tablespoon sugar-free caramel ice cream topping

     Fat-free frozen whipped dessert topping, thawed (optional)

     Chocolate-covered espresso beans, coarsely chopped (optional)

① In a blender combine ice, milk, coffee, sugar, and ice cream topping. Cover and blend until smooth. Serve immediately. If desired, top with additional whipped topping and chocolate-covered espresso beans.

PER SERVING 57 calories; 0 g total fat; 1 mg cholesterol; 36 mg sodium; 12 g carbohydrate; 0 g fiber; 2 g protein

Wake-Me-Up Smoothies

Protein-Packed Smoothies ✪ 🕒

MAKES 4 servings **START TO FINISH** 10 minutes

- 2   cups plain fat-free yogurt
- 2   ripe medium bananas
- 2   cups sliced fresh strawberries or frozen unsweetened strawberries
- 2   tablespoons honey
- 2   tablespoons peanut butter

     Whole fresh strawberries (optional)

① In a blender combine yogurt, bananas, sliced strawberries, honey, and peanut butter. Cover and blend until smooth. Serve immediately. If desired, top with whole strawberries.

PER SERVING 223 calories; 5 g total fat (1 g sat. fat); 2 mg cholesterol; 133 mg sodium; 39 g carbohydrate; 3 g fiber; 10 g protein

Although this recipe doesn't call for frozen bananas, if you make a lot of smoothies, it's a good idea to keep a bag of peeled bananas, cut into chunks, in the freezer. Frozen bananas add creaminess and body to breakfast blender drinks.

Antioxidant Power Smoothies ✪ 🕒

MAKES 2 servings **START TO FINISH** 10 minutes

- 1   cup fresh blueberries
- 1   cup fresh blackberries
- 1   6-ounce carton blueberry fat-free yogurt
- ½   cup pomegranate juice
- 1   tablespoon honey

     Fresh blueberries and/or blackberries (optional)

① In a blender combine the 1 cup blueberries, the 1 cup blackberries, the yogurt, pomegranate juice, and honey. Cover and blend until almost smooth. If desired, press mixture through a fine-mesh sieve to remove blackberry seeds. Serve immediately. If desired, garnish with additional berries.

PER SERVING 190 calories; 1 g total fat (0 g sat. fat); 2 mg cholesterol; 54 mg sodium; 43 g carbohydrate; 6 g fiber; 5 g protein

Iced Caramel-Cream Coffee

Eat-Your-Veggies Smoothies

MAKES 4 servings **START TO FINISH** 10 minutes

- 2 cups ice cubes
- 2 cups V8 V-Fusion Light peach mango juice
- 1 medium peach, halved and pitted
- 1 medium banana
- 2 leaves Swiss chard, ribs removed
  Mango wedges (optional)

① In a blender combine ice, juice, peach, banana, and Swiss chard. Cover and blend until smooth. Serve immediately. If desired, garnish with mango wedges.

PER SERVING 68 calories; 0 g total fat; 0 mg cholesterol; 41 mg sodium; 17 g carbohydrate; 1 g fiber; 1 g protein

Iced Caramel-Cream Coffee

MAKES 2 servings **START TO FINISH** 5 minutes

- 2 cups cold strong-brewed coffee
- 2 tablespoons no-sugar-added French vanilla-flavor instant breakfast mix
- 2 tablespoons sugar-free caramel ice cream topping
  Ice cubes
- 2 tablespoons frozen light whipped dessert topping, thawed
- 2 teaspoons sugar-free caramel ice cream topping
  Coarsely crushed chocolate-covered coffee beans (optional)

① In a blender combine coffee, instant breakfast mix, and 2 tablespoons ice cream topping. Cover and blend until smooth. Pour over ice in two glasses. Top with dessert topping and drizzle with 2 teaspoons ice cream topping. If desired, sprinkle with coarsely crushed coffee beans.

PER SERVING 87 calories; 1 g total fat (1 g sat. fat); 1 mg cholesterol; 62 mg sodium; 20 g carbohydrate; 1 g fiber; 2 g protein

Save a significant number of pennies—and calories—by making iced caramel coffee at home rather than buying it at the nearest chain coffee shop.

Citrus Mock Mimosas

MAKES 4 servings **PREP** 10 minutes **CHILL** 2 hours

- ¾ cup fresh orange juice
- ½ cup fresh grapefruit juice
- ¼ cup fresh lime juice
- 1 to 2 tablespoons honey
- 1 12-ounce bottle sparkling water, chilled
  Long, thin strips of orange peel, grapefruit peel, and/or lime peel, curled (optional)

① In a 2-cup glass measure combine orange juice, grapefruit juice, lime juice, and honey. Stir until honey is dissolved. Cover and chill mixture for at least 2 hours or up to 24 hours to blend flavors.

② To serve, pour juice mixture into four champagne glasses. Add sparkling water and stir lightly to mix. If desired, garnish with citrus peel strips.

PER SERVING 53 calories; 0 g total fat (0 g sat. fat); 0 mg cholesterol; 19 mg sodium; 13 g carbohydrate; 0 g fiber; 1 g protein

Citrus Mock Mimosas

Warm Fruit Bowls with Toasted Almonds ⭐ ㉚

MAKES 6 servings **START TO FINISH** 20 minutes

- 1 medium red-skin cooking apple, cored and coarsely chopped
- ¼ cup water
- ¼ teaspoon apple pie spice
- 1 medium mango, seeded, peeled, and cubed, or 1 cup coarsely chopped fresh pineapple
- 1 cup coarsely chopped fresh strawberries or whole raspberries
- ¾ cup fresh blueberries
- 1 tablespoon sugar
- ½ teaspoon vanilla
- ¼ cup sliced almonds, toasted

① In a medium saucepan combine apple, the water, and apple pie spice. Bring to boiling over medium heat, stirring occasionally. Reduce heat; simmer, covered, for 4 to 5 minutes or just until apple is tender, stirring occasionally.

② Stir in mango, strawberries, and blueberries. Cook, uncovered, for 2 to 3 minutes or until heated through, gently stirring occasionally. Remove from heat and stir in sugar and vanilla. Spoon fruit mixture into six serving bowls. Sprinkle with almonds and serve warm.

PER SERVING 88 calories; 2 g total fat (0 g sat. fat); 0 mg cholesterol; 2 mg sodium; 18 g carbohydrate; 3 g fiber; 1 g protein

Some apple varieties are best eaten raw, out of hand, while others hold up well to heat—and even have their flavors intensified by it. Good cooking apples include (but aren't limited to) Cortland, Rome Beauty, Jonathan, Pippin, and Winesap.

Layered Fruit Salad ⭐ ㉚

MAKES 6 servings **START TO FINISH** 25 minutes

- ½ an 8-ounce tub light cream cheese
- 1 6-ounce carton plain nonfat Greek yogurt
- 1 tablespoon honey
- 1 teaspoon finely shredded lemon peel
- 1 teaspoon finely shredded orange peel
- 1 medium orange, peeled and sectioned
- 3 medium kiwifruit, peeled and sliced
- 1 medium mango, seeded, peeled, and cubed
- 1 cup fresh blueberries

① In a medium mixing bowl beat cream cheese with an electric mixer on medium speed until smooth. Beat in yogurt and honey until smooth. Stir in lemon peel and orange peel.

② Divide fruit among six serving dishes; top with cream cheese mixture. Serve immediately or cover loosely and chill for up to 4 hours.

PER SERVING 131 calories; 3 g total fat (2 g sat. fat); 9 mg cholesterol; 102 mg sodium; 23 g carbohydrate; 3 g fiber; 5 g protein

Cranberry-Orange Hot Cereal ⭐ ㉚

MAKES 4 servings **PREP** 10 minutes **COOK** 12 minutes

- 2 cups water
- 1 cup fat-free milk
- 1 cup uncooked seven-grain hot cereal
- ⅛ teaspoon salt
- ½ cup fresh cranberries
- ¼ cup light or sugar-free maple-flavor syrup
- 2 tablespoons water
- 1 medium orange, peeled and sectioned

① In a medium saucepan combine the 2 cups water, milk, cereal, and salt. Bring to boiling; reduce heat. Simmer, uncovered, for 10 minutes or until cereal is tender, stirring occasionally.

② Meanwhile, in a small saucepan combine cranberries, syrup, and the 2 tablespoons water. Cook and stir over medium heat until boiling. Boil gently, uncovered, for 3 to 5 minutes or until cranberries pop and syrup is slightly thickened. Stir in orange sections. Spoon cooked cereal into four serving bowls. Top with cranberry syrup.

PER SERVING 177 calories; 2 g total fat (0 g sat. fat); 1 mg cholesterol; 134 mg sodium; 36 g carbohydrate; 3 g fiber; 6 g protein

Pumpkin-Apple Quick Oatmeal

Pumpkin-Apple Quick Oatmeal ✪ ③⓪

MAKES 4 servings **START TO FINISH** 15 minutes

- 1⅓ cups water
- ⅔ cup apple juice
- ½ cup canned pumpkin
- ⅓ cup chopped dried apples
- 1¼ cups quick-cooking rolled oats
- 1 tablespoon packed brown sugar
- 1 teaspoon ground cinnamon
- ¼ teaspoon ground nutmeg
- ½ cup vanilla fat-free yogurt
  Ground cinnamon (optional)

① In a saucepan combine the water, apple juice, pumpkin, and dried apples. Bring to boiling. In a bowl combine oats, brown sugar, 1 teaspoon cinnamon, and nutmeg; add to boiling water mixture. Cook for 1 minute, stirring occasionally.

② Divide hot oatmeal among four bowls. Top each serving with a spoonful of yogurt and, if desired, garnish with additional cinnamon.

PER SERVING 168 calories; 2 g total fat (0 g sat. fat); 1 mg cholesterol; 30 mg sodium; 35 g carbohydrate; 4 g fiber; 5 g protein

Pumpkin puree doesn't just add color and flavor to this autumnal oatmeal; it adds nutrition too. Pumpkin is a great source of vitamins A, C, and K, as well as potassium, iron, and dietary fiber.

Raspberry-Swirled Cheesy Oatmeal ✪ ③⓪

MAKES 4 servings **START TO FINISH** 25 minutes

- ¾ cup frozen unsweetened raspberries, thawed and undrained*
- 1¼ cups water
- 1 cup fat-free milk
- 2 teaspoons sugar
- ⅛ teaspoon salt
- 1 cup rolled oats
- ¼ cup tub-style light cream cheese, softened
- 1 teaspoon vanilla
- ¼ cup fresh raspberries (optional)

① Place thawed raspberries and any juice in a blender or food processor. Cover and blend or process until smooth; set aside. In a medium saucepan bring the water, milk, sugar, and salt to boiling. Stir in oats. Reduce heat. Simmer, uncovered, for 3 minutes (for quick oats) or 5 minutes (for regular oats), stirring occasionally (watch carefully and reduce heat as necessary to prevent milk mixture from boiling over). Remove from heat. Stir in cream cheese and vanilla. Cover and let stand for 2 minutes.

② Stir oatmeal and divide among four shallow serving bowls. Spoon 2 tablespoons of the pureed raspberries on the oatmeal. Use a thin metal spatula to swirl the pureed raspberries into the oatmeal. If desired, garnish with fresh raspberries.

***Tip:** Measure raspberries while frozen. Place in a small bowl to thaw so the juice doesn't drain off.

PER SERVING 226 calories; 5 g total fat (2 g sat. fat); 9 mg cholesterol; 177 mg sodium; 35 g carbohydrate; 6 g fiber; 10 g protein

With fruit, spices, and yogurt or cream cheese, oatmeal tastes like dessert but is still good for you.

menu

Sweet Potato and
Turkey Sausage Hash

Melon wedges and
red grapes

Spiced Apple-Berry
Oatmeal
[below]

Orange juice

Spiced Apple-Berry Oatmeal ✪

MAKES 6 servings **PREP** 15 minutes **COOK** 30 minutes

- 2 **cups water**
- 1¾ **cups apple juice**
- 1 **cup steel-cut oats**
- 1 **medium apple, cored and chopped**
- ½ **teaspoon apple pie spice**
- ¼ **teaspoon salt**
- ½ **cup blueberries, raspberries, or blackberries**
- 1 **cup fat-free milk**
- ¼ **cup chopped pecans or almonds, toasted (optional)**

① In a large saucepan bring the water and apple juice to boiling. Stir in oats, apple, apple pie spice, and salt. Return mixture to a simmer; reduce heat. Simmer, uncovered, stirring occasionally, for 30 minutes or until oats are tender and desired consistency. Stir in berries. Serve with milk and, if desired, pecans.

PER SERVING 164 calories; 2 g total fat (0 g sat. fat); 1 mg cholesterol; 120 mg sodium; 34 g carbohydrate; 4 g fiber; 6 g protein

Smoked Salmon Breakfast Wraps ㉚

MAKES 4 servings **START TO FINISH** 20 minutes

- ⅓ **cup light cream cheese spread**
- 1 **tablespoon snipped fresh chives**
- 1 **teaspoon finely shredded lemon peel**
- 1 **tablespoon lemon juice**
- 4 **6- to 7-inch whole wheat flour tortillas**
- 3 **ounces thinly sliced, smoked salmon (lox-style), cut into strips**
- 1 **small zucchini, trimmed**
- **Lemon wedges (optional)**

① In a small bowl stir together cream cheese, chives, lemon peel, and lemon juice until smooth. Spread evenly over tortillas, leaving a ½-inch border around edges.

② Divide salmon among tortillas, placing it on one half of each tortilla. To make zucchini ribbons, draw a sharp vegetable peeler lengthwise along zucchini to cut very thin slices. Place zucchini ribbons on salmon. Starting from one edge, roll up tortillas. Cut each wrap in half. If desired, serve with lemon wedges.

PER SERVING 124 calories; 6 g total fat (2 g sat. fat); 15 mg cholesterol; 451 mg sodium; 14 g carbohydrate; 9 g fiber; 12 g protein

Smoked Salmon Breakfast Wraps

Spiced Apple Berry Oatmeal

Tomato-Arugula Omelets

Tomato-Arugula Omelets 🕙

MAKES 4 servings **START TO FINISH** 25 minutes

Nonstick cooking spray

2 cups refrigerated or frozen egg product, thawed, or 8 eggs, lightly beaten

⅛ teaspoon black pepper

1 cup torn fresh arugula or spinach

1 cup seeded, chopped tomato

½ cup crumbled reduced-fat feta cheese (2 ounces)

¼ cup pitted kalamata olives, sliced

Whole wheat toast (optional)

① Coat an 8-inch flared-side nonstick skillet with cooking spray. Heat skillet over medium heat.

② In a medium bowl combine the eggs and pepper. Pour one-fourth of the egg mixture into prepared skillet. Immediately begin stirring the eggs gently and continuously with a wooden or plastic spatula until small pieces of cooked egg are surrounded by liquid egg. Stop stirring. Cook for 30 to 60 seconds more or until egg is set and shiny.

③ When egg is set and still shiny, sprinkle one-fourth of the arugula, one-fourth of the tomato, one-fourth the cheese, and one-fourth of the olives over half of the egg. With a spatula, lift and fold the other half over filling. Transfer omelet to a serving plate. (If necessary, wipe out skillet with a clean paper towel and recoat with nonstick cooking spray between omelets.) Repeat with remaining egg mixture, arugula, tomato, cheese, and olives to make three more omelets. If desired, serve with whole wheat toast.

PER SERVING 118 calories; 4 g total fat (2 g sat. fat); 5 mg cholesterol; 562 mg sodium; 5 g carbohydrate; 1 g fiber; 16 g protein

Bacon and Blue Cheese Frittata

MAKES 4 servings **PREP** 10 minutes **COOK** 20 minutes
STAND 5 minutes

¾ cup chopped onion

1 tablespoon olive oil

1 cup sliced fresh cremini or button mushrooms

¼ teaspoon black pepper

⅛ teaspoon salt

1½ cups coarsely chopped fresh spinach

1½ cups refrigerated or frozen egg product, thawed, or 6 eggs, lightly beaten

¼ cup crumbled blue cheese

2 slices turkey bacon, cooked according to package directions and chopped

① Preheat broiler. In an 8-inch broilerproof nonstick skillet cook onion in hot oil over medium heat for 5 minutes, stirring occasionally. Add mushrooms, pepper, and salt; cook about 10 minutes more or until mushrooms are tender and onions are lightly browned, stirring occasionally. Stir in spinach.

② Pour egg in skillet with vegetables. Cook over medium heat. As mixture sets, run a spatula around edge of skillet, lifting egg mixture so uncooked portion flows underneath. Continue cooking and lifting edge until egg mixture is almost set and surface is just slightly moist (5 to 8 minutes).

③ Broil 4 inches from the heat for 1 to 2 minutes or until top is lightly browned and center is set. Sprinkle with cheese and bacon. Let stand for 5 minutes before cutting in wedges.

PER SERVING 142 calories; 7 g total fat (3 g sat. fat); 14 mg cholesterol; 464 mg sodium; 6 g carbohydrate; 1 g fiber; 13 g protein

Protein-rich eggs loaded with fresh vegetables and a little cheese make for a great start to the day.

Zucchini-Ham Alfredo Casserole

MAKES 8 servings **PREP** 30 minutes **BAKE** 45 minutes
STAND 10 minutes **OVEN** at 325°F

- 1 medium zucchini, halved lengthwise and thinly sliced
- 1 small red sweet pepper, cut into thin bite-size strips
- ½ cup chopped onion
- 1 tablespoon olive oil
  Nonstick cooking spray
- 5 whole wheat English muffins, torn into bite-size pieces (10 ounces)
- 4 ounces low-fat, reduced-sodium cooked boneless ham, chopped (⅔ cup)
- 4 eggs, lightly beaten
- ¾ cup light alfredo sauce
- ¾ cup fat-free milk
- 1 teaspoon snipped fresh rosemary or ¼ teaspoon dried rosemary, crushed
- ¼ teaspoon black pepper
- ½ cup shredded reduced-fat Italian blend cheeses (2 ounces)

① Preheat oven to 325°F. In a large skillet cook zucchini, sweet pepper, and onion in hot oil over medium heat for 5 minutes, stirring occasionally. Meanwhile, coat a 2-quart rectangular baking dish with cooking spray. Arrange the English muffin pieces in dish. Top muffin pieces with the vegetable mixture, then the chopped ham. Set aside.

② In a large bowl whisk together the eggs, alfredo sauce, milk, rosemary, and black pepper. Pour egg mixture evenly over the layers in the dish.

③ Bake, uncovered, for 35 minutes. Sprinkle with cheese then bake for 10 to 15 minutes more or until a knife inserted near the center comes out clean. Let stand 10 minutes before serving.

PER SERVING 221 calories; 9 g total fat (3 g sat. fat); 122 mg cholesterol; 584 mg sodium; 23 g carbohydrate; 3 g fiber; 14 g protein

Eggs Benedict ③⓪

MAKES 6 servings **START TO FINISH** 25 minutes

- ½ cup light sour cream
- 2 tablespoons fat-free milk
- 1 tablespoon Dijon mustard
- 6 eggs
- 3 whole wheat English muffin, split
- 6 ounces thinly sliced reduced-sodium cooked ham
- 6 tomato slices
  Snipped fresh chives (optional)

① Preheat broiler. For sauce, in a medium bowl combine sour cream, milk, and mustard; set aside.

② Lightly grease a large skillet. Fill the skillet halfway with water. Bring water to boiling; reduce heat to simmering (bubbles should begin to break the surface of the water). Break one of the eggs into a small dish. Carefully slide egg into simmering water, holding the lip of the dish as close to the water as possible. Repeat with the remaining eggs, allowing each egg an equal amount of space. Simmer, uncovered, for 3 to 5 minutes or until egg whites are completely set and yolks begin to thicken but are not hard.

③ Meanwhile, place muffin halves, cut sides up, on a baking sheet. Broil 3 to 4 inches from the heat for 1 to 2 minutes or until toasted. Top muffin halves with ham and tomato slices. Broil about 1 minute more or until toppings are heated through.

④ To serve, use a slotted spoon to remove eggs from skillet; place eggs on tomato slices. Spoon sauce over eggs and, if desired, sprinkle with chives.

PER SERVING 198 calories; 8 g total fat (3 g sat. fat); 230 mg cholesterol; 500 mg sodium; 17 g carbohydrate; 2 g fiber; 15 g protein

This "cheater's Hollandaise" made with light sour cream, skim milk, and Dijon mustard is not only much simpler than real Hollandaise but also much healthier than the egg yolk and butter version. (And it's pretty darn good too!)

Upside-Down Crab Quiche

Upside-Down Crab Quiche

MAKES 6 servings **PREP** 25 minutes **BAKE** 30 minutes
STAND 10 minutes **OVEN** at 325°F/450°F

Nonstick cooking spray

2 cups refrigerated or frozen egg product, thawed, or 8 eggs

½ cup light sour cream

½ cup fat-free milk

¼ teaspoon black pepper

1 6-ounce can lump crabmeat, drained, flaked, and cartilage removed

⅓ cup bottled roasted red sweet peppers, drained and chopped

2 tablespoons snipped fresh parsley

1 recipe Pastry Cut-Outs

① Preheat oven to 325°F. Coat six 6-ounce custard cups, shallow ramekins, or quiche dishes with cooking spray. Set aside. In a large bowl whisk together eggs, sour cream, milk, and black pepper. Stir in crabmeat, roasted peppers, and parsley.

② Divide egg mixture among prepared custard cups. Place cups on a baking sheet. Bake for 30 to 35 minutes or until a knife inserted in centers comes out clean. Remove from oven.

③ Meanwhile, prepare Pastry Cut-Outs. Place cut-outs on a baking sheet. After quiches have baked, increase oven temperature to 450°F. Bake Pastry Cut-outs for 8 to 10 minutes or until tops are lightly browned. Place a baked cut-out on top of a quiche. Let stand for 10 minutes before serving.

Pastry Cut-Outs: In a bowl stir together ¼ cup all-purpose flour, 2 tablespoons whole wheat pastry flour, and a dash of salt. Using a pastry blender, cut in 1½ tablespoons chilled vegetable oil spread until pieces are pea size. Sprinkle 1 tablespoon cold water over part of the flour mixture; gently toss with a fork. Push moistened dough to the side of the bowl. Repeat moistening flour mixture, using 1 teaspoon cold water at a time, until all the flour mixture is moistened (3 to 4 teaspoons cold water total). Form dough into a disk. On a lightly floured surface, roll dough from center to edges to ⅛-inch thickness. Using 3- to 4-inch cookie cutters, cut six shapes from dough. Brush cut-outs with a mixture of 1 tablespoon refrigerated or frozen egg product, thawed, and 1 tablespoon water.

PER SERVING 148 calories; 5 g total fat (2 g sat. fat); 34 mg cholesterol; 302 mg sodium; 10 g carbohydrate; 1 g fiber; 16 g protein

Bacon and Egg Breakfast Wraps ✪ ㉚

MAKES 4 wraps **START TO FINISH** 25 minutes

4 slices bacon, chopped

1 cup chopped fresh mushrooms

½ cup chopped green sweet pepper

¼ teaspoon chili powder

¼ teaspoon black pepper

⅛ teaspoon salt

1 cup refrigerated egg product

¼ cup chopped seeded tomato

Few drops bottled hot pepper sauce

4 8-inch flour tortillas, warmed*

① In a large nonstick skillet cook bacon over medium heat until crisp. Using a slotted spoon, remove bacon and drain on paper towels, reserving 1 tablespoon of the drippings in skillet. Discard remaining drippings.

② Add mushrooms, sweet pepper, chili powder, black pepper, and salt to the reserved drippings. Cook and stir about 3 minutes or until vegetables are tender.

③ Pour in egg product. Using a spatula or large spoon, lift and fold egg mixture so the uncooked portion flows underneath. Continue cooking over medium heat about 2 minutes or until egg is cooked through yet still glossy and moist. Stir in cooked bacon, tomato, and hot pepper sauce. Divide egg mixture among tortillas; roll up tortillas.

***Tip:** To warm tortillas, preheat oven to 350°F. Wrap tortillas tightly in foil. Bake about 10 minutes or until heated through.

PER WRAP 195 calories; 9 g total fat (3 g sat. fat); 11 mg cholesterol; 462 mg sodium; 18 g carbohydrate; 1 g fiber; 11 g protein

Sweet Potato and Turkey Sausage Hash ✪

MAKES 4 servings **PREP** 25 minutes **BAKE** 20 minutes
OVEN at 400°F

- 2 medium russet potatoes, peeled, if desired, and diced
- 1 medium sweet potato, peeled, if desired, and diced
  Nonstick cooking spray
- ½ of a 14-ounce ring smoked turkey sausage, halved lengthwise and sliced ½ inch thick
- 1 small green sweet pepper, chopped
- 1 medium onion, chopped
- 1 tablespoon snipped fresh sage or 1 teaspoon dried sage, crushed
- ¼ teaspoon black pepper

① Preheat oven to 400°F. Place russet and sweet potatoes in a 15 x 10 x 1-inch shallow baking pan. Lightly coat with cooking spray and toss to coat.

② Bake about 20 minutes or until tender and lightly browned, turning once with a spatula.

③ Meanwhile, in a large nonstick skillet cook sausage, sweet pepper, and onion for 8 to 10 minutes or until tender, stirring occasionally. Stir in sweet potato mixture, sage, and black pepper.

PER SERVING 170 calories; 5 g total fat (1 g sat. fat); 33 mg cholesterol; 493 mg sodium; 22 g carbohydrate; 3 g fiber; 10 g protein

Grilled Peanut Butter, Banana, and Berry Sandwiches ✪ ③⁰

MAKES 4 sandwiches **START TO FINISH** 20 minutes

- ¼ cup peanut butter
- 8 slices whole grain cinnamon-raisin bread
- 1 medium banana, cut in 16 slices
- 4 fresh strawberries, each cut in 4 slices (16 slices total)
- 4 teaspoons grated bittersweet or semisweet chocolate
- 1 tablespoon butter

① Spread peanut butter evenly on one side of each bread slice. Arrange four banana slices and four strawberry slices on each of half the prepared bread slices. Sprinkle with grated chocolate. Top with the remaining bread slices, peanut butter sides down.

② In a very large skillet* or on a large griddle melt butter over medium heat. Cook sandwiches about 4 minutes or until crisp and golden brown, turning once halfway through cooking.

***Tip:** If all the sandwiches will not fit at once, do in two batches, using half the butter for each batch.

PER SANDWICH 375 calories; 16 g total fat (5 g sat. fat); 8 mg cholesterol; 374 mg sodium; 49 g carbohydrate; 8 g fiber; 13 g protein

Thinking outside of the cereal box gives you a delicious reason to get out of bed in the morning.

Sweet Potato and Turkey Sausage Hash

Spiced Waffles with Pumpkin Cream

Spiced Waffles with Pumpkin Cream ✪ 30

MAKES 4 servings **PREP** 20 minutes
BAKE per waffle baker directions

- 1¼ cups whole wheat pastry flour or whole wheat flour
- ¼ cup all-purpose flour
- 2 tablespoons flaxseed meal
- 1 tablespoon sugar
- 1½ teaspoons baking powder
- ½ teaspoon pumpkin pie spice
- ⅛ teaspoon salt
- ¼ cup refrigerated or frozen egg product, thawed, or 1 egg, lightly beaten
- 1 cup fat-free milk
- 2 tablespoons canola oil
- 1 recipe Pumpkin Cream
- 4 tablespoons finely chopped, toasted hazelnuts* (optional)

① In a medium bowl stir together whole wheat flour, all-purpose flour, flaxseed meal, sugar, baking powder, pumpkin pie spice, and salt. Make a well in the center of flour mixture; set aside.

② In a small bowl whisk together egg, milk, and oil. Add egg mixture all at once to flour mixture. Stir just until moistened (batter will be thick and slightly lumpy). If desired, fold in 2 tablespoons of the hazelnuts.

③ Lightly grease and preheat a regular waffle baker. Pour 1 to 1¼ cups batter onto grids, spreading to cover. Close lid quickly; do not open until done. Bake according to manufacturer's directions. When done, use a fork to lift waffle off grid. Repeat with remaining batter.

④ Meanwhile, prepare Pumpkin Cream. Divide waffles among four serving plates. Top with Pumpkin Cream and, if desired, sprinkle with 2 tablespoons of the hazelnuts.

Pumpkin Cream: In a bowl combine ⅓ cup canned pumpkin and ⅛ teaspoon pumpkin pie spice. Fold in 1 cup thawed frozen light whipped dessert topping.

*Tip: To toast hazelnuts, preheat oven to 350°F. Spread nuts in a single layer in a shallow baking pan. Bake for 8 to 10 minutes or until lightly toasted, stirring occasionally. Place the warm nuts on a clean kitchen towel. Rub nuts with the towel to remove the loose skins.

PER SERVING 292 calories; 11 g total fat (3 g sat. fat); 1 mg cholesterol; 265 mg sodium; 41 g carbohydrate; 5 g fiber; 9 g protein

Cornmeal Waffles with Blueberry Compote ✪ 30

MAKES 8 servings **PREP** 15 minutes
BAKE per waffle baker directions

- ¾ cup all-purpose flour
- ½ cup cornmeal
- 2 tablespoons brown sugar
- 1 teaspoon baking powder
- ¼ teaspoon salt
- 1 cup buttermilk
- ½ cup fat-free milk
- 3 tablespoons canola oil
- 2 egg yolks
- ½ teaspoon vanilla
- 2 egg whites
- 1 recipe Blueberry Compote

① In a large bowl combine flour, cornmeal, brown sugar, baking powder, and salt.

② In a medium bowl combine buttermilk, milk, oil, egg yolks, and vanilla. Whisk to combine. Whisk mixture into flour mixture just until combined (do not overmix).

③ In a large mixing bowl beat egg whites with an electric mixer on medium-high until soft peaks form. Gently fold egg whites into batter.

④ Pour about ¾ cup batter onto grids of a preheated, well-greased waffle baker. Close lid quickly; do not open until done. Bake according to manufacturer's directions. Repeat with remaining batter. Serve warm with Blueberry Compote.

Blueberry Compote: In a medium saucepan bring 1 cup apple juice and 1 tablespoon lemon juice to boiling. Reduce heat and simmer, uncovered, 8 to 10 minutes or until reduced by half. Stir in 2 cups fresh blueberries, ½ teaspoon finely shredded lemon peel, and ⅛ teaspoon ground cinnamon. Return to boiling. Reduce heat and simmer, uncovered, 5 minutes more. Makes 1⅔ cups.

PER SERVING 204 calories; 7 g total fat (1 g sat. fat); 54 mg cholesterol; 176 mg sodium; 31 g carbohydrate; 2 g fiber; 5 g protein

Smothered Cornbread Waffles ✪

MAKES 8 servings **PREP** 30 minutes
BAKE per waffle baker directions **OVEN** at 300°F

¾	cup yellow cornmeal
½	cup whole wheat pastry flour
¼	cup all-purpose flour
1	tablespoon sugar
1½	teaspoons baking powder
⅛	teaspoon salt
¼	cup refrigerated or frozen egg product, thawed, or 1 egg, lightly beaten
1	cup fat-free milk
3	tablespoons canola oil
	Nonstick cooking spray
8	eggs
	Black pepper
½	cup shredded reduced-fat cheddar cheese (2 ounces)
1	recipe Tomato Topping

① In a medium bowl stir together cornmeal, whole wheat flour, all-purpose flour, sugar, baking powder, and salt. Make a well in the center of flour mixture; set aside.

② In a small bowl whisk together egg, milk, and oil. Add egg mixture all at once to flour mixture. Stir just until moistened (batter will be thick and slightly lumpy).

③ Lightly grease and preheat a regular waffle baker. Pour about 1 to 1¼ cups batter onto grids, spreading to cover (use the amount of batter recommended by manufacturer's directions). Close lid quickly; do not open until done. Bake according to manufacturer's directions. When done, use a fork to lift waffle off grid. Repeat with remaining batter. Keep baked waffles warm in a 300°F oven while baking remaining waffles.

④ Meanwhile, coat a large nonstick skillet with cooking spray; heat over medium heat. Break 4 eggs into skillet. Sprinkle with pepper. Reduce heat to low; cook eggs for 3 to 4 minutes or until whites are completely set and yolks start to thicken. Turn the eggs and cook 30 seconds more for over-easy or 1 minute more for over-hard. Remove eggs from skillet and keep warm; repeat with remaining 4 eggs.

⑤ To serve, divide waffles in squares and place one square on each of eight serving plates. Top each with a fried egg, sprinkle with cheese, and top with ¼ cup of the Tomato Topping.

Tomato Topping: In a medium bowl combine 1½ cups chopped, seeded tomatoes; 3 green onions, thinly sliced; 1 fresh jalapeño chile pepper, finely chopped (see tip, page 8) and, if desired, 3 tablespoons snipped fresh cilantro. Makes about 2 cups.

PER SERVING 246 calories; 12 g total fat (3 g sat. fat); 216 mg cholesterol; 234 mg sodium; 23 g carbohydrate; 2 g fiber; 13 g protein

Pear-Ginger Pancakes ✪ ⑳

MAKES 4 servings **PREP** 20 minutes **COOK** 2 minutes per batch
OVEN at 300°F

½	cup all-purpose flour
½	cup whole wheat flour
1	tablespoon packed brown sugar
2	teaspoons baking powder
¼	teaspoon ground ginger
⅛	teaspoon salt
¾	cup fat-free milk
¼	cup refrigerated or frozen egg product, thawed, or 1 egg
2	tablespoons canola oil
½	cup finely chopped pear
1	recipe Apricot-Pear Syrup

① In a medium bowl stir together all-purpose flour, whole wheat flour, brown sugar, baking powder, ginger, and salt. Make a well in the center of flour mixture; set aside. In a small bowl whisk together milk, egg, and oil; stir in chopped pear. Add egg mixture all at once to flour mixture; stir just until moistened.

② For each pancake, pour ¼ cup of the batter onto a hot, lightly greased griddle or heavy skillet, spreading batter evenly if necessary. Cook over medium heat for 2 to 4 minutes or until pancakes are golden, turning when pancakes have bubbly surfaces and edges are slightly dry. Keep pancakes warm in a 300°F oven while cooking remaining pancakes. Serve pancakes with warm Apricot-Pear Syrup.

Apricot-Pear Syrup: In a small saucepan combine ½ cup finely chopped pear and 1 tablespoon lemon juice. Stir in 2 tablespoons low-sugar apricot preserves, 1 tablespoon water, and ⅛ teaspoon ground ginger. Heat over low heat until preserves are melted and mixture is warm, stirring occasionally. Makes about ½ cup.

PER SERVING 242 calories; 7 g total fat (1 g sat. fat); 1 mg cholesterol; 243 mg sodium; 39 g carbohydrate; 4 g fiber; 7 g protein

Hazelnut Coffee Cake

Hazelnut Coffee Cake

MAKES 1 loaf (12 slices) **PREP** 25 minutes **BAKE** 35 minutes
COOL 10 minutes **OVEN** at 350°F

- ¼ cup rolled oats
- 1 tablespoon packed brown sugar
- ¼ teaspoon ground cinnamon
- 1 tablespoon vegetable oil spread
- ¼ cup chopped hazelnuts, toasted*
- 1⅓ cups all-purpose flour
- ½ cup granulated sugar
- ½ teaspoon baking powder
- ¼ teaspoon baking soda
- ⅛ teaspoon salt
- 1 egg, lightly beaten
- ½ cup light sour cream
- ¼ cup water
- 3 tablespoons canola oil
- 2 tablespoons unsweetened cocoa powder
- 1 tablespoon fat-free milk
- ½ teaspoon vanilla

① Preheat oven to 350°F. Grease an 8 x 4 x 2-inch loaf pan; set aside. For topping, in a small bowl combine oats, brown sugar, and cinnamon. Using a pastry blender, cut in vegetable oil spread until mixture is crumbly. Stir in hazelnuts. Set aside.

② In a medium bowl combine flour, granulated sugar, baking powder, baking soda, and salt. In a small bowl combine egg, sour cream, the water, and oil. Add to flour mixture; stir just until combined. Place ½ cup of the batter in a small clean bowl. Stir in cocoa powder, milk, and vanilla until smooth. Spoon half the light-color batter into prepared pan, spreading evenly. Spoon half the chocolate batter in small mounds over batter in pan. Repeat layers with remaining batter. Using a thin metal spatula, slightly marble batters. Sprinkle with topping.

③ Bake for 35 to 40 minutes or until a toothpick inserted in the center comes out clean. Cool in pan on a wire rack for 10 minutes; serve warm.

*Tip: To toast hazelnuts, preheat oven to 350°F. Spread nuts in a single layer in a shallow baking pan. Bake for 8 to 10 minutes or until lightly toasted, stirring once to toast evenly. Cool nuts slightly. Place the warm nuts on a clean kitchen towel; rub with the towel to remove the loose skins.

PER SLICE 170 calories; 7 g total fat (1 g sat. fat); 20 mg cholesterol; 81 mg sodium; 23 g carbohydrate; 1 g fiber; 3 g protein

Zucchini-Chocolate Chip Scones ✪

MAKES 12 scones **PREP** 25 minutes **BAKE** 13 minutes
OVEN at 400°F

- 1½ cups all-purpose flour
- 1 cup whole wheat flour
- 3 tablespoons sugar
- 1½ teaspoons baking powder
- ½ teaspoon ground cinnamon
- ¼ teaspoon ground nutmeg
- ¼ teaspoon baking soda
- ¼ teaspoon salt
- ¼ cup butter, cut up
- ½ cup refrigerated or frozen egg product, thawed, or 2 eggs, lightly beaten
- ½ cup buttermilk or fat-free sour milk*
- 1 cup shredded zucchini
- ½ cup miniature semisweet chocolate pieces

① Preheat oven to 400°F. In a large bowl stir together all-purpose flour, whole wheat flour, sugar, baking powder, cinnamon, nutmeg, baking soda, and salt. Using a pastry blender, cut in butter until mixture resembles coarse crumbs. Make a well in center of the flour mixture.

② In a small bowl combine egg and buttermilk; stir in zucchini and chocolate pieces. Add the buttermilk mixture all at once to the flour mixture. Using a fork, stir just until moistened.

③ Turn dough out onto a lightly floured surface. Knead dough by folding and gently pressing for 10 to 12 strokes or until nearly smooth. Pat or lightly roll dough to an 8-inch circle. Cut dough in 12 wedges.

④ Place dough wedges 2 inches apart on an ungreased baking sheet. Bake for 13 to 15 minutes or until edges are light brown. Remove scones from baking sheet; serve warm.

*Tip: To make ½ cup fat-free sour milk, place 1½ teaspoons lemon juice or vinegar in a glass measuring cup. Add enough fat-free milk to equal ½ cup total; stir. Let stand for 5 minutes before using.

PER SCONE 202 calories; 7 g total fat (4 g sat. fat); 11 mg cholesterol; 179 mg sodium; 30 g carbohydrate; 2 g fiber; 5 g protein

menu

Upside-Down Crab Quiche

Layered Fruit Salad

Ginger-Peach Tea Biscuits [below]

Hot coffee and tea

Ginger-Peach Tea Biscuits

MAKES 12 biscuits **PREP** 20 minutes **BAKE** 12 minutes **OVEN** at 375°F

Nonstick cooking spray
1 cup all-purpose flour
½ cup whole wheat pastry flour or whole wheat flour
2 tablespoons sugar
1 tablespoon loose leaf green or white tea, crushed
2 teaspoons baking powder
1 teaspoon ground ginger
¼ teaspoon salt
¼ cup butter
½ cup finely chopped dried peaches
1 6-ounce carton plain low-fat yogurt
¼ cup refrigerated or frozen egg product, thawed, or 1 egg, lightly beaten

① Preheat oven to 375°F. Coat a large baking sheet with cooking spray or line with parchment paper; set aside. In a large bowl stir together flours, sugar, tea, baking powder, ginger, and salt. Using a pastry blender, cut in butter until mixture resembles coarse crumbs. Stir in peaches. Make a well in the center of the flour mixture.

② In a small bowl combine yogurt and egg. Add yogurt mixture all at once to flour mixture. Using a fork, stir until combined. Drop dough into 12 mounds 2 inches apart on prepared baking sheet.

③ Bake for 12 to 15 minutes or until tops are lightly browned. Transfer biscuits to wire racks; serve warm.

PER BISCUIT 121 calories; 4 g total fat (3 g sat. fat); 11 mg cholesterol; 157 mg sodium; 18 g carbohydrate; 1 g fiber; 3 g protein

Cranberry-Almond Bread ✪

MAKES 1 loaf (12 slices) **PREP** 20 minutes **BAKE** 50 minutes **COOL** 10 minutes **STAND** overnight **OVEN** at 350°F

1½ cups whole wheat pastry flour
½ cup all-purpose flour
½ cup granulated sugar
1 tablespoon baking powder
¼ teaspoon salt
⅓ cup almond paste
¼ cup refrigerated or frozen egg product, thawed, or 1 egg, lightly beaten
3 tablespoons canola oil
1 cup fat-free milk
⅔ cup fresh cranberries, chopped
⅓ cup chopped almonds, toasted
2 teaspoons powdered sugar (optional)

① Preheat oven to 350°F. Grease the bottom and ½ inch up the sides of an 8 x 4 x 2-inch loaf pan; set aside. In a large bowl stir together whole wheat flour, all-purpose flour, sugar, baking powder, and salt. Make a well in the center of the flour mixture; set aside.

② In a medium bowl stir together almond paste, egg, and oil until smooth. Stir in milk. Add milk mixture all at once to flour mixture; stir just until moistened (batter should be lumpy). Fold in cranberries and almonds. Spoon batter into prepared loaf pan.

③ Bake for 50 to 55 minutes or until a toothpick inserted near the center comes out clean. Cool in pan on a wire rack for 10 minutes. Remove from pan. Cool completely on wire rack. Wrap and store overnight before slicing. If desired, sprinkle lightly with powdered sugar before serving.

PER SLICE 177 calories; 7 g total fat (1 g sat. fat); 0 mg cholesterol; 158 mg sodium; 27 g carbohydrate; 2 g fiber; 4 g protein

Almond paste and marzipan are similar but slightly different. Almond paste is generally used as a filling. The almonds are more coarsely ground than those in marzipan, which is sweeter and which is primarily used for decorating baked goods.

Cranberry-Almond Bread

Cranberry-Pistachio Muffins

Cranberry-Pistachio Muffins ✪

MAKES 12 muffins **PREP** 15 minutes **BAKE** 15 minutes
COOL 5 minutes **OVEN** at 375°F

	Nonstick cooking spray
1¼	cups all-purpose flour
½	cup whole wheat pastry flour
2	teaspoons baking powder
¼	teaspoon salt
⅛	teaspoon ground cardamom
¼	cup refrigerated or frozen egg product, thawed, or 1 egg, lightly beaten
¾	cup fat-free milk
½	cup sugar
3	tablespoons canola oil
1	teaspoon vanilla
¾	cup coarsely chopped fresh cranberries
¼	cup chopped pistachio nuts

① Preheat oven to 375°F. Line twelve 2½-inch muffin cups with paper bake cups. Lightly coat cups with cooking spray; set aside. In a medium bowl stir together all-purpose flour, whole wheat pastry flour, baking powder, salt, and cardamom. Make a well in the center of the flour mixture; set aside.

② In another medium bowl combine egg, milk, sugar, oil, and vanilla. Add milk mixture all at once to flour mixture. Stir just until moistened (batter should be lumpy). Gently stir in cranberries.

③ Spoon batter into prepared muffin cups, filling each about two-thirds full. Sprinkle with pistachio nuts. Bake for 15 to 18 minutes or until a toothpick inserted in centers comes out clean. Cool in muffin cups on wire rack for 5 minutes. Remove from muffin cups; serve warm.

PER MUFFIN 149 calories; 5 g total fat (0 g sat. fat); 0 mg cholesterol; 126 mg sodium; 24 g carbohydrate; 1 g fiber; 3 g protein

Cinnamon-Almond Chocolate Crescents ✪

MAKES 16 rolls **PREP** 45 minutes **RISE** 1½ hours
BAKE 14 minutes **OVEN** at 375°F

3½	to 4 cups flour
1	package active dry yeast
1¼	cups fat-free milk
3	tablespoons granulated sugar
2	tablespoons vegetable oil spread
1	teaspoon salt
1	teaspoon instant espresso coffee powder
¼	cup refrigerated or frozen egg product, thawed, or 1 egg
½	cup unsweetened cocoa powder
¼	cup flaxseed meal
½	teaspoon ground cinnamon
	Nonstick cooking spray
½	cup chopped almonds, toasted
2	teaspoons powdered sugar (optional)

① In a large mixing bowl combine 1½ cups of the flour and the yeast; set aside. In a small saucepan heat and stir milk, 2 tablespoons of the granulated sugar, the vegetable oil spread, salt, and espresso powder just until warm (120°F to 130°F). Add milk mixture to flour mixture along with egg. Beat with an electric mixer on low for 30 seconds. Beat on high for 3 minutes. Using a wooden spoon, stir in cocoa powder and as much of the remaining flour as you can.

② Turn dough out onto a lightly floured surface. Knead in enough of the remaining flour to make a moderately soft dough that is smooth and elastic (3 to 5 minutes total). Shape dough into a ball. Place in a greased bowl, turning once to grease surface of dough. Cover; let rise in a warm place until double in size (about 1 hour).

③ Punch dough down. Turn dough out onto a lightly floured surface. Divide dough in half. Cover; let rest for 10 minutes. Lightly grease two large baking sheets; set aside. In a small bowl combine flaxseed meal, remaining 1 tablespoon granulated sugar, and cinnamon; set aside.

④ On a lightly floured surface, roll each dough half into a 12-inch circle. Lightly coat circles with cooking spray. Sprinkle evenly with flaxseed meal mixture and almonds. Cut each dough circle into eight wedges. To shape rolls, begin at wide end of each wedge and roll toward the point. Place, point sides down, 2 to 3 inches apart on prepared baking sheets. Cover and let rise in a warm place until nearly double in size (about 30 minutes).

⑤ Preheat oven to 375°F. Bake for 14 to 18 minutes or until rolls sound hollow when tapped. Immediately transfer rolls to wire racks. Cool slightly and serve warm. If desired, sprinkle with powdered sugar just before serving.

PER ROLL 162 calories; 4 g total fat (1 g sat. fat); 0 mg cholesterol; 171 mg sodium; 27 g carbohydrate; 3 g fiber; 6 g protein

Cinnamon Streusel Rolls ✪ (photo page 64)

MAKES 15 rolls **PREP** 45 minutes **RISE** 1½ hours
BAKE 25 minutes **COOL** 5 minutes **OVEN** at 375°F

- 1 cup fat-free milk
- 2 tablespoons packed brown sugar
- 2 tablespoons vegetable oil spread
- 1 teaspoon salt
- ¼ cup warm water (110°F to 115°F)
- 1 package active dry yeast
- ¼ cup refrigerated or frozen egg product, thawed, or 1 egg, lightly beaten
- 4 to 4½ cups all-purpose flour
- ½ cup rolled oats, toasted*
- 2 teaspoons ground cinnamon
- 2 tablespoons vegetable oil spread
- ¼ cup chopped pecans, toasted
- 1 recipe Sour Cream Icing

① In a saucepan heat and stir milk, brown sugar, 2 tablespoons vegetable oil spread, and the salt until warm (110°F to 115°F). In a bowl combine the warm water and yeast; let stand for 10 minutes. Add egg and milk mixture to yeast mixture. Stir in as much of the flour as you can.

② Turn dough out onto a lightly floured surface. Knead in enough of the remaining flour to make a moderately soft dough that is smooth and elastic (3 to 5 minutes total). Shape dough into a ball. Place in a lightly greased bowl, turning once to grease surface of dough. Cover; let rise in a warm place until double in size (about 1 hour). Punch dough down. Turn out onto a lightly floured surface. Cover; let rest for 10 minutes.

③ Meanwhile, lightly grease a 13 x 9 x 2-inch baking pan; set aside. In a medium bowl combine oats and cinnamon. Using your fingers, blend in 2 tablespoons vegetable oil spread until mixture is crumbly. Stir in pecans.

④ Roll dough into a 15 x 8-inch rectangle. Sprinkle with oat mixture, leaving a 1-inch space along one of the long sides. Starting from the long side with topping, roll dough into a spiral. Pinch dough to seal seam. Slice into 15 equal pieces. Arrange pieces, cut sides up, in prepared baking pan. Cover and let rise in a warm place until nearly double in size (about 30 minutes).

⑤ Preheat oven to 375°F. Bake for 25 to 30 minutes or until golden. Cool in pan on a wire rack for 5 minutes. Remove rolls from pan. Drizzle with Sour Cream Icing.

Sour Cream Icing: In a small bowl combine ⅓ cup light sour cream, ¼ cup powdered sugar, ¼ teaspoon vanilla, and enough fat-free milk (2 to 3 teaspoons) to make a drizzling consistency.

*Tip: To toast oats, place rolled oats in a large skillet; heat over medium heat for 4 to 5 minutes or until lightly toasted, stirring frequently.

PER ROLL 196 calories; 5 g total fat (1 g sat. fat); 2 mg cholesterol; 199 mg sodium; 33 g carbohydrate; 2 g fiber; 5 g protein

Banana-Coconut Bread ✪

MAKES 1 loaf (12 slices) **PREP** 30 minutes **BAKE** 45 minutes
COOL 10 minutes **STAND** overnight **OVEN** at 350°F

- 1 cup all-purpose flour
- ½ cup whole wheat pastry flour or whole wheat flour
- 2 teaspoons baking powder
- ½ teaspoon pumpkin pie spice
- ¼ teaspoon baking soda
- ¼ teaspoon salt
- 1 cup mashed bananas (2 to 3 medium)
- ½ cup packed brown sugar
- ⅓ cup unsweetened light coconut milk
- ¼ cup refrigerated or frozen egg product, thawed, or 1 egg, lightly beaten
- 2 tablespoons canola oil
- ¼ cup chopped macadamia nuts or sliced almonds
- ¼ cup raw chip coconut or shredded coconut

① Preheat oven to 350°F. Grease the bottom and ½ inch up the sides of an 8 x 4 x 2-inch loaf pan; set aside.

② In a bowl stir together all-purpose flour, whole wheat flour, baking powder, pumpkin pie spice, baking soda, and salt. Make a well in the center of the flour mixture.

③ In a medium bowl combine mashed bananas, brown sugar, coconut milk, egg, and oil. Add banana mixture all at once to flour mixture; stir just until moistened (batter should be lumpy). Spoon batter into prepared loaf pan. Sprinkle with macadamia nuts and coconut.

④ Bake for 45 to 50 minutes or until a toothpick inserted near center comes out clean, covering loaf loosely with foil during the last 20 minutes of baking to prevent overbrowning. Cool in pan on a wire rack for 10 minutes. Remove from pan. Cool completely on wire rack. Wrap and store overnight before slicing.

PER SLICE 154 calories; 6 g total fat (1 g sat. fat); 0 mg cholesterol; 130 mg sodium; 24 g carbohydrate; 2 g fiber; 3 g protein

Baked Spiced Apple
Mini Doughnuts

Baked Spiced Apple Mini Doughnuts ✪

MAKES 36 mini doughnuts (3 mini doughnuts per serving)
PREP 30 minutes **BAKE** 6 minutes **OVEN** at 325°F

	Nonstick cooking spray
¾	cup all-purpose flour
½	cup whole wheat pastry flour
1	teaspoon apple pie spice
½	teaspoon baking soda
¼	teaspoon baking powder
⅛	teaspoon salt
¾	cup unsweetened applesauce
½	cup sugar
¼	cup refrigerated or frozen egg product, thawed, or 1 egg, lightly beaten
3	tablespoons canola oil
1	recipe Spiced Sugar Coating, Powdered Sugar Coating, or Vanilla Icing

① Preheat oven to 325°F. Coat a 12-indentation, 2-inch doughnut pan with cooking spray; set aside. In a medium bowl combine the flours, apple pie spice, baking soda, baking powder, and salt. Make a well in center of flour mixture; set aside.

② In another medium bowl combine applesauce, sugar, egg, and oil. Add applesauce mixture all at once to flour mixture. Stir until nearly smooth. Spoon batter into a large resealable plastic bag. Cut off a corner and squeeze batter into prepared indentations, filling each about two-thirds full.

③ Bake for 6 to 8 minutes or until tops spring back when lightly touched. Cool in pan on rack for 3 minutes. Remove from pans and place on a wire rack. Coat with Spiced Sugar Coating* or Powdered Sugar Coating,* or drizzle with Vanilla Icing. Repeat with the remaining batter, cooling pan and coating it with cooking spray between each batch.

Spiced Sugar Coating: In a small bowl combine 3 tablespoons granulated sugar, 3 tablespoons ground flaxseed meal, and ¼ teaspoon apple pie spice.

Powdered Sugar Coating: In a small bowl combine 3 tablespoons powdered sugar and 3 tablespoons cornstarch.

Vanilla Icing: Soften 2 tablespoons tub-style light cream cheese in a small bowl. Stir until smooth. Gradually stir in ¼ cup fat-free vanilla yogurt with artificial sweetener until mixture is smooth. Makes ⅓ cup.

*Tip: If coating with Spiced Sugar Coating, coat doughnuts while warm. If coating with Powdered Sugar Coating, coat doughnuts after they are cool. Place coating in a large resealable plastic bag. Add doughnuts in batches. Seal bag and toss gently to coat. Remove doughnuts, shaking off excess coating.

PER SERVING 181 calories; 6 g total fat (0 g sat. fat); 0 mg cholesterol; 126 mg sodium; 31 g carbohydrate; 2 g fiber; 3 g protein

You can still eat doughnuts even if you're trying to be healthy—if they're baked instead of fried.

Ginger Chicken with Rice Noodles, page 70

Pleasing Poultry

menu

Farmer's Market
Salad Platter

Spanish-Style Rice

Baked Chicken Planks
[below]

Banana Cream Pie
Squares

Baked Chicken Planks ★

MAKES 4 servings **PREP** 20 minutes **BAKE** 15 minutes
OVEN at 400°F

Nonstick cooking spray

4 skinless, boneless chicken breast halves
(1 to 1¼ pounds total)

2 egg whites, lightly beaten

1 tablespoon water

1 teaspoon finely shredded lemon peel

½ cup seasoned fine dry bread crumbs

¼ cup finely shredded Parmesan cheese

¼ cup bottled low-calorie barbecue sauce
(optional)

① Preheat oven to 400°F. Lightly coat a large baking sheet with cooking spray; set aside. Cut each chicken breast half lengthwise into three strips.

② In a small bowl beat together egg whites, the water, and lemon peel. In another small bowl stir together bread crumbs and cheese. Dip chicken strips in egg white mixture, then in bread crumb mixture, turning to coat. Arrange strips on prepared baking sheet. Lightly coat tops of chicken strips with additional cooking spray.

③ Bake about 15 minutes or until chicken is no longer pink (170°F), turning once halfway through baking. If desired, serve with barbecue sauce.

PER SERVING 207 calories; 3 g total fat (1 g sat. fat); 70 mg cholesterol; 534 mg sodium; 11 g carbohydrate; 0 g fiber; 32 g protein

Chicken Romano

MAKES 4 servings **PREP** 20 minutes **BAKE** 18 minutes
OVEN at 400°F

Nonstick cooking spray

4 skinless, boneless chicken breast halves
(1¼ to 1½ pounds total)

1 egg white

1 tablespoon water

1¼ cups cornflakes, crushed (about ½ cup)

2 tablespoons grated Romano cheese

½ teaspoon dried Italian seasoning, basil, or
oregano, crushed

⅛ teaspoon black pepper

4 ounces dried multigrain spaghetti

1⅓ cups low-sodium tomato spaghetti sauce

Shaved or grated Romano cheese (optional)

Snipped fresh parsley (optional)

① Preheat oven to 400°F. Lightly coat a 15 x 10 x 1-inch baking pan with cooking spray; set aside. Place each piece of chicken between two pieces of plastic wrap. Pound lightly with the flat side of a meat mallet until about ½ inch thick. Remove plastic wrap.

② In a shallow dish combine egg white and the water. In another shallow dish combine crushed cornflakes, 2 tablespoons cheese, Italian seasoning, and pepper. Dip chicken pieces, one at a time, into egg mixture, then into crumb mixture to coat. Place coated chicken in the prepared baking pan.

③ Bake, uncovered, about 18 minutes or until chicken is tender and no longer pink (170°F). Meanwhile, cook spaghetti according to package directions; drain. In a small saucepan cook spaghetti sauce until heated through, stirring occasionally.

④ To serve, divide cooked spaghetti among four plates. Top with chicken and spaghetti sauce. If desired, sprinkle with additional cheese and parsley.

PER SERVING 362 calories; 6 g total fat (1 g sat. fat); 85 mg cholesterol; 405 mg sodium; 34 g carbohydrate; 4 g fiber; 41 g protein

Baked Chicken Planks

Curry-Lime Chicken Kabobs

Curry-Lime Chicken Kabobs

MAKES 4 servings **PREP** 30 minutes **MARINATE** 4 hours **GRILL** 18 minutes

- 1 pound skinless, boneless chicken breast halves, cut into 1½-inch pieces
- 1 6-ounce carton plain yogurt
- ¼ cup snipped fresh cilantro
- 1 teaspoon finely shredded lime peel
- 2 tablespoons lime juice
- 2 tablespoons olive oil or vegetable oil
- 1 tablespoon honey
- 1 tablespoon Dijon mustard
- 2 cloves garlic, minced
- ½ teaspoon curry powder
- ¼ teaspoon salt
- ¼ teaspoon black pepper
- 2 medium green and/or red sweet peppers, cut into 1-inch pieces
- 1 medium zucchini, cut into ½-inch slices
- 8 yellow or red cherry tomatoes

① Place chicken in a resealable plastic bag set in a large bowl. For marinade, in a small bowl combine yogurt, cilantro, lime peel, lime juice, oil, honey, mustard, garlic, curry powder, salt, and black pepper. Pour marinade over chicken. Seal bag; turn to coat chicken. Marinate in the refrigerator for 4 to 24 hours, turning bag occasionally. Drain chicken, reserving marinade.

② On eight metal skewers, alternately thread chicken, sweet peppers, and zucchini, leaving ¼ inch between pieces. Brush vegetables with reserved marinade.

③ For a charcoal grill, arrange medium-hot coals around a drip pan. Test for medium heat above pan. Place chicken skewers on grill rack over drip pan. Cover and grill for 18 to 20 minutes or until chicken is no longer pink, turning once halfway through grilling and threading a tomato onto each skewer during the last 1 minute of grilling. (For a gas grill, preheat grill. Reduce heat to medium. Adjust for indirect cooking. Grill as above.)

PER SERVING 263 calories; 9 g total fat (2 g sat. fat); 68 mg cholesterol; 336 mg sodium; 15 g carbohydrate; 2 g fiber; 30 g protein

Curried Chicken with Cabbage, Apple, and Onion 30

MAKES 4 servings **START TO FINISH** 30 minutes

- 1 teaspoon curry powder
- ¼ teaspoon salt
- ¼ teaspoon black pepper
- 4 small skinless, boneless chicken breast halves (1 to 1¼ pounds total)
- 2 teaspoons olive oil
- 2 teaspoons butter
- 1 medium onion, sliced and separated into rings
- 3 cups shredded cabbage
- 2 red-skin cooking apples (such as Rome or Jonathan), cored and thinly sliced
- ½ cup apple juice

① In a small bowl combine ½ teaspoon of the curry powder, the salt, and pepper. Sprinkle spice mixture evenly over chicken; rub in with your fingers.

② In a large nonstick skillet heat oil over medium-high heat. Add chicken. Cook for 8 to 12 minutes or until no longer pink (170°F), turning once. Transfer chicken to a platter. Cover to keep warm.

③ Melt butter in the hot skillet. Add onion. Cook about 5 minutes or until onion is tender, stirring occasionally. Stir in cabbage, apple, and apple juice. Sprinkle with the remaining ½ teaspoon curry powder. Cook for 3 to 4 minutes or just until apples and vegetables are tender, stirring occasionally.

④ To serve, divide chicken and cabbage mixture among four dinner plates.

PER SERVING 237 calories; 6 g total fat (2 g sat. fat); 71 mg cholesterol; 231 mg sodium; 19 g carbohydrate; 4 g fiber; 27 g protein

Curry powder comes in different degrees of hotness. Standard curry powder is generally fairly mild. Curry powder labeled "Madras" is generally hotter. Curry powder quickly loses its pungency. Buy it in small quantities and store it no longer than 2 months.

Ginger Chicken with Rice Noodles (photo page 64)

MAKES 4 servings **PREP** 20 minutes **GRILL** 12 minutes

¼   cup very finely chopped green onions
1   tablespoon grated fresh ginger
6   cloves garlic, minced
4   teaspoons olive oil
¼   teaspoon salt
4   small skinless, boneless chicken breast halves (1 to 1¼ pounds total)
4   ounces dried rice noodles
2   cups broccoli florets
1   cup chopped carrots
1   teaspoon finely shredded lime peel
2   tablespoons lime juice
2   to 3 tablespoons snipped fresh cilantro
3   tablespoons coarsely chopped peanuts
     Snipped fresh cilantro (optional)

① For rub, in a small bowl combine green onions, ginger, garlic, 2 teaspoons of the oil, and the salt. Sprinkle evenly over chicken; rub in with your fingers.

② For a charcoal grill, place chicken on the rack of an uncovered grill directly over medium coals. Grill for 12 to 15 minutes or until tender and no longer pink (170°F), turning once halfway through grilling. (For a gas grill, preheat grill. Reduce heat to medium. Place chicken on grill rack over heat. Cover and grill as above.) Thinly slice chicken diagonally; set aside.

③ Meanwhile, in a large saucepan cook rice noodles, broccoli, and carrots in a large amount of boiling water for 3 to 4 minutes or just until noodles are tender; drain. Rinse with cold water; drain again. Using kitchen scissors, snip noodles into short lengths. In a bowl stir together lime peel, lime juice, and the remaining 2 teaspoons oil. Add noodle mixture and the 2 to 3 tablespoons cilantro; toss gently to coat.

④ Divide noodle mixture among four serving bowls; add chicken slices. Sprinkle with peanuts and, if desired, additional cilantro. Serve immediately.

PER SERVING 347 calories; 10 g total fat (2 g sat. fat); 66 mg cholesterol; 351 mg sodium; 34 g carbohydrate; 3 g fiber; 31 g protein

Asian Barbecued Chicken

MAKES 4 servings **PREP** 20 minutes **GRILL** 35 minutes

¼   cup bottled plum sauce
2   tablespoons water
1   tablespoon bottled hoisin sauce
1   tablespoon reduced-sodium soy sauce
1   tablespoon honey
1   teaspoon sesame seeds
1   teaspoon grated fresh ginger
1   clove garlic, minced
⅛   teaspoon five-spice powder
⅛   teaspoon crushed red pepper
4   medium bone-in chicken breast halves, skin removed
1   medium sweet onion (such as Vidalia or Walla Walla), thinly sliced

① In a small saucepan combine plum sauce, the water, hoisin sauce, soy sauce, honey, sesame seeds, ginger, garlic, five-spice powder, and crushed red pepper. Cook over medium heat until bubbly, stirring frequently. Reduce heat. Cover and simmer for 5 minutes. Remove from heat; set aside.

② Tear off four 24 x 18-inch pieces of heavy-duty foil. Fold each in half to make an 18 x 12-inch rectangle. Place a chicken breast half on each foil rectangle. Top with plum sauce mixture and sweet onion.

③ For each packet, bring up two opposite edges of the foil and seal with a double fold. Fold remaining ends to completely enclose the food, allowing space for steam to build.

④ For a charcoal grill, grill foil packets on the rack of an uncovered grill directly over medium coals for 35 to 40 minutes or until done (170°F), turning packets once halfway through cooking and carefully opening packets to check doneness. (For a gas grill, preheat grill. Reduce heat to medium. Place foil packets on grill rack over heat. Cover and grill as above.)

Oven Method: Preheat oven to 350°F. Prepare as directed through Step 3. Bake packets directly on the oven rack for 35 to 40 minutes or until chicken is done (170°F), carefully opening packets to check doneness.

PER SERVING 251 calories; 3 g total fat (1 g sat. fat); 82 mg cholesterol; 410 mg sodium; 21 g carbohydrate; 1 g fiber; 34 g protein

Asian Barbecued Chicken

Cheese-and-Date-Stuffed Chicken Breasts

Cheese and Date Stuffed Chicken Breasts

MAKES 4 servings **PREP** 20 minutes **BAKE** 15 minutes
OVEN at 375°F

2	tablespoons pitted whole dates, chopped
4	small chicken breast halves (2 to 2½ pounds total), skinned
2	ounces goat cheese (chèvre), softened
2	tablespoons slivered almonds, toasted and chopped
1	teaspoon snipped fresh thyme or rosemary
¼	teaspoon salt
¼	teaspoon black pepper
	Nonstick cooking spray
1	tablespoon honey
1	tablespoon lemon juice
	Fresh thyme sprigs (optional)

① Preheat oven to 375°F. Place dates in a small bowl; add enough boiling water to just cover dates. Let stand for 5 minutes. Meanwhile, using a sharp knife, cut a pocket in each chicken breast by cutting horizontally through the thickest portion to, but not through, the opposite side.

② Drain liquid off dates. Add goat cheese, almonds, and thyme to dates and stir until combined. Spoon cheese mixture into pockets in chicken. If necessary, secure openings with wooden toothpicks. Sprinkle chicken with the salt and pepper.

③ Coat an unheated oven-going large nonstick skillet with cooking spray. Heat skillet over medium heat. Add chicken pieces to skillet, meaty sides down. Cook for 3 to 4 minutes or until browned. Turn chicken pieces. Bake for 15 to 18 minutes or until chicken is no longer pink (170°F). Meanwhile, in a small bowl combine honey and lemon juice. Brush over chicken for the last 2 to 3 minutes of baking. If desired, garnish with thyme sprigs.

PER SERVING 250 calories; 6 g total fat (3 g sat. fat); 92 mg cholesterol; 294 mg sodium; 10 g carbohydrate; 1 g fiber; 37 g protein

Goat cheese is a smart choice for those who are trying to eat healthfully. It's lower in both fat and calories than most cow's milk cheeses—and because it has a distinctive flavor, just a little bit goes a long way.

Chicken and Tomato Orzo

MAKES 4 servings **PREP** 25 minutes **COOK** 15 minutes
STAND 5 minutes

1	tablespoon olive oil
12	ounces skinless, boneless chicken breast halves, cut into 1-inch pieces
1	cup sliced fresh mushrooms
½	cup chopped onion
⅔	cup dried orzo pasta (rosamarina)
2	cloves garlic, minced
1	14-ounce can reduced-sodium chicken broth
1	tablespoon no-salt-added tomato paste
¼	teaspoon black pepper
2	medium tomatoes, seeded and cut into wedges
¼	cup pitted kalamata olives, halved
¼	cup crumbled feta cheese (1 ounce)
2	tablespoons snipped fresh parsley

① In a large saucepan heat oil over medium-high heat. Add chicken, mushrooms, and onion; cook and stir until chicken is no longer pink and onion is tender. Stir in orzo and garlic. Cook and stir about 2 minutes more or until orzo is lightly browned. Remove from heat.

② Carefully stir in broth, tomato paste, and pepper. Bring to boiling; reduce heat. Simmer, covered, about 15 minutes or until orzo is tender but still firm. Remove saucepan from heat; stir in tomatoes and olives. Cover and let stand for 5 minutes.

③ Sprinkle each serving with cheese and parsley.

PER SERVING 297 calories; 8 g total fat (2 g sat. fat); 56 mg cholesterol; 476 mg sodium; 29 g carbohydrate; 3 g fiber; 27 g protein

Chicken and Tomato Orzo

Chicken-Pasta Toss ③⓪

MAKES 6 servings **START TO FINISH** 30 minutes

- 12 ounces skinless, boneless chicken breast halves
- 6 ounces dried multigrain or whole grain penne pasta
- 1 tablespoon olive oil or canola oil
- 4 cloves garlic, minced
- ¼ teaspoon crushed red pepper
- 2 cups broccoli florets
- 1 14.5-ounce can diced tomatoes with green pepper, celery, and onions, undrained
- 1 tablespoon snipped fresh basil or oregano
  Shaved Parmesan cheese (optional)

① Cut chicken into bite-size strips; set aside. Cook pasta according to package directions. Drain.

② Meanwhile, in a large nonstick skillet heat oil over medium-high heat. Add garlic and crushed red pepper; cook and stir for 30 seconds. Add broccoli; cook and stir for 3 minutes more. Remove broccoli from skillet.

③ Add chicken to the hot skillet; cook and stir for 3 to 4 minutes or until no longer pink. Return broccoli to the skillet. Add undrained tomatoes and drained pasta. Cook, stirring occasionally, until heated through.

④ To serve, divide pasta mixture among four shallow bowls. Sprinkle with basil and, if desired, Parmesan cheese.

PER SERVING 221 calories; 4 g total fat (0 g sat. fat); 33 mg cholesterol; 242 mg sodium; 27 g carbohydrate; 3 g fiber; 20 g protein

Chicken and Pepper Saute ③⓪

MAKES 4 servings **START TO FINISH** 30 minutes

- ¼ cup all-purpose flour
- ¼ teaspoon salt
- ¼ teaspoon black pepper
- 4 small skinless, boneless chicken breast halves (1 to 1¼ pounds total)
- 1 tablespoon canola oil or olive oil
- 2 small red and/or green sweet peppers, seeded and cut into bite-size strips
- 1 small onion, halved and sliced
- 2 cloves garlic, minced
- 3 plum tomatoes, seeded and chopped (1 cup)
- ⅔ cup dry white wine or reduced-sodium chicken broth
- 1 tablespoon lemon juice
- 2 tablespoons snipped fresh parsley

① In a shallow dish combine flour, salt, and black pepper. Dip chicken breast halves in flour mixture, turning to coat both sides.

② In a large skillet heat oil over medium heat. Add chicken to skillet. Cook for 8 to 12 minutes or until chicken is no longer pink (170°F), turning once. Remove chicken from skillet and cut up, if desired; cover to keep warm.

③ Add sweet peppers, onion, and garlic to skillet. Cook and stir for 2 minutes. Remove skillet from heat. Add tomatoes, wine, and lemon juice to skillet. Return to heat. Bring to boiling; reduce heat. Boil gently about 4 minutes more or until liquid is slightly thickened. Stir in parsley.

④ Serve pepper mixture and chicken in shallow bowls.

PER SERVING 236 calories; 5 g total fat (1 g sat. fat); 66 mg cholesterol; 138 mg sodium; 12 g carbohydrate; 2 g fiber; 28 g protein

With just a few ingredients, mild-tasting chicken transforms into interesting eating.

Chicken Fettuccine Alfredo

{ *menu*

Orange, Lemon, and
Olive Salad with
Cranberry Vinaigrette

Chicken Fettuccine
Alfredo
[below]

Berry Tart with
Lemon Cookie Crust

}

Chicken Fettuccine Alfredo ✪ ③⓪

MAKES 6 servings **START TO FINISH** 30 minutes

6	ounces dried whole wheat fettuccine
12	ounces packaged pretrimmed fresh green beans, trimmed and cut into 1- to 2-inch pieces
1	small onion, halved and thinly sliced (1 cup)
1	tablespoon olive oil
12	ounces chicken breast strips
3	cloves garlic, minced
1	10-ounce container refrigerated light Alfredo pasta sauce
¼	cup chicken broth
½	teaspoon dried thyme, crushed
	Cracked black pepper

① In a 4-quart saucepan cook fettuccine according to package directions, omitting any salt and adding green beans the last 5 to 6 minutes of cooking. Drain and return to pan.

② In a large nonstick skillet cook onion, covered, in hot oil over medium heat for 7 to 8 minutes or until starting to brown, stirring occasionally. Add chicken and garlic. Cook, uncovered, for 4 to 6 minutes more or until chicken is no longer pink and onion is very tender, stirring frequently. Reduce heat to low. Add Alfredo sauce, chicken broth, and thyme. Cook and stir until heated through.

③ Add chicken mixture to cooked fettuccine; toss to coat. Divide fettuccine mixture among six serving plates. Sprinkle with pepper.

PER SERVING 276 calories; 8 g total fat (3 g sat. fat); 45 mg cholesterol; 354 mg sodium; 31 g carbohydrate; 2 g fiber; 22 g protein

Pesto Chicken with Summer Squash ③⓪

MAKES 4 servings **PREP** 5 minutes **BROIL** 10 minutes

1	pound skinless, boneless chicken breast halves
2	small zucchini (12 ounces total), halved lengthwise
2	small yellow summer squash (12 ounces total), halved lengthwise
¼	teaspoon salt
¼	teaspoon black pepper
¼	cup purchased basil pesto

① Preheat broiler. Sprinkle chicken, zucchini, and yellow squash with salt and black pepper. Place chicken breast halves on the unheated rack of a broiler pan. Broil about 5 inches from the heat for 5 minutes.

② Turn chicken; place vegetables on rack with chicken. Spoon pesto over chicken and vegetables. Broil 5 to 7 minutes more or until chicken is no longer pink (170°F) and vegetables are tender.

③ Slice chicken and serve with zucchini and yellow squash pieces.

PER SERVING 230 calories; 9 g total fat (2 g sat. fat); 71 mg cholesterol; 364 mg sodium; 8 g carbohydrate; 3 g fiber; 30 g protein

Pesto Chicken with Summer Squash

Mexican Chicken Salad Stacks

MAKES 4 servings **PREP** 30 minutes **BROIL** 6 minutes

- 4 small skinless, boneless chicken breast halves (1 to 1¼ pounds total)
- 1 teaspoon ancho chile powder or chili powder
- ½ teaspoon dried oregano, crushed
- ½ teaspoon dried thyme, crushed
- ⅛ teaspoon salt
- ⅛ teaspoon black pepper
- 2 tablespoons orange juice
- 1 tablespoon olive oil
- 1 tablespoon white wine vinegar
- 1 teaspoon honey
- 4 cups shredded romaine lettuce
- 1 small avocado, halved, seeded, peeled, and sliced
- 2 oranges, peeled and sectioned
- 1 ounce queso fresco cheese, crumbled, or Monterey Jack cheese, shredded (¼ cup)

① Place each chicken breast half between two pieces of plastic wrap. Using the flat side of a meat mallet, pound chicken until about ½ inch thick. Remove plastic wrap.

② Preheat broiler. In a small bowl stir together chile powder, oregano, thyme, salt, and black pepper. Sprinkle spice mixture evenly over chicken pieces; rub in with your fingers.

③ Place chicken on the unheated rack of a broiler pan. Broil 4 to 5 inches from the heat for 6 to 8 minutes or until chicken is tender and no longer pink (170°F), turning once halfway through broiling. Slice chicken.

④ Meanwhile, in a medium bowl whisk together the orange juice, oil, vinegar, and honey. Add lettuce; toss to coat. To assemble, divide lettuce mixture among four dinner plates. Top with sliced chicken, avocado, and orange sections. Sprinkle with cheese.

PER SERVING 276 calories; 11 g total fat (2 g sat. fat); 68 mg cholesterol; 153 mg sodium; 16 g carbohydrate; 6 g fiber; 30 g protein

Chicken Salad Lettuce Cups ③⓪

MAKES 4 servings **START TO FINISH** 25 minutes

- ¼ cup light mayonnaise
- 2 tablespoons white balsamic vinegar or regular balsamic vinegar
- 1 large clove garlic, minced
- ⅛ teaspoon salt
- 3 cups coarsely chopped, cooked chicken breast
- 1 large red-skin apple, cored and coarsely chopped
- 1 cup coarsely chopped, seeded cucumber
- 1 cup chopped Bibb or Boston lettuce or red leaf lettuce
- ½ cup chopped bottled roasted red sweet peppers
- ¼ cup thinly sliced green onions
- 12 large leaves Bibb or Boston lettuce or red leaf lettuce
- 2 tablespoons pine nuts, toasted

① In a large bowl whisk together mayonnaise, vinegar, garlic, and salt. Add chicken, apple, cucumber, chopped lettuce, roasted sweet peppers, and green onions. Toss to coat.

② To serve, divide lettuce leaves among serving plates. Spoon about ½ cup of the chicken mixture into each lettuce leaf. Sprinkle chicken mixture with pine nuts.

PER SERVING 297 calories; 11 g total fat (2 g sat. fat); 95 mg cholesterol; 257 mg sodium; 14 g carbohydrate; 2 g fiber; 35 g protein

Mexican Chicken Salad Stacks

Chicken Salad Lettuce Cups

Chicken and Noodles

Chicken and Noodles ✪

MAKES 8 servings **PREP** 20 minutes **COOK** 7 hours (low) or 3 hours (high) + 1 to 1½ hours (high) **STAND** 5 minutes

- 3 medium carrots, peeled and cut into 1-inch pieces
- 2 medium parsnips, peeled and cut into 1-inch pieces
- 1 cup pearl onions* or frozen small whole onions
- 2 stalks celery, cut into 1-inch pieces
- 3 whole chicken legs (drumsticks and thighs) (about 3 pounds), skinned
- ½ teaspoon dried thyme, crushed
- ½ teaspoon dried sage, crushed
- 2 cloves garlic, minced
- ½ teaspoon salt
- ¼ teaspoon black pepper
- 2 14-ounce cans reduced-sodium chicken broth
- ¼ cup dry sherry or reduced-sodium chicken broth
- 1 12-ounce package frozen egg noodles
- ¾ cup frozen peas
- 4 or 5 fresh sage leaves (optional)

① In a 5- to 6-quart slow cooker place carrots, parsnips, onions, and celery. Top with chicken; sprinkle with thyme, sage, garlic, salt, and pepper. Pour chicken broth and sherry over all in cooker.

② Cover and cook on low-heat setting for 7 hours or on high-heat setting for 3 hours. Stir in noodles. If using low-heat setting, turn to high-heat setting. Cover and cook for 1 to 1½ hours more or until noodles are tender.

③ Remove chicken. When cool enough to handle, remove meat from bones. Coarsely shred chicken and stir into mixture in cooker. Add peas; cover and let stand for 5 minutes. If desired, garnish with fresh sage leaves.

*Tip: If using fresh onions, cook in enough boiling water to cover for 30 to 60 seconds; drain and rinse with cold water. Cut off root ends and slip off peels.

PER SERVING 301 calories; 5 g total fat (1 g sat. fat); 127 mg cholesterol; 497 mg sodium; 35 g carbohydrate; 4 g fiber; 26 g protein

Cacciatore-Style Chicken

MAKES 6 servings **PREP** 25 minutes **COOK** 7 hours (low) or 3 (high) + 15 minutes (high)

- 2 cups fresh mushrooms, halved or quartered
- 2 medium onions, cut into wedges
- 2 stalks celery, sliced
- 2 medium carrots, chopped
- 4 cloves garlic, minced
- 3 tablespoons quick-cooking tapioca, crushed
- 1 teaspoon dried oregano, crushed
- ¼ teaspoon salt
- ¼ teaspoon black pepper
- 2 bay leaves
- 12 chicken drumsticks (about 3 pounds total), skinned
- ½ cup reduced-sodium chicken broth
- ¼ cup dry white wine or reduced-sodium chicken broth
- 1 14.5-ounce can diced tomatoes, undrained
- 1 medium yellow, red, or green sweet pepper, cut into strips
- ⅓ cup tomato paste
- 2 cups hot cooked spaghetti
- ¼ cup shredded fresh basil

① In a 5- to 6-quart slow cooker combine mushrooms, onions, celery, carrots, and garlic. Sprinkle with tapioca, oregano, salt, black pepper, and bay leaves. Add chicken. Pour broth and wine over all in cooker.

② Cover and cook on low-heat setting for 7 to 8 hours or on high-heat setting for 3 to 3½ hours.

③ If using low-heat setting, turn to high-heat setting. Stir in undrained tomatoes, sweet pepper, and tomato paste. Cover and cook for 15 minutes more. Discard bay leaves.

④ Serve chicken and tomato mixture over hot cooked spaghetti. Top with fresh basil.

PER SERVING 324 calories; 5 g total fat (1 g sat. fat); 98 mg cholesterol; 408 mg sodium; 35 g carbohydrate; 4 g fiber; 33 g protein

Almond Chicken Salad 🕥

MAKES 4 servings **START TO FINISH** 15 minutes

- 12 ounces refrigerated grilled chicken breast strips
- 1 11-ounce can mandarin orange sections, drained
- 1 6-ounce package baby spinach
- 1 cup seedless red grapes, halved
- ¼ cup sliced almonds
- ½ cup orange juice
- 2 tablespoons balsamic vinegar
- 1 tablespoon toasted sesame oil
- ¼ teaspoon black pepper

① In a very large bowl combine chicken, orange sections, spinach, grapes, and almonds. In a screw-top jar combine orange juice, balsamic vinegar, sesame oil, and pepper; shake to combine.

② Pour dressing over salad; toss to combine. Divide among four serving plates. Serve immediately.

PER SERVING 249 calories; 8 g total fat (1 g sat. fat); 55 mg cholesterol; 431 mg sodium; 25 g carbohydrate; 3 g fiber; 22 g protein

Almond Chicken Salad

Wilted Chicken Salad with Pomegranate Dressing 🕥

MAKES 4 servings **START TO FINISH** 30 minutes

- ¾ cup pomegranate juice
- 1 14- to 16-ounce package chicken tenderloins
- 2 tablespoons olive oil
- ½ of a medium red onion, cut lengthwise into thin wedges
- 1 tablespoon snipped fresh oregano or ½ teaspoon dried oregano, crushed
- ¾ teaspoon coarsely ground black pepper
- ½ teaspoon salt
- 2 tablespoons red wine vinegar
- 2 6-ounce packages fresh baby spinach
- ½ cup pomegranate seeds
- ¼ cup slivered almonds, toasted (see tip, page 15)

① In a small saucepan bring pomegranate juice to boiling; boil gently, uncovered, for 5 to 8 minutes or until reduced to ¼ cup. Remove from heat; set aside. Meanwhile, in a 12-inch skillet cook chicken in 1 tablespoon hot oil over medium-high heat for 6 to 8 minutes or until chicken is no longer pink (170°F), turning occasionally. Remove chicken from skillet. Keep warm.

② Add onion, remaining oil, dried oregano (if using), pepper, and salt to skillet; cook for 3 to 5 minutes or until onion is just tender, stirring occasionally. Stir in reduced pomegranate juice and vinegar; bring to boiling. Boil 1 minute. Remove from heat and stir in fresh oregano (if using). Gradually add spinach, tossing just until spinach is wilted.

③ Transfer mixture to a large shallow dish. Top with chicken, pomegranate seeds, and almonds. Serve immediately.

PER SERVING 292 calories; 11 g total fat (2 g sat. fat); 58 mg cholesterol; 425 mg sodium; 21 g carbohydrate; 4 g fiber; 27 g protein

Wilted Chicken Salad with Pomegranate Dressing

Southwestern Chicken and Black Bean Salad

menu

Vegetable Turkey
"Sushi"

Fresh mango wedges

Southwestern
Chicken and Black
Bean Salad
[below]

No-Bake Apricot-
Almond Balls

Southwestern Chicken and Black Bean Salad 30

MAKES 4 servings **START TO FINISH** 25 minutes

10	cups torn romaine lettuce leaves
1	15-ounce can no-salt-added black beans, rinsed and drained
1½	cups chopped cooked chicken or turkey breast
1½	cups red and/or yellow cherry tomatoes, halved
½	cup bottled light Caesar salad dressing
1½	teaspoons chili powder
½	teaspoon ground cumin
½	cup broken baked tortilla chips (about 1 ounce)
2	tablespoons snipped fresh cilantro or parsley
	Fresh cilantro sprigs (optional)

① In a large bowl combine romaine, black beans, chicken, and tomatoes.

② For dressing, in a small bowl whisk together salad dressing, chili powder, and cumin. Pour dressing over salad; toss gently to coat. Sprinkle with tortilla chips and snipped cilantro. If desired, garnish with cilantro sprigs.

PER SERVING 293 calories; 7 g total fat (2 g sat. fat); 55 mg cholesterol; 445 mg sodium; 31 g carbohydrate; 9 g fiber; 26 g protein

Mediterranean Chicken Salad 30

MAKES 6 servings **START TO FINISH** 20 minutes

⅓	cup lemon juice
2	tablespoons snipped fresh mint
2	tablespoons snipped fresh basil
2	tablespoons olive oil
1	tablespoon honey
¼	teaspoon black pepper
5	cups shredded romaine lettuce
2	cups cut-up cooked chicken breast
2	plum tomatoes, cut into wedges
1	15-ounce can garbanzo beans (chickpeas), rinsed and drained
2	tablespoons pitted kalamata olives, quartered
2	tablespoons crumbled reduced-fat feta cheese
12	whole kalamata olives

① For dressing, in a screw-top jar combine lemon juice, mint, basil, oil, honey, and pepper. Cover and shake well.

② Place lettuce on a large platter. Top with chicken, tomatoes, beans, the quartered olives, and cheese. Drizzle with dressing. Garnish individual servings with whole olives.

PER SERVING 252 calories; 9 g total fat (1 g sat. fat); 41 mg cholesterol; 422 mg sodium; 24 g carbohydrate; 5 g fiber; 19 g protein

Mediterranean Chicken Salad

Moo Shu Chicken Wraps ③⓪

MAKES 4 servings **START TO FINISH** 25 minutes
OVEN at 350°F

12	ounces skinless, boneless chicken breast halves
4	7- to 8-inch whole grain tortillas
2	teaspoons canola oil or olive oil
2	cups small broccoli florets
1	medium onion, chopped
½	teaspoon ground ginger
¼	teaspoon ground black pepper
3	tablespoons bottled hoisin sauce

① Preheat oven to 350°F. Cut chicken into thin bite-size strips; set aside. Stack tortillas and wrap in foil. Bake about 10 minutes or until heated through and softened.

② Meanwhile, in a large nonstick skillet heat 1 teaspoon of the oil over medium-high heat. Add broccoli, onion, ginger, and pepper. Cook and stir for 3 to 5 minutes or just until vegetables are tender; remove vegetable mixture from skillet. Add chicken and the remaining 1 teaspoon oil. Cook for 3 to 5 minutes or until chicken is no longer pink, stirring occasionally. Add vegetable mixture and hoisin sauce to chicken mixture. Heat through.

③ To assemble, use a slotted spoon to spoon chicken mixture onto tortillas, placing about ¾ cup of the mixture to one side of each tortilla. Roll up tortillas; cut in half to serve. If desired, serve skillet juices as a dipping sauce.

PER SERVING 294 calories; 7 g total fat (2 g sat. fat); 50 mg cholesterol; 574 mg sodium; 25 g carbohydrate; 12 g fiber; 30 g protein

Chicken-Spinach Focaccia Sandwich ③⓪

MAKES 6 servings **START TO FINISH** 25 minutes

1	8- to 9-inch Italian flatbread (focaccia)
¼	cup light mayonnaise
¼	cup chopped bottled roasted red sweet peppers
1	teaspoon capers, drained (optional)
2	cups fresh baby spinach and/or arugula
2	cups shredded cooked chicken breast (10 ounces)
1	medium tomato, quartered and thinly sliced
¼	cup thinly sliced red onion, cooked if desired
2	hard-cooked eggs, chopped

① Halve focaccia horizontally. Wrap and save the top half for another use. Set the bottom half aside. In a small bowl combine mayonnaise, roasted red peppers, and, if using, capers. Spread mayonnaise mixture over the cut side of the focaccia half.

② Arrange spinach atop the mayonnaise mixture. Top with chicken, tomato, red onion, and eggs. Cut into wedges.

Ciabatta Sandwiches: Substitute 6 multigrain ciabatta rolls, split, for the focaccia. Spread mayonnaise mixture on cut sides of rolls. Fill rolls with spinach, chicken, tomato, red onion, and eggs.

PER SERVING 241 calories; 8 g total fat (2 g sat. fat); 114 mg cholesterol; 132 mg sodium; 21 g carbohydrate; 2 g fiber; 21 g protein

Here are two takes on the chicken sandwich: an Asian-style wrap and open-face Italian focaccia .

Chicken-Spinach Focaccia Sandwich

Mediterranean Chicken Panini

Mediterranean Chicken Panini

MAKES 4 servings **PREP** 25 minutes **COOK** 8 minutes

Olive oil nonstick cooking spray

2 small skinless, boneless chicken breast halves (about 8 ounces total)

1 recipe Dried Tomato-Pepper Spread

4 miniature squares whole wheat bagel bread or multigrain ciabatta rolls, split

1 small zucchini

① Lightly coat an unheated panini griddle, covered indoor electric grill, or large nonstick skillet with nonstick cooking spray. Preheat over medium heat or heat according to manufacturer's directions. Add chicken. If using griddle or grill, close lid and grill for 6 to 7 minutes or until chicken is no longer pink. (If using skillet, cook chicken for 10 to 12 minutes or until chicken is no longer pink, turning once.) Cool chicken slightly; split each chicken piece in half horizontally and cut crosswise into 2-inch-wide slices.

② Spread the Dried Tomato-Pepper Spread on cut sides of bagel bread squares. Place chicken on bottoms of the bread squares. Using a vegetable peeler, cut very thin lengthwise strips from the zucchini. Place zucchini strips on top of the chicken. Place bagel square tops on top of the zucchini, spread sides down. Press down lightly. Lightly coat the top and bottom of each sandwich with nonstick cooking spray.

③ Place sandwiches on griddle, grill, or skillet, adding in batches if necessary. If using griddle or grill, close lid and grill for 2 to 3 minutes or until bread is toasted. (If using skillet, place a heavy saucepan or skillet on top of sandwiches. Cook for 1 to 2 minutes or until bottoms are toasted. Carefully remove saucepan or top skillet—it may be hot. Turn sandwiches; top again with the saucepan or skillet. Cook for 1 to 2 minutes more or until bread is toasted.)

Dried Tomato-Pepper Spread: In a small bowl combine ¼ cup dried tomatoes (not oil-pack) and 2 tablespoons boiling water. Cover and let stand for 5 minutes. Transfer undrained tomato mixture to a food processor. Add ¼ cup drained bottled roasted red sweet peppers; 1 tablespoon balsamic vinegar; ½ teaspoon snipped fresh oregano or ¼ teaspoon dried oregano, crushed; 1 clove garlic, minced; and dash ground black pepper. Cover and process until smooth. Makes ⅓ cup.

PER SERVING 238 calories; 2 g total fat (0 g sat. fat); 33 mg cholesterol; 354 mg sodium; 35 g carbohydrate; 5 g fiber; 21 g protein

Chicken, Kraut, and Apple Panini 30

MAKES 4 sandwiches **PREP** 15 minutes **COOK** 12 minutes

1 cup canned sauerkraut

8 slices very thin sliced firm-texture whole wheat bread

Nonstick cooking spray

12 ounces sliced, cooked chicken breast

1 apple, cored and thinly sliced

4 thin slices reduced-fat Swiss cheese (2 to 3 ounces total)

① Place sauerkraut in a colander and rinse with cold water. Drain well, using a spoon to press out excess liquid. Set aside.

② Lightly coat one side of each bread slice with cooking spray. Place four bread slices, coated sides down, on a work surface. Top with chicken, sauerkraut, apple slices, and cheese. Top with the remaining four bread slices, coated sides up.

③ Coat an unheated grill pan or large skillet with cooking spray. Preheat over medium-low heat for 1 to 2 minutes. Add sandwiches, in batches if necessary. Place a heavy skillet on sandwiches. Cook over medium-low heat for 6 to 8 minutes or until bottoms are toasted. Using hot pads, carefully remove top skillet. Turn sandwiches and top again with skillet. Cook for 6 to 8 minutes more or until bottoms are toasted.

PER SANDWICH 283 calories; 7 g total fat (3 g sat. fat); 79 mg cholesterol; 457 mg sodium; 21 g carbohydrate; 4 g fiber; 34 g protein

Cooked chicken breast is a handy thing to have in your refrigerator for quick sandwiches, salads, and pasta dishes. Chicken cooked on the bone will be juicier and more flavorful. Roast bone-in, skin on chicken breast at 350°F for 35 to 45 minutes, or until the juices run clear and a meat thermometer inserted into the breast registers 160°F. Let the chicken cool slightly, then wrap it tightly and refrigerate it. Use it within 3 to 4 days.

Glazed Roast Turkey

MAKES 16 servings **PREP** 20 minutes **ROAST** 2¾ hours
STAND 15 minutes **OVEN** at 325°F

- 1 **10- to 12-pound turkey**
- 1 **tablespoon butter, melted**
- 1 **recipe Raspberry Glaze**

   Halved fresh plum, red seedless grapes, arugula, and/or fresh herb sprigs (optional)

① Preheat oven to 325°F. Rinse inside of the turkey; pat dry with paper towels. Pull the neck skin to the back; fasten with a skewer.

② Tuck the ends of the drumsticks under the band of skin across the tail. If there is no band of skin, tie the drumsticks securely to the tail. Twist wing tips under the back.

③ Place turkey, breast side up, on a rack in a shallow roasting pan. Brush with the butter. If desired, insert an ovenproof meat thermometer into the center of an inside thigh muscle not touching bone. Cover turkey loosely with foil.

④ Roast for 2¾ to 3 hours Remove foil the last 45 minutes of roasting. Cut band of skin or string between drumsticks so thighs cook evenly. During the last 15 minutes of roasting, brush twice with the Raspberry Glaze. Roast until the thermometer registers 180°F. (The juices should run clear and drumsticks should move easily in their sockets.)

⑤ Remove turkey from oven. Let stand for 15 to 20 minutes before carving. Remove and discard skin before consuming. If desired, garnish platter with plums, grapes, arugula, and/or herb sprigs. Carve turkey.

Raspberry Glaze: In a small saucepan combine ½ cup low-sugar raspberry preserves, 1 tablespoon lemon juice, 1 teaspoon dry mustard, 1 teaspoon Worcestershire sauce, and ¼ teaspoon black pepper. Heat and stir until preserves are melted.

PER SERVING 225 calories; 4 g total fat (1 g sat. fat); 138 mg cholesterol; 94 mg sodium; 3 g carbohydrate; 0 g fiber; 42 g protein

Indian-Spiced Chicken Pitas 30

MAKES 4 pita halves **START TO FINISH** 30 minutes

- 1 **cup plain fat-free yogurt**
- 1 **teaspoon garam masala**
- ½ **teaspoon bottled hot pepper sauce**
- ¼ **teaspoon salt**
- 12 **ounces skinless, boneless chicken breast halves, cut into bite-size strips**

   Nonstick cooking spray

- 2 **whole wheat pita bread rounds, halved crosswise**
- 1 **cup refrigerated mango and papaya slices, drained and coarsely chopped**
- 1 **tablespoon tiny fresh mint leaves**

① In a small bowl combine yogurt, garam masala, hot pepper sauce, and salt. Pour three-fourths of the mixture into a resealable plastic bag; refrigerate the remaining yogurt mixture until serving time. Add chicken to plastic bag. Seal bag; turn to coat chicken. Marinate in the refrigerator for 15 minutes. Drain chicken, discarding marinade.

② Coat an unheated large nonstick skillet with cooking spray. Heat skillet over medium heat. Add chicken to hot skillet; cook about 5 minutes or until tender and no longer pink, turning once.

③ To serve, divide chicken evenly among pita bread halves. Drizzle with the reserved yogurt mixture. Top with chopped fruit; sprinkle with fresh mint.

PER PITA HALF 249 calories; 2 g total fat (0 g sat. fat); 51 mg cholesterol; 430 mg sodium; 32 g carbohydrate; 3 g fiber; 26 g protein

Indian-Spiced Chicken Pitas

Rosemary Turkey with Vegetables

Rosemary Turkey with Vegetables

MAKES 8 servings **PREP** 30 minutes **COOK** 9 hours (low) or 4½ hours (high) **STAND** 15 minutes

- 1 teaspoon dried rosemary, crushed
- ¼ teaspoon salt
- ¼ teaspoon garlic powder
- ¼ teaspoon dried thyme, crushed
- ¼ teaspoon black pepper
- 1 2¾- to 3¼-pound turkey breast half with bone, skinned
- 1 tablespoon vegetable oil
- Nonstick cooking spray
- 1¼ pounds new potatoes, halved
- 8 medium carrots, peeled and cut into 2- to 3-inch long pieces
- 1 large onion, cut into ½-inch wedges
- ½ cup reduced-sodium chicken broth
- ¼ cup flour
- Black pepper

① In a small bowl combine rosemary, salt, garlic powder, thyme, and pepper. Rub over turkey breast. In a very large skillet brown turkey breast on all sides in hot oil over medium heat. Lightly coat the inside of a 5- to 6-quart slow cooker with cooking spray. In prepared cooker place potatoes, carrots, onion, and ¼ cup of the broth. Top with turkey.

② Cover and cook on low-heat setting for 9 hours or on high-heat setting for 4½ hours.

③ Transfer turkey to a cutting board. Cover turkey loosely with foil and let stand for 15 minutes. Meanwhile, using a slotted spoon, transfer vegetables to a serving platter; keep warm.

④ For gravy, strain cooking liquid into a 2-cup measure. Add enough additional broth to equal 1¾ cups. In a medium saucepan whisk together the remaining ¼ cup broth and the flour until smooth; whisk in remaining broth mixture. Cook and stir over medium heat until thickened and bubbly; cook and stir for 1 minute more. Season to taste with additional pepper.

⑤ Cut turkey meat off the bone. Slice turkey and serve with vegetables and gravy.

PER SERVING 256 calories; 3 g total fat (0 g sat. fat); 76 mg cholesterol; 272 mg sodium; 23 g carbohydrate; 4 g fiber; 34 g protein

Barbecue-Glazed Turkey ★ ③⓪

MAKES 4 servings **START TO FINISH** 30 minutes

- ⅔ cup reduced-sugar ketchup
- ¼ cup orange juice
- 3 tablespoons snipped fresh cilantro
- 1 clove garlic, minced
- ¼ teaspoon ground cumin
- ¼ teaspoon black pepper
- 1 large turkey breast tenderloin (about 1 pound), split in half horizontally; or 4 skinless, boneless chicken breast halves (1- to 1¼-pounds total); or 4 small bone-in chicken breast halves (1¾- to 2-pounds total), skin removed

① For sauce, in a small saucepan combine ketchup, orange juice, 2 tablespoons of the cilantro, the garlic, cumin, and black pepper. Bring to boiling over medium heat, stirring constantly. Reduce heat. Simmer, uncovered, for 5 minutes. Transfer ⅓ cup of the sauce to a small bowl and keep remaining sauce warm.

② For a charcoal grill, place turkey pieces on the rack of an uncovered grill directly over medium coals. Grill for 12 to 16 minutes (12 to 15 minutes for boneless, skinless chicken and 25 to 35 minutes for bone-in chicken) or until no longer pink, turning once halfway through grilling and brushing with the ⅓ cup sauce for the last 2 minutes of grilling. (For a gas grill, preheat grill. Reduce heat to medium. Place poultry pieces on grill rack over heat. Cover and grill as above.)

③ Slice turkey and serve with remaining sauce. Garnish with remaining 1 tablespoon cilantro.

PER SERVING 163 calories; 1 g total fat (0 g sat. fat); 70 mg cholesterol; 298 mg sodium; 10 g carbohydrate; 0 g fiber; 28 g protein

The difference in the fat and calorie content of skinless vs. skin-on chicken breast is significant. A 4-ounce chicken breast with skin has about 190 calories and 11 grams of fat. A comparably sized skinless breast has 120 calories and about 1.5 grams of fat.

Turkey and Pasta Primavera ✪

MAKES 6 servings **PREP** 15 minutes **COOK** 4 hours (low) or 2 hours (high)

- 1½ **pounds turkey breast tenderloins or skinless, boneless chicken breast halves, cut into 1-inch pieces**
- 1 **16-ounce package frozen stir-fry vegetables (sugar snap peas, carrots, onions, and mushrooms)**
- 1½ **teaspoons dried basil, oregano, or Italian seasoning, crushed**
- 1 **10-ounce container refrigerated light Alfredo pasta sauce**
- 8 **ounces dried linguine or spaghetti, broken**
- ¼ **cup shredded Parmesan cheese (1 ounce)**

① In a 3½- to 5-quart slow cooker combine turkey and frozen vegetables. Sprinkle with basil. Stir in Alfredo sauce.

② Cover and cook on low-heat setting for 4 hours or on high-heat setting for 2 hours.

③ Cook pasta according to package directions; drain. Stir pasta into mixture in slow cooker. Sprinkle individual servings with Parmesan cheese.

PER SERVING 373 calories; 7 g total fat (4 g sat. fat); 84 mg cholesterol; 394 mg sodium; 36 g carbohydrate; 2 g fiber; 38 g protein

Turkey and Pasta Primavera

Ham and Apricot Turkey Spirals

MAKES 6 servings **PREP** 30 minutes **ROAST** 35 minutes
OVEN at 425°F

- 2 **12-ounce turkey breast tenderloins**
- 4 **ounces thinly sliced reduced-sodium cooked ham**
- ½ **cup finely chopped dried apricot halves**
- 2 **tablespoons Dijon mustard**
- 1 **tablespoon snipped fresh rosemary or 1 teaspoon dried rosemary, crushed**
- 1 **teaspoon honey**
- 1 **egg white, beaten**
- ½ **teaspoon black pepper**
- ½ **cup whole wheat panko (Japanese-style bread crumbs)**

① Preheat oven to 425°F. Using a sharp knife, split each tenderloin almost in half horizontally, cutting to within ½ inch of the opposite side. Open each tenderloin like a book and place each between two pieces of plastic wrap so it lays almost flat. Using the flat side of a meat mallet, pound each tenderloin to ½ inch thick. Remove top pieces of plastic wrap.

② Layer ham slices evenly on turkey pieces. In a small bowl combine apricots, mustard, rosemary, and honey. Spread evenly over ham. Starting with a short side, roll up each turkey piece into a spiral. Tie each spiral at 2-inch intervals with clean 100-percent-cotton kitchen string.

③ Brush egg white over turkey spirals. Sprinkle with pepper. Sprinkle panko in an even layer on a piece of waxed paper. Roll each turkey spiral in the panko to coat. Place turkey spirals on a rack in a shallow roasting pan. Roast for 35 minutes or until turkey is no longer pink (170°F). Slice to serve.

PER SERVING 214 calories; 2 g total fat (1 g sat. fat); 81 mg cholesterol; 372 mg sodium; 13 g carbohydrate; 2 g fiber; 34 g protein

Although panko bread crumbs are relatively new to the shelves of American grocery stores, they have hit big. These Japanese-style bread crumbs have a flakier, lighter, and airier texture than regular bread crumbs, so they get crispier when cooked. Panko is used in Japanese cooking as a breading for fried foods.

Ham and Apricot Turkey Spirals

Tandoori-Style Turkey Kabobs

menu

Tomato-Basil Soup
with Toasted Cheese
Croutons

Green Beans
with Peppers and
Pineapple

Tandoori-Style
Turkey Kabobs
[below]

Tandoori-Style Turkey Kabobs

MAKES 4 servings **PREP** 30 minutes **MARINATE** 4 hours
GRILL 14 minutes **CHILL** 1 hour

- ¾ cup plain low-fat yogurt
- 2 teaspoons finely shredded lime peel
- 3 tablespoons lime juice
- 1 tablespoon bottled minced garlic
- 1 tablespoon bottled minced ginger
- ½ of a fresh serrano chile pepper, seeded and finely chopped (see tip, page 8)
- 2 teaspoons paprika
- 1 teaspoon ground cumin
- ½ teaspoon ground coriander
- ½ teaspoon ground cardamom
- ¼ teaspoon cayenne pepper
- 1½ pounds turkey tenderloins, cut into 1½-inch cubes
- 1 recipe Carrot-Radish Salad
  Lime wedges (optional)
  Green onion strips (optional)

① For marinade, in a small bowl combine yogurt, lime peel, lime juice, minced garlic, minced ginger, serrano pepper, paprika, cumin, coriander, cardamom, and cayenne. Mix well.

② Place turkey cubes in a large resealable plastic bag set in a shallow dish. Add marinade. Seal bag and turn to coat cubes well. Marinate in the refrigerator for at least 4 hours or up to 24 hours. Prepare Carrot-Radish Salad; cover and chill.

③ Remove turkey from marinade, discarding marinade. Thread cubes on bamboo skewers that have been soaked in water for at least 30 minutes, leaving ¼-inch space between cubes.

④ For a charcoal grill, place kabobs on the rack of an uncovered grill directly over medium coals. Grill for 14 to 16 minutes or until turkey is no longer pink (170°F). (For a gas grill, preheat grill. Reduce heat to medium. Place kabobs on grill rack over heat. Cover and grill as above.) Serve immediately with Carrot-Radish Salad, and, if desired, lime wedges and onion strips.

Carrot-Radish Salad: In a medium bowl stir together 1½ cups shredded carrots; ½ cup shredded radishes; ½ cup golden raisins; and 2 green onions, bias-sliced. In a small bowl stir together ⅓ cup plain low-fat yogurt, ¼ teaspoon finely shredded lime peel, 1 tablespoon lime juice, 1 tablespoon honey, and ¼ teaspoon ground coriander. Stir into carrot mixture until well combined. Cover and chill 1 to 4 hours. Stir well before serving. Makes 2½ cups.

PER SERVING 346 calories; 3 g total fat (1 g sat. fat); 109 mg cholesterol; 170 mg sodium; 34 g carbohydrate; 4 g fiber; 47 g protein

Honey-Cranberry Turkey ✪

MAKES 4 servings **START TO FINISH** 20 minutes

- 2 turkey breast tenderloins, halved horizontally (about 1¼ pounds)
  Salt and ground black pepper
- 1 tablespoon butter
- ½ cup whole cranberry sauce
- 1 tablespoon honey
- ½ teaspoon finely shredded lemon peel
- 1 tablespoon lemon juice

① Sprinkle turkey with salt and pepper. In a very large skillet cook turkey in hot butter over medium-high heat for 12 to 15 minutes or until no longer pink (170°F), turning once. Transfer to a serving platter; reserve drippings in skillet. Cover turkey to keep warm.

② Stir cranberry sauce, honey, lemon peel, and lemon juice into reserved drippings in skillet. Cook and stir until heated through. Spoon over turkey.

PER SERVING 252 calories; 4 g total fat (2 g sat. fat); 96 mg cholesterol; 246 mg sodium; 18 g carbohydrate; 0 g fiber; 35 g protein

Bacon-Wrapped Turkey Tenderloins

MAKES 6 servings **PREP** 20 minutes **GRILL** 12 minutes
COOK 10 minutes

- 1   teaspoon black pepper
- 1   teaspoon ground coriander
- 1   teaspoon ground cumin
- ½   teaspoon salt
- 3   turkey breast tenderloins (2 to 2½ pounds)
- 12   slices packaged ready-to-serve cooked bacon
- 3   medium plums, pitted and sliced
- ¼   cup plum jelly
- 1   tablespoon cider vinegar

① In a small bowl stir together pepper, coriander, cumin, and salt; sprinkle mixture evenly on both sides of turkey tenderloins. Cut each tenderloin crosswise into quarters to make 12 total pieces. Wrap each turkey piece with a slice of bacon and secure with a wooden toothpick.

② For a charcoal grill, grill turkey on the rack of an uncovered grill directly over medium coals for 12 to 15 minutes or until turkey is no longer pink (170°F), turning once halfway through grilling. (For a gas grill, preheat grill. Reduce heat to medium. Place turkey on grill rack over heat. Cover and grill as directed.)

③ Meanwhile, in a medium saucepan stir together plum slices, jelly, and vinegar. Bring to boiling over medium heat, stirring frequently; reduce heat. Simmer, uncovered, for 4 to 6 minutes or until plums are tender. Serve over turkey pieces.

PER 2-PIECE SERVING 270 calories; 5 g total fat (2 g sat. fat); 104 mg cholesterol; 453 mg sodium; 14 g carbohydrate; 1 g fiber; 40 g protein

Turkey Steaks with Spinach, Pears, and Blue Cheese ㉚

MAKES 4 servings **START TO FINISH** 20 minutes

- 2   turkey breast tenderloins (1 to 1¼ pounds)
- 1   teaspoon dried sage, crushed
      Salt
      Freshly ground black pepper
- 2   tablespoons butter
- 1   6-ounce package fresh baby spinach
- 1   large pear, cored and thinly sliced
- ¼   cup crumbled blue cheese

① Horizontally split tenderloins to make four ½-inch-thick steaks. Rub turkey with sage; sprinkle with salt and pepper. In extra-large skillet cook steaks in 1 tablespoon of the butter over medium-high heat 14 to 16 minutes or until no longer pink (170°F), turning once. (Reduce heat to medium if turkey browns too quickly.) Remove from skillet. Add spinach to skillet. Cook and stir just until wilted.

② Meanwhile, in small skillet cook pear slices in remaining 1 tablespoon butter over medium to medium-high heat, stirring occasionally for 5 minutes or until tender and lightly browned.

③ Serve steaks with spinach and pears. Top with blue cheese.

PER SERVING 240 calories; 9 g total fat (5 g sat. fat); 92 mg cholesterol; 380 mg sodium; 8 g carbohydrate; 2 g fiber; 31 g protein

If you don't like the stems on spinach leaves and don't want to spend the time destemming them, buy baby spinach. The stems are so tender—if they are present at all—they're not the least bit bothersome.

Ginger Turkey Mini Burgers

Ginger Turkey Mini Burgers ③⓪

MAKES 4 burgers **PREP** 20 minutes **GRILL** 10 minutes

- 1 egg white, beaten, or 2 tablespoons refrigerated or frozen egg product, thawed
- 2 tablespoons snipped fresh cilantro
- 2 tablespoons quick-cooking rolled oats
- 2 cloves garlic, minced
- ½ teaspoon grated fresh ginger
- ¼ teaspoon reduced-sodium soy sauce
- 8 ounces uncooked ground turkey breast
- ¼ of a medium avocado
- 2 tablespoons chopped tomato
- 4 whole grain cocktail-size hamburger buns, split

  Thinly sliced red onion and/or torn dark leafy greens (optional)

① In a medium bowl combine egg white, cilantro, rolled oats, half of the garlic, the ginger, and soy sauce. Add ground turkey breast; mix well. Using damp hands, shape into four ¾-inch-thick patties.

② For a charcoal grill, grill patties on the greased rack of an uncovered grill directly over medium coals for 10 to 12 minutes or until done (165°F), turning once. (For a gas grill, preheat grill. Reduce heat to medium. Place patties on grill rack over heat. Cover and grill as above.)

③ Meanwhile, in a small bowl use a fork to coarsely mash avocado. Stir in chopped tomato and the remaining garlic. To serve burgers, spread a thin layer of the avocado mixture on bottom half of each bun. Add patties. If desired, top with red onion and/or dark leafy greens.

PER BURGER 165 calories; 3 g total fat (0 g sat. fat); 35 mg cholesterol; 142 mg sodium; 15 g carbohydrate; 4 g fiber; 20 g protein

Turkey Mango Sandwich ③⓪

MAKES 4 sandwiches **START TO FINISH** 15 minutes

- ¼ cup light mayonnaise or salad dressing
- 1 green onion, thinly sliced
- 1 tablespoon snipped fresh cilantro
- ½ teaspoon finely shredded lime peel
- 4 1-ounce slices whole grain bakery bread
- 1 cup fresh spinach leaves
- 6 ounces packaged lower-sodium sliced, cooked turkey breast
- 1 medium mango, seeded, peeled, and thinly sliced
- 1 small fresh poblano chile pepper,* stemmed, seeded, and thinly sliced into rings

① In a small bowl stir together mayonnaise, green onion, cilantro, and lime peel. Spread on one side of each of the bread slices.

② To assemble, layer four bread slices, spread sides up, with spinach, turkey, mango slices, and pepper slices. Serve on plates with knife and fork.

*Tip: Because chile peppers contain volatile oils that can burn your skin and eyes, avoid direct contact with them as much as possible. When working with chile peppers, wear plastic or rubber gloves. If your bare hands do touch the peppers, wash your hands and nails well with soap and warm water.

PER SANDWICH 211 calories; 7 g total fat (1 g sat. fat); 28 mg cholesterol; 470 mg sodium; 25 g carbohydrate; 4 g fiber; 14 g protein

A perfectly seasoned turkey breast slider is fun food you can eat with a perfectly clear conscience.

menu

Crusty whole grain
bread

Orange, Fennel, and
Olive Salad with
Cranberry Vinaigrette

Lasagna Roll-Ups
[below]

Lemon Meringue
Sandwich Cookies

Lasagna Roll-Ups with Roasted Pepper-Tomato Sauce ★

MAKES 8 servings **PREP** 45 minutes **BAKE** 35 minutes
STAND 10 minutes **OVEN** at 350°F

1	medium red onion
	Nonstick cooking spray
4	cloves garlic, minced
1	14½-ounce can no-salt-added diced tomatoes, undrained
1	12-ounce jar roasted red sweet peppers, drained
¼	cup no-salt-added tomato paste
2	tablespoons balsamic vinegar
8	dried whole wheat or regular lasagna noodles (7 ounces)
8	ounces smoked turkey sausage, quartered lengthwise and thinly sliced
1	medium red sweet pepper, cut into thin strips
1	medium zucchini, quartered lengthwise and thinly sliced
2	egg whites, lightly beaten
1⅓	cups shredded reduced-fat mozzarella cheese (about 5½ ounces)
1	cup light ricotta cheese
¼	cup snipped fresh basil or 2 teaspoons dried basil, crushed

① Preheat oven to 350°F. Chop half of the red onion. Cut remaining half into thin slivers; set aside. For Pepper-Tomato Sauce, lightly coat an unheated medium nonstick skillet with cooking spray; heat skillet over medium heat. Add chopped red onion and the garlic; cook for 5 minutes or until onion is tender, stirring occasionally. Transfer onion mixture to a blender or food processor. Add undrained tomatoes, roasted peppers, tomato paste, and vinegar. Cover and blend or process until smooth. Set aside.

② Cook lasagna noodles according to package directions. Drain; rinse with cold water. Drain again. Place noodles in a single layer on a sheet of foil; set aside.

③ Lightly coat an unheated large nonstick skillet with cooking spray; heat over medium heat. Add red onion slivers, the sausage, and sweet pepper. Cook for 5 minutes or until onion is tender, stirring occasionally. Add zucchini; cook for 3 to 4 minutes more or until zucchini is just softened, stirring occasionally.

④ In a medium bowl combine egg whites, 1 cup of the mozzarella cheese, the ricotta cheese, and 2 tablespoons of the fresh basil (if using) or 2 teaspoons dried basil (if using).

⑤ Lightly coat a 3-quart rectangular baking dish with nonstick spray. Spread half of the tomato sauce in prepared dish; set aside. Spread a scant ¼ cup of the cheese mixture on each lasagna noodle. Top with a scant ⅓ cup of the turkey mixture. Starting from a short end, roll up each noodle. Place the lasagna rolls, seam sides down, in the prepared baking dish. Spoon the remaining sauce over the lasagna rolls.

⑥ Bake, covered, about 30 minutes or until lasagna rolls are heated through. Uncover and sprinkle with remaining ⅓ cup mozzarella cheese. Bake, uncovered, 5 to 10 minutes more or until cheese melts. Let stand for 10 minutes before serving. Sprinkle each serving with some of the remaining 2 tablespoons fresh basil (if using).

PER SERVING 268 calories; 8 g total fat (3 g sat. fat); 33 mg cholesterol; 455 mg sodium; 30 g carbohydrate; 6 g fiber; 19 g protein

If you don't have time to make the Roasted Red Pepper-Tomato Sauce, substitute a 16-ounce jar of prepared marinara or fire-roasted tomato pasta sauce.

Lasagna Roll-Ups with Roasted Pepper-Tomato Sauce

Mushroom-Sausage Flatbreads

Mushroom-Sausage Flatbreads

MAKES 8 servings **PREP** 25 minutes **BAKE** 13 minutes
OVEN at 425°F

- 6 ounces uncooked turkey Italian sausage links, with casings removed
- 2 cups sliced fresh mushrooms
- 2 medium tomatoes, chopped
- ½ of a 16-ounce package frozen (yellow, green, and red) peppers and onion stir-fry vegetables (2 cups)
- 3 cloves garlic, minced
- 4 multigrain low-fat wraps
- ¾ cup shredded reduced-fat mozzarella cheese (3 ounces)
- 2 tablespoons shredded Parmesan cheese (1 ounce)

① Preheat oven to 425°F. In a large skillet cook sausage and mushrooms over medium heat until sausage is browned and mushrooms are tender, stirring to break up sausage as it cooks. Drain mixture in a colander; set aside.

② In the same large skillet cook chopped tomatoes, stir-fry vegetables, and garlic over medium heat until boiling, stirring occasionally. Reduce heat. Simmer, uncovered, about 5 minutes or until most of the liquid is evaporated and vegetables are very tender, stirring occasionally.

③ Place wraps on a very large baking sheet. Bake for 5 minutes. Spread vegetable mixture over hot wraps. Top with sausage mixture and tomatoes. Sprinkle with mozzarella and Parmesan cheeses. Bake for 8 to 10 minutes or until cheese is melted and just starting to brown. To serve, cut each flatbread into quarters.

PER SERVING 128 calories; 5 g total fat (2 g sat. fat); 20 mg cholesterol; 440 mg sodium; 12 g carbohydrate; 6 g fiber; 12 g protein

Baked Cavatelli

Baked Cavatelli ✪

MAKES 8 servings **PREP** 30 minutes **BAKE** 40 minutes
COOK 15 minutes **OVEN** at 350°F

- 8 ounces dried cavatelli or dried multigrain penne pasta
- 12 ounces uncooked ground Italian turkey sausage
- 1 cup chopped eggplant or zucchini
- 1 cup chopped fresh cremini or button mushrooms
- 1 medium red sweet pepper, chopped
- 1 medium onion, chopped
- 2 cloves garlic, minced
- 1 14.5-ounce can no-salt-added diced tomatoes, undrained
- 1 8-ounce can no-salt-added tomato sauce
- ¼ cup snipped fresh basil or 1 tablespoon dried basil, crushed
- 1 tablespoon snipped fresh oregano or 1 teaspoon dried oregano, crushed
- ¼ teaspoon salt
- ¼ teaspoon black pepper
- 1 cup shredded reduced-fat Italian blend cheese (4 ounces)

① Preheat oven to 350°F. Cook pasta according to package directions, omitting any salt or oil. Drain; set aside.

② Meanwhile, in a very large skillet cook sausage, eggplant, mushrooms, sweet pepper, onion, and garlic over medium heat just until sausage is browned and vegetables are tender, stirring to break up sausage as it cooks. Drain off any fat and discard. Add tomatoes, tomato sauce, dried basil (if using), dried oregano (if using), salt, and black pepper. Bring to boiling; reduce heat. Simmer, covered, for 10 minutes, stirring occasionally. Stir in fresh basil (if using) and fresh oregano (if using).

③ In a very large bowl stir together pasta and sausage mixture. Spoon mixture into a 3-quart baking dish.

④ Bake, covered, for 35 to 40 minutes or until heated through. Uncover; sprinkle with cheese. Bake 5 minutes more or until cheese is melted.

PER SERVING 254 calories; 7 g total fat (3 g sat. fat); 34 mg cholesterol; 492 mg sodium; 30 g carbohydrate; 3 g fiber; 17 g protein

Honey-Ancho-Glazed
Beef Tenderloin, page 115

Marvelous Meats

Pot Roast and Onions ✪

MAKES 8 servings **PREP** 15 minutes
COOK 8 hours (low) or 4 hours (high)

1   2- to 2½-pound boneless beef chuck pot roast

2   medium onions, cut into wedges

1   8-ounce can tomato sauce

¼   cup water

1   tablespoon yellow mustard

1   to 2 teaspoons prepared horseradish

½   teaspoon salt

¼   teaspoon black pepper

2   tablespoons flour

2   tablespoons cold water

① Trim fat from roast. If necessary, cut roast to fit in a 3½- or 4-quart slow cooker. Place roast in the cooker. Top with onions. In a small bowl combine tomato sauce, the ¼ cup water, the mustard, horseradish, salt, and pepper; pour over all in cooker.

② Cover and cook on low-heat setting for 8 to 10 hours or on high-heat setting for 4 to 5 hours.

③ Transfer meat and onions to a serving platter. Cover to keep warm. For sauce, transfer cooking liquid to a small saucepan. Skim off fat. In a small bowl stir together flour and the 2 tablespoons cold water. Stir into mixture in saucepan. Cook and stir over medium heat until thickened and bubbly; cook and stir for 1 minute more. Serve with roast and onions.

PER SERVING 170 calories; 5 g total fat (2 g sat. fat); 67 mg cholesterol; 376 mg sodium; 5 g carbohydrate; 1 g fiber; 25 g protein

Pot Roast with Chipotle-Fruit Sauce

MAKES 8 servings **PREP** 15 minutes
COOK 10 hours (low) or 5 hours (high)

1   2½- to 3-pound boneless beef chuck pot roast

2   teaspoons garlic-pepper seasoning

1   7-ounce package mixed dried fruit

½   cup water

1   tablespoon finely chopped canned chipotle peppers in adobo sauce

1   tablespoon cold water

2   teaspoons cornstarch

Couscous (optional)

① Trim fat from roast. If necessary, cut roast to fit in a 3½- or 4-quart slow cooker. Sprinkle both sides of roast with garlic-pepper seasoning. Place roast in the cooker. Add fruit, the ½ cup water, and chipotle peppers.

② Cover and cook on low-heat setting for 10 to 11 hours or on high-heat setting for 5 to 5½ hours.

③ Transfer roast and fruit to a serving platter. Cover to keep warm. Transfer cooking liquid to a bowl or measuring cup; skim off fat. In a medium saucepan combine the 1 tablespoon cold water and cornstarch; add cooking liquid. Cook and stir over medium heat until thickened and bubbly; cook and stir for 2 minutes more. To serve, spoon sauce over meat and fruit, and, if desired, couscous.

PER SERVING 251 calories; 6 g total fat (2 g sat. fat); 62 mg cholesterol; 189 mg sodium; 17 g carbohydrate; 1 g fiber; 32 g protein

The aroma of pot roast bubbling away in the slow cooker is like a big, warm hug and welcome home.

Pot Roast with Chipotle-Fruit Sauce

Cowboy Beef

{

menu

Iceberg wedge with
low-fat blue cheese
dressing

Roasted Garlic Herb
Bread

Cowboy Beef
[below]

Layered Brownies

}

Cowboy Beef ✪

MAKES 8 servings **PREP** 10 minutes
COOK 10 hours (low) or 5 hours (high)

1 2- to 2½-pound boneless beef chuck pot roast

1 15-ounce can chili beans in chili gravy, undrained

1 11-ounce can whole kernel corn with sweet peppers, drained

1 10-ounce can diced tomatoes and green chiles, undrained

1 to 2 teaspoons finely chopped canned chipotle peppers in adobo sauce

① Trim fat from meat. If necessary, cut meat to fit into a 3½- or 4-quart slow cooker. Place meat in the cooker. In a medium bowl stir together the beans, drained corn, undrained tomatoes, and the chipotle peppers. Pour bean mixture over meat in cooker.

② Cover and cook on low-heat setting for 10 to 12 hours or on high-heat setting for 5 to 6 hours.

③ Transfer meat to a cutting board. Pull meat into pieces and arrange in a shallow serving bowl. Using a slotted spoon, spoon bean mixture into bowl with meat. Drizzle some of the cooking liquid over meat and bean mixture to moisten.

PER SERVING 223 calories; 5 g total fat (2 g sat. fat); 50 mg cholesterol; 473 mg sodium; 14 g carbohydrate; 4 g fiber; 29 g protein

Rib Roast with Dijon-Sour Cream Sauce

MAKES 8 servings **PREP** 25 minutes **MARINATE** 6 hours
ROAST 1¾ hours **STAND** 15 minutes **OVEN** at 350°F

1 4-pound beef rib roast, trimmed of fat

¾ cup dry red wine or lower-sodium beef broth

¼ cup lemon juice

2 teaspoons dried rosemary, crushed

2 teaspoons dried marjoram, crushed

¼ teaspoon garlic salt

1 recipe Dijon-Sour Cream Sauce

① Place meat in a large resealable plastic bag set in a shallow dish. For marinade, in a small bowl combine wine, lemon juice, rosemary, marjoram, and garlic salt. Pour over meat. Seal bag; turn to coat meat. Marinate in the refrigerator for at least 6 hours or up to 24 hours, turning bag occasionally. Drain meat, discarding marinade.

② Preheat oven to 350°F. Place roast, fat side up, in an ungreased 13 x 9 x 2-inch baking pan or 3-quart baking dish. Insert an ovenproof meat thermometer into the center of the roast. The thermometer should not touch the bone.

③ Roast, uncovered, until desired doneness. Allow 1¾ to 2¼ hours for medium-rare (135°F) or 2¼ to 2¾ hours for medium (150°F). Cover with foil; let stand 15 minutes. The temperature of the meat after standing should be 145°F for medium-rare or 160°F for medium. Carve roast and serve with Dijon-Sour Cream Sauce.

Dijon-Sour Cream Sauce: In a small bowl stir together one 8-ounce carton light sour cream, 2 tablespoons Dijon mustard, and ½ teaspoon sodium-free lemon-pepper seasoning. Cover and chill until serving time.

PER SERVING 258 calories; 12 g total fat (6 g sat. fat); 80 mg cholesterol; 263 mg sodium; 2 g carbohydrate; 0 g fiber; 30 g protein

Brisket in Onion-Ale Sauce

MAKES 10 servings   **PREP** 15 minutes
COOK 10 hours (low) or 5 hours (high)

1	3½- to 4-pound fresh beef brisket
2	medium onions, thinly sliced and separated into rings
1	bay leaf
1	12-ounce can beer
¼	cup bottled chili sauce
1	clove garlic, minced
½	teaspoon dried thyme, crushed
¼	teaspoon salt
¼	teaspoon black pepper
2	tablespoons cornstarch
2	tablespoons cold water

① Trim fat from meat. If necessary, cut meat to fit into a 3½- to 5-quart slow cooker. In the cooker combine onions and bay leaf; add meat. In a medium bowl combine beer, chili sauce, garlic, thyme, salt, and pepper. Pour over meat in cooker.

② Cover and cook on low-heat setting for 10 to 11 hours or high-heat setting for 5 to 5½ hours.

③ Using a slotted spoon, transfer meat and onions to a serving platter. Slice meat across the grain; cover and keep warm. Discard bay leaf.

④ For sauce, pour enough of the cooking liquid into a 4-cup glass measuring cup to equal 2½ cups; skim off fat. (Discard the remaining cooking liquid.) In a medium saucepan combine cornstarch and the cold water; stir in the 2½ cups cooking liquid. Cook and stir over medium heat until thickened and bubbly. Cook and stir for 2 minutes more. Serve meat and onions with sauce.

PER SERVING 283 calories; 12 g total fat (4 g sat. fat); 79 mg cholesterol; 266 mg sodium; 6 g carbohydrate; 1 g fiber; 33 g protein

Brisket is an inexpensive cut of beef that requires a long, slow cooking time to get really tender—perfect for the slow cooker. You'll find it as either flat cut or point cut. The flat cut is leaner, but the point cut has more flavor because it has a little more fat.

Espresso-Rubbed Beef Sirloin with Mushroom-Onion au Jus

MAKES 12 servings   **PREP** 25 minutes   **COOK** 30 minutes
ROAST 45 minutes   **STAND** 10 minutes   **OVEN** at 425°F

1	tablespoon instant espresso coffee powder
2	teaspoons dried thyme, crushed
1	teaspoon paprika
½	teaspoon garlic powder
½	teaspoon salt
½	teaspoon freshly ground black pepper
1	3-pound boneless beef top sirloin steak, cut 2 inches thick, trimmed of fat
2	tablespoons canola oil
2	large sweet onions, halved and thinly sliced
12	ounces fresh button or cremini mushrooms, sliced (4½ cups)
2	14-ounce cans lower-sodium beef broth
1	teaspoon instant espresso coffee powder

① Preheat oven to 425°F. In a small bowl combine the 1 tablespoon espresso powder, thyme, paprika, garlic powder, salt, and pepper. Sprinkle evenly on both sides of steak, rubbing in with your fingers.

② In a very large skillet heat 1 tablespoon of the oil over medium-high heat. Add steak. Cook for 5 to 10 minutes or until browned, turning to brown both sides.

③ Transfer steak to a rack in a shallow roasting pan. Insert an ovenproof meat thermometer so tip is centered in thickest part of beef, not resting in fat. Roast steak in oven, uncovered, for 45 to 55 minutes or until meat thermometer registers 140°F for medium-rare.

④ Meanwhile, add remaining oil to the same skillet. Add onions. Cook over medium heat for 10 minutes, stirring occasionally. Add mushrooms and cook for 10 to 15 minutes more or until onions are very tender and lightly browned, stirring occasionally. Remove from heat and add beef broth and the 1 teaspoon espresso powder. Bring to boiling over high heat, stirring to scrape up any browned bits from bottom of skillet. Reduce heat; simmer, uncovered, for 10 minutes to blend flavors.

⑤ Transfer steak to a cutting board. Cover tightly with foil; let stand for 10 minutes. The temperature of the meat after standing should be 145°F. Slice steak across the grain and serve with mushroom-onion mixture.

Per serving 209 calories; 8 g total fat (2 g sat. fat); 53 mg cholesterol; 291 mg sodium; 7 g carbohydrate; 1 g fiber; 27 g protein

Espresso-Rubbed Beef Sirloin with
Mushroom-Onion au Jus

Fennel and Lime-Crusted Beef Tenderloin

Fennel and Lime-Crusted Beef Tenderloin

MAKES 12 servings **PREP** 40 minutes **ROAST** 50 minutes **STAND** 10 minutes **OVEN** at 425°F

- ¼ cup fennel seeds
- ¼ cup snipped fresh tarragon
- ¼ cup finely shredded lime peel (5 or 6 limes)
- 3 tablespoons olive oil
- 2 teaspoons freshly ground black pepper
- ½ teaspoon salt
- 1 3-pound center-cut beef tenderloin, trimmed of fat
- 1 pound peeled onions (such as cipollini onions, pearl onions, and/or cut-up yellow onions)
- 3 cups sliced fennel
- ½ cup dry red wine or lower-sodium beef broth
- 1 pound fresh green beans, trimmed

① In a bowl combine fennel seeds, tarragon, lime peel, 2 tablespoons of the oil, the pepper, and salt. Coat tenderloin with the seed mixture. Place meat on a nonreactive tray; cover loosely with foil. Refrigerate for at least 30 minutes or up to 1 hour.

② Preheat oven to 425°F. Place meat on a roasting rack in an ungreased 13 x 9 x 2-inch baking pan. Return any coating left on tray to meat. In a bowl toss together onions and 1½ teaspoons of the oil. Place onions alongside the meat on half of the pan. Roast, uncovered, for 30 minutes.

③ Meanwhile, toss together fennel and the remaining 1½ teaspoons oil. Stir onions. Add fennel alongside the meat on the other half of pan. Roast, uncovered, for 20 to 30 minutes more or until thermometer registers 135°F for medium-rare.

④ Transfer meat to a cutting board; cover with foil. Let stand for 10 to 15 minutes. The temperature of the meat after standing should be 145°F for medium-rare.

⑤ For the sauce, pour any drippings from the pan or dish into a small saucepan, scraping and including the crusty browned bits. Add red wine; cook until bubbly, stirring constantly to dissolve browned bits.

⑥ To serve, cook green beans in a small amount of boiling water about 5 minutes or until crisp-tender. Drain. Toss green beans with the sauce. Arrange beans on serving platter. Slice tenderloin and arrange on beans. Serve with roasted onions and fennel.

PER SERVING 248 calories; 11 g total fat (3 g sat. fat); 57 mg cholesterol; 167 mg sodium; 9 g carbohydrate; 4 g fiber; 25 g protein

Honey-Ancho-Glazed Beef Tenderloin (photo page 106)

MAKES 10 servings **PREP** 20 minutes **GRILL** 40 minutes **STAND** 10 minutes

- 2 to 3 cups cherry wood chips
- ¼ cup honey
- 1 tablespoon ground ancho chile pepper or chili powder
- 2 teaspoons canola oil
- 1 2½- to 3-pound beef tenderloin, trimmed of fat
- 1 teaspoon black pepper
- ½ teaspoon salt

  Watercress, key limes, kumquats, and/or tangerine wedges (optional)

① At least 1 hour before grilling, soak wood chips in enough water to cover. Drain before using.

② In a small saucepan combine honey and chile pepper. Heat and stir over medium-low heat until heated through. Remove from heat; stir in oil. Brush some of the mixture over the beef tenderloin. Season beef with black pepper and salt.

③ For a charcoal grill arrange preheated coals around a drip pan. Test for medium heat above the drip pan. Sprinkle wood chips over coals. Pour 1 inch of water into the drip pan. Place roast on grill rack directly over the drip pan. Cover and grill for 40 to 50 minutes or until an instant-read thermometer inserted near the center of the roast registers 135°F, brushing with honey mixture occasionally during the first 20 minutes of grilling. Discard any remaining honey mixture.

④ Remove meat from grill; cover with foil. Let stand for 10 to 15 minutes before slicing. The temperature after standing should be 145°F for medium-rare. Transfer to a serving platter. If desired, garnish with watercress, key limes, kumquats, and/or tangerine wedges.

*Tip: To grind ancho chile peppers, place dried, seeded, and stemmed ancho chile peppers in a blender. Cover and blend until ground.

PER SERVING 168 calories; 7 g total fat (2 g sat. fat); 52 mg cholesterol; 164 mg sodium; 7 g carbohydrate; 0 g fiber; 18 g protein

Wine-Glazed Steak ⏱

MAKES 2 servings **START TO FINISH** 30 minutes

- 1 boneless beef top sirloin steak, cut ½ to ¾ inch thick (8 to 10 ounces total)
- 2 teaspoons olive oil
- 1 cup sliced fresh mushrooms
- 2 cloves garlic, minced
- ⅛ teaspoon crushed red pepper
- ¼ cup dry red wine or low-calorie cranberry juice*
- 2 tablespoons balsamic vinegar
- 1 tablespoon reduced-sodium soy sauce
- 1 teaspoon honey*

① Trim fat from steak; cut steak into two equal portions. In a large skillet heat oil over medium-high heat. Add steaks. Reduce heat to medium; cook for 10 to 13 minutes or until desired doneness (145°F for medium-rare or 160°F for medium), turning steaks occasionally. If steaks brown too quickly, reduce heat to medium-low. Transfer steaks to a serving platter; keep warm.

② Add mushrooms, garlic, and crushed red pepper to skillet; cook and stir for 2 minutes. Remove skillet from heat. Carefully add wine. Return to heat. Boil gently, uncovered, for 3 to 5 minutes or until most of the liquid is evaporated. Add balsamic vinegar, soy sauce, and honey; return to simmering. Cook and stir about 2 minutes or until slightly thickened. Spoon over steaks.

*Tip:** If using the cranberry juice option, omit the honey.

PER SERVING 267 calories; 9 g total fat (2 g sat. fat); 48 mg cholesterol; 336 mg sodium; 11 g carbohydrate; 1 g fiber; 28 g protein

Wine-Glazed Steak

Tropical Fiesta Steak

MAKES 4 servings **PREP** 30 minutes **MARINATE** 30 minutes
GRILL 14 minutes

- ⅓ cup mango, pear, or apricot nectar
- ¼ cup snipped fresh mint or basil or 1 tablespoon dried mint, crushed
- ¼ cup sliced green onions
- 3 tablespoons Pickapeppa sauce or spicy brown mustard
- 1 tablespoon cooking oil
- 1 tablespoon lemon juice
- ⅛ teaspoon salt
  Several dashes bottled hot pepper sauce
- 1 1-pound boneless beef top sirloin steak, cut 1 inch thick
- ½ cup chopped red sweet pepper
- ½ cup chopped red apple or pear
- ½ cup chopped peeled mango, unpeeled peach, or unpeeled nectarine
- ¼ cup sliced celery
  Fresh mint sprigs (optional)

① For marinade, in a small bowl stir together nectar, snipped or dried mint, 2 tablespoons of the green onions, the Pickapeppa sauce, oil, lemon juice, salt, and hot pepper sauce. Remove ¼ cup of the marinade; cover and refrigerate until serving time.

② Place steak in a resealable plastic bag set in a shallow bowl. Pour remaining marinade over steak. Seal bag; turn to coat steak. Marinate in the refrigerator for 12 to 24 hours, turning bag occasionally.

③ For fruit relish, in a small bowl combine sweet pepper, apple, mango, celery, and the remaining 2 tablespoons green onions. Cover and refrigerate for up to 24 hours.

④ Drain steak, discarding marinade. Place steak on rack of an uncovered grill directly over medium coals. Grill until desired doneness, turning once halfway through grilling. Allow 14 to 18 minutes for medium-rare (145°F) or 18 to 22 minutes for medium (160°F).

⑤ To serve, thinly slice steak across the grain. Serve with fruit relish and drizzle with the reserved ¼ cup marinade. If desired, garnish with mint sprigs.

PER SERVING 211 calories; 7 g total fat (2 g sat. fat); 48 mg cholesterol; 166 mg sodium; 10 g carbohydrate; 1 g fiber; 26 g protein

Tropical Fiesta Steak

Philly Steak Sandwiches

Philly Steak Sandwiches ✪

MAKES 4 servings **PREP** 20 minutes **BROIL** 17 minutes

- 1   12-ounce boneless beef top sirloin steak, cut 1 inch thick
- ½   teaspoon garlic-pepper seasoning
  Nonstick cooking spray
- 2   medium red and/or green sweet peppers, seeded and cut into thin strips
- 1   large onion, thinly sliced and separated into rings
- 4   whole wheat frankfurter buns, split
- ½   cup shredded reduced-fat cheddar or reduced-fat Monterey Jack cheese (2 ounces)

① Preheat broiler. Trim fat from steak. Sprinkle steak with garlic-pepper seasoning. Place seasoned steak on the unheated rack of a broiler pan. Broil 3 to 4 inches from heat until desired doneness. Allow 15 to 17 minutes for medium-rare doneness (145°F) or 20 to 22 minutes for medium doneness (160°F).

② Meanwhile, coat an unheated very large nonstick skillet with nonstick cooking spray. Preheat skillet over medium heat. Add sweet peppers and onion. Cover and cook for 5 minutes. Uncover and cook about 5 minutes more or just until tender, stirring occasionally.

③ Place split buns on a large baking sheet. Broil 4 to 5 inches from heat for 1 to 2 minutes or until lightly toasted. Remove bun tops from baking sheet; set aside. Slice steak into bite-size strips. Divide steak strips and sweet pepper mixture among bun bottoms. Sprinkle with cheese. Broil 4 to 5 inches from the heat for 1 to 2 minutes or until cheese is melted. Top with bun tops.

PER SERVING 295 calories; 8 g total fat (3 g sat. fat); 46 mg cholesterol; 416 mg sodium; 29 g carbohydrate; 4 g fiber; 27 g protein

With calorie counts for a restaurant-style Philly cheese steak ranging from 500 to 1,200, this 295-calorie version makes for guilt-free noshing.

Pepper-Steak Quesadillas

MAKES 4 servings **PREP** 30 minutes **MARINATE** 30 minutes **COOK** 6 minutes **OVEN** at 300°F

- 8   ounces beef sirloin steak or boneless beef top round steak
- 1   teaspoon finely shredded lime peel
- 2   cloves garlic, minced
- ¼   teaspoon ground cumin
- 4   7- to 8-inch whole wheat tortillas
  Nonstick cooking spray
- 1   medium red sweet pepper, seeded and cut into thin bite-size strips
- ¼   cup thinly sliced green onions
- ½   cup chopped peeled jicama
- 2   ounces reduced-fat Monterey Jack cheese, shredded (½ cup)
- 8   lime wedges (optional)

① Trim fat from beef. Thinly slice beef across the grain into bite-size strips. In a medium bowl combine steak strips, lime peel, garlic, and cumin. Cover and marinate in the refrigerator for 30 minutes to 4 hours.

② Preheat oven to 300°F. Lightly coat one side of each tortilla with nonstick cooking spray. Place tortillas, coated sides down, on a tray or clean work surface. Coat an unheated extra-large nonstick skillet with nonstick cooking spray. Preheat skillet over medium heat. Add steak strips, sweet pepper, and green onions to hot skillet. Cook for 3 to 5 minutes or until steak is browned and pepper is crisp-tender, stirring occasionally. Remove from heat. Stir in jicama.

③ Divide steak and pepper mixture among tortillas, placing the mixture on one half of each tortilla. Sprinkle beef mixture with cheese. Fold tortillas over filling; press down lightly.

④ Coat a clean, unheated extra-large nonstick skillet or griddle with nonstick cooking spray. Preheat skillet or griddle over medium-high heat; reduce heat to medium. Cook quesadillas, half at a time, in hot skillet or griddle about 3 minutes or until tortillas are browned, turning once halfway through cooking. Place quesadillas on a baking sheet; keep warm in the oven while cooking the remaining quesadillas.

⑤ Cut each quesadilla into three wedges. If desired, serve with lime wedges.

PER SERVING 267 calories; 9 g total fat (4 g sat. fat); 34 mg cholesterol; 475 mg sodium; 20 g carbohydrate; 11 g fiber; 25 g protein

Grilled Steak Fajitas ✪

MAKES 4 servings **PREP** 25 minutes **GRILL** 20 minutes

- 3 red, yellow and/or green sweet peppers, sliced
- 1 large onion, sliced
- 1 tablespoon olive oil
- 1½ teaspoons fajita seasoning
- 3 cloves garlic, minced
- 1 pound boneless beef top sirloin steak, cut 1 inch thick
- ¼ teaspoon crushed red pepper (optional)
- 4 8-inch whole wheat tortillas
  Snipped fresh cilantro (optional)
  Purchased salsa (optional)
  Sour cream (optional)

① Fold a 36 x 18-inch piece of heavy foil in half crosswise. Place sweet peppers and onion in the center of the foil. Drizzle with oil; sprinkle with ½ teaspoon of the fajita seasoning and the garlic. Bring up the opposite edges of the foil; seal with a double fold. Fold in remaining edges, leaving space for steam to build. Set aside.

② Sprinkle the remaining 1 teaspoon fajita seasoning and the crushed red pepper on both sides of steak; rub in with your fingers. For a charcoal grill, place steak and the vegetable packet on the rack of an uncovered grill directly over medium coals. Grill steak until desired doneness, turning once halfway through grilling. Allow 14 to 18 minutes for medium-rare (145°F) or 18 to 22 minutes for medium (160°F). Remove steak and keep warm. Grill vegetables about 20 minutes or until tender, turning once halfway through grilling. (For a gas grill, preheat grill. Reduce heat to medium. Place steak and vegetable packet on grill rack over heat. Cover and grill as above.)

③ Meanwhile, wrap tortillas in foil. Place tortilla packet next to steak on grill rack; grill about 10 minutes or until tortillas are heated through, turning once halfway through grilling. Slice meat into thin bite-size strips. Divide meat among tortillas; top with vegetables. Roll up. If desired, serve with cilantro, salsa, and sour cream.

PER SERVING 356 calories; 12 g total fat (3 g sat. fat); 48 mg cholesterol; 464 mg sodium; 25 g carbohydrate; 13 g fiber; 34 g protein

Garlic Steaks with Nectarine Relish

MAKES 2 servings **PREP** 20 minutes **MARINATE** 30 minutes **GRILL** 4 minutes

- 1 boneless beef top loin steak, cut 1 inch thick (about 10 ounces)
- 3 cloves garlic, thinly sliced
- ⅛ teaspoon salt
- ⅛ teaspoon black pepper
- 1 medium onion, coarsely chopped
- 1 teaspoon olive oil
- 1 tablespoon cider vinegar
- 1 teaspoon honey
- 1 small nectarine, pitted and chopped
- 1 teaspoon snipped fresh mint
  Fresh mint sprigs (optional)

① Trim fat from steak. With the tip of a paring knife, make small slits in steak; insert half of the garlic into slits. Wrap steak in plastic wrap; chill for 30 minutes. Sprinkle with salt and pepper.

② Meanwhile, for relish, in a large nonstick skillet cook onions and remaining garlic in hot oil over medium heat for 5 to 10 minutes or until onions are golden, stirring occasionally. Stir in vinegar and honey. Stir in nectarine and the snipped mint; heat through.

③ Preheat indoor electric grill. Place steaks on the grill rack. If using a covered grill, close lid. Grill until steaks are desired doneness. (For a covered grill, allow 4 to 6 minutes for medium-rare (145°F) or 6 to 8 minutes for medium (160°F). For an uncovered grill, allow 8 to 12 minutes for medium-rare (145°F) or 12 to 15 minutes for medium (160°F), turning once halfway through grilling.) If using a charcoal grill place steak on grill rack directly over medium coals. Grill to desired doneness, turning once. Allow 10 to 12 minutes for medium-rare (145°F) and 12 to 15 minutes for medium (160°F). If using a gas grill, preheat grill. Reduce temperature to medium. Place steak on grill rack over heat; cover and grill as above. Serve the steaks with relish. If desired, garnish with mint sprigs.

PER SERVING 274 calories; 13 g total fat (4 g sat. fat); 60 mg cholesterol; 200 mg sodium; 15 g carbohydrate; 2 g fiber; 24 g protein

Garlic Steaks with Nectarine Relish

Grilled Beef and Avocado Salad
with Cilantro-Lime Vinaigrette

Grilled Beef and Avocado Salad with Cilantro-Lime Vinaigrette

MAKES 4 servings **PREP** 20 minutes **MARINATE** 24 hours **GRILL** 17 minutes

- 12   ounces beef flank steak
- ½   cup bottled reduced-calorie clear Italian salad dressing
- ½   teaspoon finely shredded lime peel
- ¼   cup lime juice
- 2   tablespoons snipped fresh cilantro
- ¼   cup chopped onion
- ¼   teaspoon salt
- ¼   teaspoon black pepper
- 6   cups torn mixed salad greens
- 2   small red and/or yellow tomatoes, cut into wedges
- 1   small avocado, halved, seeded, peeled, and sliced (optional)

① Score both sides of steak in a diamond pattern by making shallow diagonal cuts at 1-inch intervals. Place steak in a resealable plastic bag set in a shallow dish. Set aside.

② In a screw-top jar combine salad dressing, lime peel, lime juice, and cilantro. Cover and shake well. Pour half of the salad dressing mixture into a small bowl; cover and chill until serving time. Add onion to remaining salad dressing mixture in jar. Cover and shake well; pour mixture over steak in bag. Seal bag; turn to coat steak. Marinate in the refrigerator for 24 hours, turning bag occasionally.

③ Drain beef, discarding marinade. Sprinkle with salt and pepper. Grill steak on the rack of an uncovered grill directly over medium coals for 17 to 21 minutes for medium (160°F), turning once. [Or place steak on the unheated rack of a broiler pan. Broil 3 to 4 inches from the heat for 15 to 18 minutes for medium (160°F), turning once.]

④ To serve, thinly slice beef across grain. Arrange salad greens, tomatoes, and, if desired, avocado on 4 salad plates. Top with beef. Drizzle reserved dressing over individual salads.

PER SERVING 164 calories; 7 g total fat (3 g sat. fat); 35 mg cholesterol; 477 mg sodium; 6 g carbohydrate; 2 g fiber; 20 g protein

Espresso-Marinated Flank Steak

MAKES 4 servings **PREP** 20 minutes **MARINATE** 4 hours **GRILL** 17 minutes

- 1   1½- to 2-pound beef flank steak
- 1   cup espresso coffee, chilled
- ¼   cup finely chopped red onion
- 2   tablespoons packed brown sugar
- 2   tablespoons Dijon mustard
- 2   tablespoons balsamic vinegar
- 1   tablespoon olive oil
- 1   teaspoon cracked black pepper
- 2   cloves garlic, minced
- 1   teaspoon instant espresso coffee powder
- ¼   teaspoon salt
- ¼   teaspoon black pepper

① Trim fat from steak. Score both sides of steak in a diamond pattern by making shallow diagonal cuts at 1-inch intervals. Place steak in a large resealable plastic bag set in a shallow dish.

② For marinade, in a small bowl combine coffee, onion, brown sugar, mustard, vinegar, oil, cracked pepper, and garlic. Pour marinade over steak in bag; seal bag. Turn to coat steak. Marinate in the refrigerator for 4 to 12 hours, turning bag occasionally.

③ Drain steak, discarding marinade. Sprinkle espresso coffee powder evenly over both sides of steak; rub in with your fingers.

④ For a charcoal grill, grill steak on the rack of an uncovered grill directly over medium coals for 17 to 21 minutes for medium (160°F), turning once halfway through grilling. (For a gas grill, preheat grill. Reduce heat to medium. Place steak on grill rack over heat. Cover and grill as directed.)

⑤ Sprinkle steak with salt and pepper. Thinly slice steak diagonally across the grain.

PER STEAK 271 calories; 12 g total fat (5 g sat. fat); 60 mg cholesterol; 253 mg sodium; 1 g carbohydrate; 0 g fiber; 36 g protein

French Dip Sandwiches ✪

MAKES 8 servings **PREP** 30 minutes
COOK 9 hours (low) or 4½ hours (high)

- 2   medium sweet onions (such as Vidalia, Maui, or Walla Walla), cut into ½-inch-thick slices and separated into rings (2 cups)
- 1   2½- to 3-pound fresh beef brisket or boneless beef bottom round roast
- 2   cloves garlic, minced
- 1   teaspoon dried marjoram, rosemary, or thyme, crushed
- ¼   teaspoon black pepper
- 1   14.5-ounce can lower-sodium beef broth
- ¼   cup water
- 2   tablespoons Worcestershire sauce
- 4   large whole grain hoagie rolls
- 1   recipe Roasted Pepper Relish and/or Garlic-Chive Mustard Spread (optional)

① Place onions in a 4- to 5-quart slow cooker. Trim fat from beef. If necessary, cut roast in half to fit into cooker. Place roast on onions. Sprinkle with garlic, marjoram, and pepper. Pour broth, the water, and Worcestershire sauce over all.

② Cover and cook on low-heat setting for 9 to 10 hours for brisket or 8 to 9 hours for bottom round or on high-heat setting for 4½ to 5 hours for brisket or 4 to 4½ hours for bottom round.

③ Transfer meat to a cutting board; thinly slice across the grain, removing any visible fat as you slice. Using a slotted spoon, remove onions from cooker. Cut rolls crosswise in half. Split halves horizontally. If desired, toast the rolls. Divide sliced beef and onion slices among roll bottoms. If desired, add Roasted Pepper Relish and/or Garlic-Chive Mustard Spread as directed below. Add roll tops. Skim fat from cooking juices in cooker; pass juices for dipping sandwiches.

PER SERVING 320 calories; 12 g total fat (4 g sat. fat); 88 mg cholesterol; 382 mg sodium; 20 g carbohydrate; 3 g fiber; 33 g protein

Roasted Pepper Relish: Preheat oven to 425°F. Line a 15 x 10 x 1-inch baking pan with foil; set aside. Quarter, stem, and seed 1 large red sweet pepper. Quarter, stem, and seed 1 medium fresh poblano pepper (see tip, page 8). Place pepper quarters, cut sides down, in the prepared pan. Roast, uncovered, for 20 to 25 minutes or until pepper skins are charred. Wrap foil around pepper quarters to fully enclose; let stand until cool enough to handle. Using a sharp knife, peel off and discard skin from peppers. Chop pepper pieces and combine in a bowl. Stir in 2 tablespoons thinly sliced green onions, 2 tablespoons chopped pepperoncini salad peppers, 1 teaspoon olive oil, and ⅛ teaspoon black pepper. Spoon over beef and onions on sandwiches before adding roll tops. Makes ¾ cup.

Garlic-Chive Mustard Spread: In a bowl combine ¼ cup light sour cream; ¼ cup Dijon mustard; 1 tablespoon snipped fresh chives; and 1 clove garlic, minced. Spread on cut side of roll tops before placing on top of beef and onions. Makes ½ cup.

This popular sandwich made with slow-cooked beef is perfect party fare for a casual gathering.

Cilantro-Lime Flank Steak

Cilantro-Lime Flank Steak

MAKES 4 servings PREP 15 minutes MARINATE 1 hour
GRILL 17 minutes

- 1   pound beef flank steak
- ¼   cup water
- ¼   cup lime juice
- 6   cloves garlic, minced
- 2   tablespoons snipped fresh cilantro
- 2   teaspoons snipped fresh oregano or ½ teaspoon dried oregano, crushed
- ¼   teaspoon ground chipotle chile powder or chili powder
- ¼   teaspoon salt
- ⅛   teaspoon black pepper
- 1   cup purchased pico de gallo
       Whole wheat tortillas (optional)
       Lime wedges (optional)

① Trim fat from steak. Score both sides of steak in a diamond pattern by making shallow diagonal cuts at 1-inch intervals. Place steak in a resealable plastic bag set in a shallow dish.

② For marinade, in a small bowl stir together the water, lime juice, garlic, cilantro, oregano, and chipotle chile powder. Pour marinade over steak in bag. Seal bag; turn to coat steak. Marinate in the refrigerator for 1 to 2 hours, turning bag occasionally.

③ Drain steak, reserving marinade. Sprinkle steak with salt and pepper. Place steak on the rack of an uncovered grill directly over medium coals. Grill for 17 to 21 minutes or until medium doneness (160°F), turning once and brushing with the reserved marinade halfway through grilling. Discard any remaining marinade. (For a gas grill, preheat grill. Reduce heat to medium. Place steak on grill rack over heat. Cover and grill as above.)

④ To serve, thinly slice beef across the grain; divide among four dinner plates. Top with pico de gallo. If desired, serve with tortillas and lime wedges.

PER SERVING 203 calories; 9 g total fat (3 g sat. fat); 47 mg cholesterol; 250 mg sodium; 5 g carbohydrate; 1 g fiber; 26 g protein

Look for prepared pico de gallo in the refrigerated section of your supermarket's produce department.

Brown Mustard Grilled Steak and Asparagus 30

MAKES 4 servings PREP 15 minutes GRILL 11 minutes

- 1   pound asparagus spears
- ½   teaspoon cracked black pepper
- 1   pound boneless beef ribeye steak, cut 1 inch thick
- 2   tablespoons coarse grain brown mustard
- 2   tablespoons balsamic vinegar
- 1   clove garlic, minced
- ¼   teaspoon salt
- 1   ounce pecorino or Parmesan cheese, shaved

① Snap off and discard woody bases from asparagus; set aside.

② Rub pepper into steak. In a small bowl combine mustard, vinegar, garlic, and salt. Spread half of the mixture over steaks, and toss remaining half with asparagus.

③ For a charcoal grill, grill steak on the rack of an uncovered grill directly over medium coals for 11 to 15 minutes for medium-rare or 14 to 18 minutes for medium, turning once halfway through grilling and adding asparagus for the last 8 minutes of grilling. (For a gas grill, preheat grill. Reduce heat to medium. Add steaks; cover and grill as above.)

④ Serve steak with asparagus, topped with shavings of cheese.

PER SERVING 238 calories; 11 g total fat (5 g sat. fat); 74 mg cholesterol; 485 mg sodium; 4 g carbohydrate; 1 g fiber; 27 g protein

Brown Mustard Grilled Steak and Asparagus

Sweet Asian Beef Stir-Fry

MAKES 4 servings **START TO FINISH** 40 minutes

- 3 tablespoons low-sugar orange marmalade
- 2 tablespoons light teriyaki sauce
- 2 tablespoons water
- 1 tablespoon grated fresh ginger
- ¼ to ½ teaspoon crushed red pepper
- 3 ounces dried multigrain spaghetti or soba (buckwheat) noodles
  Nonstick cooking spray
- 2 cups small broccoli florets
- ½ of a small red onion, cut into thin wedges
- 1 cup packaged julienned carrots, or 2 carrots, cut into thin bite-size strips
- 2 teaspoons canola oil
- 12 ounces boneless beef top sirloin steak, cut into thin bite-size pieces
- 3 cups shredded napa cabbage

① For sauce, in a small bowl combine marmalade, teriyaki sauce, the water, ginger, and crushed red pepper. Cook spaghetti according to package directions.

② Meanwhile, coat a large nonstick skillet with cooking spray. Preheat over medium-high heat. Add broccoli and red onion to hot skillet. Cover; cook for 3 minutes, stirring occasionally. Add carrots; cover and cook for 3 to 4 minutes or until vegetables are crisp-tender, stirring occasionally. Remove vegetables from skillet.

③ Heat oil in the same skillet. Add beef strips; cook and stir over medium-high heat for 3 to 5 minutes or until slightly pink in center. Return vegetables to the skillet along with the sauce and cabbage. Cook and stir for 1 to 2 minutes or just until heated through and cabbage is wilted.

PER SERVING 279 calories; 6 g total fat (2 g sat. fat); 36 mg cholesterol; 259 mg sodium; 30 g carbohydrate; 5 g fiber; 25 g protein

Japanese soba noodles are made from buckwheat. Try them in this stir-fry—they have a hearty texture and nutty flavor.

Beefy Pasta Salad ✪ ③⓪

MAKES 4 servings **START TO FINISH** 30 minutes

- 1 cup dried multigrain penne pasta (about 3½ ounces)
- 2 ears of corn, husks and silks removed
  Nonstick cooking spray
- 12 ounces boneless beef sirloin steak, trimmed of fat, cut into thin bite-size strips
- 1 cup cherry tomatoes, halved
- ¼ cup shredded fresh basil
- 2 tablespoons finely shredded Parmesan cheese
- 3 tablespoons white wine vinegar
- 1 tablespoon olive oil
- 1 clove garlic, minced
- ¼ teaspoon salt
- ⅛ teaspoon black pepper
- ¼ cup finely shredded Parmesan cheese

① In a 4- to 6-quart Dutch oven cook pasta according to package directions, adding corn for the last 3 minutes of cooking time. Using tongs, transfer corn to a large cutting board. Drain pasta. Rinse in cold water and drain again; set aside. Cool corn until cool enough to handle.

② Meanwhile, coat an unheated large nonstick skillet with cooking spray. Preheat skillet over medium-high heat. Add beef strips. Cook for 4 to 6 minutes or until slightly pink in the center, stirring occasionally. (If using shredded beef, cook until heated through.) Remove from heat and cool slightly.

③ On a cutting board place each ear of corn stem end down. While holding corn firmly at pointed end to keep in place, use a sharp knife to cut corn from cobs, leaving corn in planks; rotate cob as needed to cut corn from all sides. In a large bowl combine pasta, beef, tomatoes, basil, and the 2 tablespoons Parmesan cheese.

④ In a screw-top jar combine vinegar, oil, garlic, salt, and pepper. Cover and shake well. Pour over pasta mixture; toss gently to coat. Gently fold in corn planks or place corn planks on top of individual servings. Serve immediately. Garnish with ¼ cup Parmesan cheese.

PER SERVING 313 calories; 10 g total fat (3 g sat. fat); 41 mg cholesterol; 341 mg sodium; 28 g carbohydrate; 4 g fiber; 28 g protein

Beefy Pasta Salad

Weeknight Beefy Skillet

{
# *menu*

Mixed greens salad

Corn bread

Weeknight Beefy
Skillet
[below]

Ginger-Spiced
Chocolate Cake
}

Weeknight Beefy Skillet

MAKES 4 servings **START TO FINISH** 40 minutes

- 1 **pound lean ground beef**
- 1 **cup chopped celery (2 stalks)**
- ½ **cup chopped onion (1 medium)**
- 2 **cloves garlic, minced**
- 1 **15.5- to 16-ounce can butter beans, rinsed and drained**
- 1 **14.5-ounce can no-salt-added diced tomatoes**
- 1 **8-ounce can no-salt-added tomato sauce**
- 1 **medium green sweet pepper, cut in bite-size strips**
- 1 **jalapeño, seeded and finely chopped (see tip, page 8)**
- 2 **teaspoons Worcestershire sauce**
- 1 **teaspoon dried basil, crushed**
- 1 **teaspoon dried oregano, crushed**
- ½ **teaspoon bottled hot pepper sauce**
- ¼ **teaspoon black pepper**

① In a large skillet cook ground beef, celery, onion, and garlic, over medium heat until browned. Drain fat.

② Add butter beans, undrained tomatoes, tomato sauce, sweet pepper, jalapeño, Worcestershire sauce, basil, oregano, hot pepper sauce, and black pepper. Bring to boiling. Reduce heat and simmer, uncovered, 10 to 15 minutes or until desired consistency.

PER SERVING 342 calories; 12 g total fat (5 g sat. fat); 74 mg cholesterol; 499 mg sodium; 33 g carbohydrate; 9 g fiber; 30 g protein

Sesame Ginger Beef Stir-Fry 30

MAKES 4 servings **START TO FINISH** 30 minutes

- 12 **ounces beef sirloin**
- 1 **cup reduced-sodium chicken broth**
- 1 **tablespoon grated fresh ginger or 1 teaspoon ground ginger**
- 1 **tablespoon cornstarch**
- 2 **cloves garlic, minced**
- 1 **teaspoon ground coriander**
- ⅛ **to ¼ teaspoon crushed red pepper**
- 2 **teaspoons sesame oil**
- 1 **medium onion, halved and sliced**
- 2 **cups broccoli florets**
- 1 **medium red sweet pepper, cut in bite-size strips**
- 1⅓ **cups hot cooked brown rice**
- 1 **teaspoon sesame seeds, toasted (optional)**

① If desired, partially freeze beef for easier slicing. Trim fat from meat. Thinly slice meat across the grain into bite-size strips. Set aside.

② For sauce, in a small bowl stir together chicken broth, ginger, cornstarch, garlic, coriander, and crushed red pepper; set aside.

③ In a wok or large skillet heat sesame oil over medium-high heat. Add onion and cook and stir in hot oil for 2 minutes. Add broccoli and sweet pepper. Cook and stir for 1 to 2 minutes more or until vegetables are crisp-tender. Remove from wok.

④ Add beef strips to hot wok. (Lightly coat skillet with nonstick cooking spray if needed.) Cook and stir for 2 to 3 minutes or until meat is slightly pink in center. Push meat from center of wok.

⑤ Stir sauce. Add sauce to center of wok. Cook and stir until thickened and bubbly. Return cooked vegetables to wok; stir to coat all ingredients with sauce. Cook and stir for 1 to 2 minutes more or until heated through. Serve immediately with rice. Sprinkle with sesame seeds, if desired.

PER SERVING 255 calories; 7 g total fat (2 g sat. fat); 36 mg cholesterol; 212 mg sodium; 25 g carbohydrate; 4 g fiber; 23 g protein

Roast Beef Panini ✪ ③⓪

MAKES 4 servings **PREP** 25 minutes **COOK** 3 minutes

Nonstick cooking spray
8   slices marble rye, rye, or pumpernickel bread
1   recipe Horseradish Spread
8   ounces leftover cooked roast beef, sliced
1   cup watercress or baby arugula
2   slices havarti cheese (about 1½ ounces), halved
¼   cup thinly sliced red onion

① Lightly coat a panini maker or griddle with nonstick cooking spray. Preheat panini maker or griddle over medium heat.

② On one side of the bread slices spread Horseradish Spread. On 4 bread slices place roast beef, watercress, cheese, and red onion. Top with remaining bread slices, spread sides down.

③ Cook sandwiches 3 minutes in the panini maker or 5 minutes on a griddle, weighting with a skillet and turning once halfway through cooking time.

Horseradish Spread: In a bowl combine 2 tablespoons light mayonnaise, 1 tablespoon prepared horseradish, 1 teaspoon Dijon mustard, and ⅛ teaspoon caraway seeds.

PER SERVING 333 calories; 11 g total fat (4 g sat. fat); 60 mg cholesterol; 615 mg sodium; 32 g carbohydrate; 4 g fiber; 24 g protein

Both watercress and arugula have a pleasant, peppery bite. They can be used interchangeably in most recipes—including this one.

Middle Eastern Beef Salad ③⓪

MAKES 4 servings **START TO FINISH** 30 minutes

12   ounces beef tenderloin steaks, cut 1 inch thick
⅛   teaspoon salt
⅛   teaspoon black pepper
6   cups packaged fresh baby spinach
2   medium yellow or red tomatoes, cut into wedges
1   small cucumber, coarsely chopped
1   15-ounce can garbanzo beans (chickpeas), rinsed and drained
1   recipe Mint-Yogurt Dressing

① Trim fat from steaks. Season steaks with salt and pepper. For a charcoal grill, place steaks on the grill rack directly over medium coals. Grill, uncovered, until desired doneness, turning once halfway through. Allow 10 to 12 minutes for medium-rare (145°F) or 12 to 15 minutes for medium (160°F). (For a gas grill, preheat grill. Reduce heat to medium. Place steaks on grill rack over heat. Cover and grill as above.)

② Meanwhile, on four dinner plates arrange spinach, tomatoes, cucumber, and garbanzo beans. Set aside. Prepare Mint-Yogurt Dressing; set aside.

③ Thinly slice the grilled steak and place on top of salad. Serve with dressing.

Mint-Yogurt Dressing: In a small bowl combine ¼ cup snipped fresh parsley; ¼ cup snipped fresh mint; 3 cloves garlic, minced; 1 teaspoon olive oil; and 1 teaspoon honey. Stir in 6 tablespoons plain low-fat or fat-free yogurt until well combined. Makes about ½ cup.

PER SERVING 282 calories; 9 g total fat (3 g sat. fat); 58 mg cholesterol; 542 mg sodium; 25 g carbohydrate; 6 g fiber; 27 g protein

Roast beef and melty cheese on toasted rye make a highly satisfying sandwich.

Roast Beef Panini

Lamb Chops with Garlic and Lavender

Lamb Chops with Garlic and Lavender

MAKES 8 to 10 servings **PREP** 45 minutes **CHILL** 4 hours
GRILL 12 minutes

16	to 20 lamb rib or loin chops, cut 1 inch thick (4 to 5 pounds)
1	tablespoon dried lavender or finely shredded lemon peel
1	tablespoon dried Italian seasoning, crushed
1½	teaspoons freshly ground black pepper
1	teaspoon sea salt or salt
4	whole bulbs garlic, separated into cloves and peeled
2	tablespoons olive oil
2	lemons, halved (optional)
	Fresh lavender (optional)

① Trim fat from chops. In a small bowl combine dried lavender, Italian seasoning, pepper, and sea salt. Sprinkle evenly over both sides of chops; rub in with your fingers. Cover and chill chops for up to 4 hours.

② In a medium skillet cook garlic cloves in hot oil over medium heat for 15 to 20 minutes or until golden and soft, stirring occasionally and reducing heat if cloves begin to brown and if oil splatters. Remove from heat; cover and keep warm.

③ Meanwhile, for a charcoal grill, grill chops on the rack of an uncovered grill directly over medium coals until desired doneness, turning once halfway through grilling. Allow 12 to 14 minutes for medium-rare (145°F) and 15 to 17 minutes for medium (160°F). (For a gas grill, preheat grill. Reduce heat to medium. Place chops on grill rack over heat. Cover; grill as directed.)

④ To serve, transfer chops to serving plates. Spoon garlic cloves on grilled chops. If desired, squeeze fresh lemon juice on chops and top with fresh lavender.

PER 2 CHOPS 215 calories; 12 g total fat (3 g sat. fat); 64 mg cholesterol; 263 mg sodium; 6 g carbohydrate; 2 g fiber; 21 g protein

Versatile Saucy Meatballs ③⓪

MAKES 4 servings **START TO FINISH** 25 minutes

⅓	cup water
¼	cup bulgur
1	egg
1	teaspoon dried Italian seasoning, chili powder, or salt-free Cajun seasoning
¼	teaspoon salt
⅛	teaspoon black pepper
1	pound uncooked extra-lean ground beef (90% lean or higher) or ground turkey
1	14½-ounce can Italian-, Mexican-, or Cajun-style stewed tomatoes, undrained, cut up
2	cups hot cooked spaghetti squash
2	tablespoons small fresh basil or cilantro leaves or thinly sliced green onion

① In a large microwave-safe bowl combine the water and bulgur. Microwave on high for 1 minute; do not drain. Cool slightly.

② Stir egg, desired seasoning, salt, and pepper into bulgur mixture. Add beef; mix well. Shape into 24 meatballs. Place in a microwave-safe 2-quart square baking dish. Cover with vented plastic wrap. Microwave on high for 4 minutes, rearranging once; drain off liquid.

③ Pour undrained stewed tomatoes over meatballs. Cover with vented plastic wrap. Microwave on high for 1 to 3 minutes more or until meatballs are no longer pink in centers (165°F). Serve meatballs over spaghetti squash. Sprinkle with basil, cilantro, or green onion.

Per serving 264 calories; 11 g total fat (3 g sat. fat); 142 mg cholesterol; 644 mg sodium; 19 g carbohydrate; 4 g fiber; 24 g protein

Seeded Pork Roast

MAKES 8 servings **PREP** 25 minutes
COOK 9 hours (low) or 4½ hours (high)

- 1   3- to 3½-pound boneless pork shoulder roast
- 1   tablespoon reduced-sodium soy sauce
- 2   teaspoons anise seeds, crushed
- 2   teaspoons fennel seeds, crushed
- 2   teaspoons caraway seeds, crushed
- 2   teaspoons dill seeds, crushed
- 2   teaspoons celery seeds, crushed
- ½   cup lower-sodium beef broth
- ⅔   cup apple juice
- 1   tablespoon cornstarch

① Trim fat from meat. If necessary, cut meat to fit into a 3½- or 4-quart slow cooker. Brush soy sauce over meat. On a large piece of foil or waxed paper combine anise seeds, fennel seeds, caraway seeds, dill seeds, and celery seeds. Roll roast in seeds to coat evenly. Place meat in cooker. Pour broth and ⅓ cup of the apple juice around meat.

② Cover and cook on low-heat setting for 9 to 10 hours or on high-heat setting for 4½ to 5 hours.

③ Transfer meat to a serving platter, reserving cooking liquid. Cover meat to keep warm.

④ For gravy, strain cooking liquid and skim off fat. Transfer liquid to a small saucepan. In a small bowl combine remaining ⅓ cup apple juice and cornstarch; stir into liquid in saucepan. Cook and stir over medium heat until thickened and bubbly. Cook and stir for 2 minutes more. Serve gravy with meat and, if desired, *egg noodles*.

PER SERVING 260 calories; 10 g total fat (4 g sat. fat); 110 mg cholesterol; 235 mg sodium; 5 g carbohydrate; 1 g fiber; 34 g protein

Seeded Pork Roast

Italian Pork with Sweet Potatoes

MAKES 4 servings **PREP** 20 minutes
COOK 8 hours (low) or 4 hours (high)

- 1   teaspoon fennel seeds, crushed
- ½   teaspoon dried oregano, crushed
- ½   teaspoon garlic powder
- ½   teaspoon paprika
- ¼   teaspoon salt
- ¼   teaspoon black pepper
- 1   1½- to 2-pound boneless pork shoulder roast
- 1   pound sweet potatoes, peeled and cut into 1-inch pieces
- 1   cup reduced-sodium chicken broth

① In a small bowl combine fennel seeds, oregano, garlic powder, paprika, salt, and pepper. Trim fat from roast. Sprinkle fennel seed mixture evenly over roast; rub in with your fingers. If necessary, cut roast to fit into a 3½- or 4-quart slow cooker. Set roast aside.

② Place sweet potatoes in cooker. Add roast. Pour broth over all in cooker.

③ Cover and cook for 8 to 10 hours on low-heat setting or 4 to 5 hours on high-heat setting.

④ Remove meat from cooker, reserving cooking liquid. Slice meat. Using a slotted spoon, transfer sweet potatoes to a platter. Serve meat with sweet potatoes.

PER SERVING 341 calories; 10 g total fat (4 g sat. fat); 110 mg cholesterol; 490 mg sodium; 24 g carbohydrate; 4 g fiber; 36 g protein

Sweet potatoes are one of the world's most nutrient-dense foods. Loaded with cancer-fighting beta-carotene, they also have antioxidant, anti-inflammatory, and blood sugar-regulating properties.

Fruit-Stuffed Pork Tenderloins
with Mustard-Cranberry Sauce

menu

Wheat ciabatta rolls

Green Beans with
Bacon and Walnuts

Fruit-Stuffed Pork
Tenderloins with
Mustard-Cranberry
Sauce [below]

Apple Spice Cake

Fruit-Stuffed Pork Tenderloins with Mustard-Cranberry Sauce

MAKES 8 servings **PREP** 45 minutes **ROAST** 50 minutes
STAND 5 minutes **OVEN** at 375°F

2	stalks celery, sliced
1	medium onion, finely chopped
1	clove garlic, minced
2	tablespoons canola oil
2	cups cooked brown rice
¼	cup dried cranberries
¼	cup snipped dried apricots
1	teaspoon finely shredded orange peel
½	teaspoon dried thyme, crushed
¼	teaspoon salt
⅛	teaspoon black pepper
¼	cup apple juice (optional)
2	1-pound pork tenderloins
¼	teaspoon salt
¼	teaspoon black pepper
1	recipe Mustard-Cranberry Sauce

① Preheat oven to 375°F. For stuffing, in a medium saucepan cook celery, onion, and garlic in hot oil over medium heat about 4 minutes or until tender. Remove from heat. Stir in rice, cranberries, apricots, orange peel, thyme, ¼ teaspoon salt, and ⅛ teaspoon pepper. Stir in apple juice to moisten, if needed. Set stuffing aside.

② Trim any fat from pork. Use a sharp knife to make a lengthwise cut down the center of each pork tenderloin, cutting to, but not through, the other side of the meat. Repeat by making two cuts on either side of the first cut. Place each tenderloin between two pieces of plastic wrap. Working from the center out to the corners, pound lightly with the flat side of a meat mallet to make a 12 x 8-inch rectangle. Remove top piece of plastic wrap. Sprinkle pork with ¼ teaspoon salt and ¼ teaspoon pepper.

③ Spoon half of the stuffing on one of the tenderloins to within 1 inch of the edges. Roll tenderloin into a spiral, beginning with a short side. Tie meat with clean 100%-cotton kitchen string. Place seam side down on a rack in a shallow roasting pan. Repeat with remaining tenderloin and remaining stuffing, placing second tenderloin next to the first on the rack.

④ Roast, uncovered, for 50 to 60 minutes or until an instant-read thermometer inserted in the stuffing registers 165°F. Cover loosely with foil and let stand 5 minutes before slicing. Remove string from meat; discard.

⑤ Meanwhile, prepare Mustard-Cranberry Sauce. Cut tenderloins into slices. Serve with sauce.

Mustard-Cranberry Sauce: In a small saucepan cook 1 clove garlic, minced, in 2 tablespoons hot canola oil over medium heat for 1 minute. Stir in 2 tablespoons flour and 1 tablespoon Dijon-style mustard until combined. Stir in 1¼ cups reduced-sodium chicken broth. Cook and stir until thickened and bubbly. Cook and stir 1 minute more. Stir in ¼ cup half-and-half or light cream and ¼ cup dried cranberries; heat through. Makes 1⅔ cups.

PER SERVING 300 calories; 11 g total fat (2 g sat. fat); 76 mg cholesterol; 355 mg sodium; 24 g carbohydrate; 2 g fiber; 26 g protein

If you don't like the strings on celery, getting rid of them is easy. Simply run a vegetable peeler down the back of each stalk. The strings will come right off.

Herb-Scented Tuscan Pork Loin ✪

MAKES 12 to 15 servings **PREP** 20 minutes **CHILL** 8 hours
ROAST 2 hours **STAND** 15 minutes **OVEN** at 325°F

- 3 tablespoons snipped fresh rosemary
- 8 cloves garlic, minced
- 4 teaspoons finely shredded lemon peel
- 1 teaspoon kosher salt
- 1 4½- to 5-pound boneless pork top loin roast (double loin, tied)
- 4 ounces thinly sliced pancetta

① In a small bowl combine rosemary, garlic, lemon peel, and salt. Set aside.

② Untie meat; trim fat from meat. Spread rosemary mixture over top of one of the loins. Place pancetta on top of the other loin. Reassemble meat, placing the pancetta-topped loin on top and positioning the rosemary mixture in the middle. Retie with clean 100%-cotton kitchen string. Wrap meat tightly in plastic wrap and chill for 8 to 24 hours.

③ Preheat oven to 325°F. Place meat on a rack in a shallow roasting pan. Insert an ovenproof meat thermometer into center of meat. Roast for 2 to 2½ hours or until meat thermometer registers 150°F.

④ Cover meat with foil and let stand for 15 minutes. The temperature of the meat after standing should be 160°F. Slice meat.

PER SERVING 286 calories; 12 g total fat (4 g sat. fat); 99 mg cholesterol; 396 mg sodium; 1 g carbohydrate; 0 g fiber; 39 g protein

Carnitas

Carnitas ✪

MAKES 6 servings **PREP** 10 minutes
COOK 10 hours (low) to 5 hours (high)

- 1 2-pound boneless pork shoulder roast, cut into 2-inch pieces
- ¼ teaspoon salt
- ¼ teaspoon black pepper
- 1 tablespoon whole black peppercorns
- 2 teaspoons cumin seeds
- 4 cloves garlic, minced
- 1 teaspoon dried oregano, crushed
- 3 bay leaves
- 2 14-ounce cans reduced-sodium chicken broth
- 2 teaspoons finely shredded lime peel
- 2 tablespoons lime juice
- 12 6-inch crisp corn tortillas
- 2 green onions, thinly sliced
- ⅓ cup light sour cream (optional)
- ⅓ cup purchased salsa (optional)

① Sprinkle pork with salt and pepper. Place in a 3½- or 4-quart slow cooker.

② To make a bouquet garni, cut a 6-inch square from a double thickness of 100%-cotton cheesecloth. Place peppercorns, cumin seeds, garlic, oregano, and bay leaves in center of cheesecloth square. Bring up corners of cheesecloth and tie with clean 100%-cotton kitchen string. Add to slow cooker. Add broth.

③ Cover and cook on low-heat setting for 10 to 12 hours or on high-heat setting for 5 to 6 hours.

④ Using a slotted spoon, remove meat from slow cooker. Discard bouquet garni and cooking liquid. Using two forks, coarsely shred meat; discard any fat. Sprinkle meat with lime peel and lime juice; toss to mix. Serve on tortillas. Top with green onions. Top with sour cream and salsa, if desired.

PER SERVING 318 calories; 10 g total fat (3 g sat. fat); 90 mg cholesterol; 377 mg sodium; 24 g carbohydrate; 4 g fiber; 32 g protein

Herb-Scented Tuscan Pork Loin

Pork Tenderloin Medallions with Plum Sauce

MAKES 4 servings **START TO FINISH** 40 minutes

- ¼ cup chopped onion
- 1 clove garlic, minced
- 1 teaspoon sesame oil
- 2 medium plums, pitted and chopped (1½ cups)
- 1½ teaspoons rice vinegar
- 1½ teaspoons grated fresh ginger, or ¼ teaspoon ground ginger
- 1 teaspoon reduced-sodium soy sauce
- 1 teaspoon honey
- ¼ teaspoon salt
- ¼ teaspoon ground coriander
- 1 1-pound pork tenderloin
  Nonstick cooking spray
- 7 cups chopped bok choy (1 head)
- ¼ cup chopped green onions (2)

① In a small saucepan cook onion and garlic in hot sesame oil over medium heat for 4 minutes or until tender. Stir in plums, vinegar, ginger, soy sauce, honey, ⅛ teaspoon of the salt, and coriander. Bring to boiling. Reduce heat; cover and simmer 5 minutes or until plums are tender. Transfer mixture to a blender or food processor. Cover and blend or process until smooth; set aside.

② Trim fat from heat. Cut meat crosswise into 1-inch slices. Press cut side of each piece with the palm of your hand to make an even thickness. Sprinkle meat with remaining ⅛ teaspoon salt. Coat a large skillet with nonstick cooking spray. Heat over medium-high heat. Add pork and cook for 2 to 3 minutes per side or until juices run clear. Remove from skillet and keep warm.

③ Add bok choy to skillet. Cover and cook for 3 minutes or until wilted, stirring occasionally. Place bok choy on a serving platter. Top with pork and some of the plum sauce. Sprinkle with green onions. Pass any remaining plum sauce.

PER SERVING 191 calories; 4 g total fat (1 g sat. fat); 74 mg cholesterol; 392 mg sodium; 12 g carbohydrate; 3 g fiber; 28 g protein

Barbecued Pork Sandwiches ✪

MAKES 6 sandwiches **PREP** 20 minutes **COOK** 15 minutes

- Nonstick cooking spray
- ½ cup chopped, onion (1 medium)
- 2 cloves garlic, minced
- ⅔ cup water
- ½ of a 6-ounce can tomato paste (⅓ cu
- 2 tablespoons red wine vinegar
- 2 tablespoon brown sugar
- 1 tablespoon chili powder
- 1 teaspoon dried oregano, crushed
- 1 teaspoon Worcestershire sauce
- ¼ teaspoon cayenne pepper
  Dash bottled hot pepper sauce
- 12 ounces pork tenderloin
- ¾ cup green sweet pepper, chopped (1 medium)
- 6 whole wheat hamburger buns, split and toasted

① For sauce, lightly coat a small saucepan with cooking spray. Heat saucepan over medium heat. Add onion and garlic; cook and stir about 5 minutes or until onion is tender. Stir in the water, tomato paste, vinegar, brown sugar, chili powder, oregano, Worcestershire sauce, cayenne pepper, and bottled hot pepper sauce. Bring to boiling; reduce heat. Simmer, uncovered, about 10 minutes or until desired consistency, stirring occasionally.

② Meanwhile, trim any fat from meat. Cut meat into bite-size strips. Lightly coat a large skillet with cooking spray. Heat skillet over medium-high heat. Add meat. Cook and stir for 2 to 3 minutes or until meat is slightly pink in center. Stir in the sauce and sweet pepper; heat through. Serve the barbecued pork on toasted buns.

PER SANDWICH 225 calories; 4 g total fat (1 g sat. fat); 37 mg cholesterol; 388 mg sodium; 29 g carbohydrate; 3 g fiber; 17 g protein

Roasted Pork with Apples

MAKES 4 servings **PREP** 15 minutes **ROAST** 20 minutes
STAND 10 minutes **OVEN** at 425°F

1	teaspoon snipped fresh sage or ½ teaspoon dried sage, crushed
¼	teaspoon salt
¼	teaspoon coarsely ground black pepper
1	1-pound pork tenderloin
1	tablespoon canola oil
1	medium red onion, cut into thin wedges
3	medium cooking apples (such as Granny Smith or Jonathan), cored and cut into ½-inch-thick wedges
⅔	cup apple juice or apple cider
	Fresh sage sprigs (optional)

① Preheat oven to 425°F. In a small bowl combine the snipped sage, salt, and pepper. Sprinkle mixture on all sides of tenderloin; rub in with your fingers. In a large skillet brown tenderloin in hot oil over medium heat, turning to brown all sides.

② Transfer pork to a shallow roasting pan. Add onion to pan around pork. Roast, uncovered, for 10 minutes. Stir in apples; roast for 10 to 15 minutes more or until pork is slightly pink in center (155°F).

③ Transfer pork and apple mixture to a serving platter; cover with foil. Let stand for 10 minutes. The temperature of the meat after standing should be 160°F. Slice meat.

④ Meanwhile, in a small saucepan bring apple juice to boiling; simmer gently, uncovered, for 8 to 10 minutes or until reduced to ¼ to ⅓ cup. Drizzle over meat and apple mixture. If desired, garnish with sage sprigs.

PER SERVING 239 calories; 6 g total fat (1 g sat. fat); 74 mg cholesterol; 209 mg sodium; 22 g carbohydrate; 3 g fiber; 24 g protein

Roasted Pork with Apples

Pork Loin with Apples and Pears

MAKES 8 servings **PREP** 25 minutes
ROAST 1 hour + 5 minutes **STAND** 10 minutes **OVEN** at 425°F

2	teaspoons black pepper
1	teaspoon garlic powder
¾	teaspoon salt
1	3-pound boneless pork top loin roast (single loin)
2	tablespoons olive oil
⅓	cup molasses
2	tablespoons red wine vinegar
1	tablespoon reduced-sodium soy sauce
3	apples, cut into halves, wedges, or slices
2	red pears, cut into halves, wedges, or slices
2	tablespoons sugar

① Preheat oven to 425°F. Line a shallow roasting pan with heavy foil; lightly oil foil. Place meat rack in pan; set aside. In a small bowl combine pepper, garlic powder, and salt. Trim fat from pork. Brush pork with 1 tablespoon of the olive oil; rub with pepper mixture. Place pork on rack in roasting pan. Roast, uncovered, for 35 minutes.

② For glaze, in a skillet combine molasses, vinegar, and soy sauce. Bring to boiling; reduce heat. Simmer 1 minute. Transfer to a bowl. Set glaze and skillet aside.

③ Brush pork with some glaze (reserve 2 tablespoons glaze for fruit). Roast for 20 minutes more, brushing with glaze halfway through roasting. Roast another 10 minutes or until an instant-read thermometer inserted into the center of the roast registers 150°F. Remove from oven; cover with foil. Let stand 10 minutes before slicing.

④ Meanwhile, in skillet used for glaze heat remaining 1 tablespoon olive oil. Toss fruit with sugar. Add fruit to skillet; cover and cook for 2 minutes. Uncover and cook for 3 minutes more or until fruit is crisp-tender. Add reserved glaze; heat through. Serve pork with fruit and drizzle with pan juices.

PER SERVING 370 calories; 10 g total fat (3 g sat. fat); 107 mg cholesterol; 371 mg sodium; 30 g carbohydrate; 3 g fiber; 39 g protein

Pork with Cherry and Wild Rice Stuffing

Pork with Cherry and Wild Rice Stuffing

MAKES 8 servings   **PREP** 1 hour   **ROAST** 1 hour 45 minutes
STAND 15 minutes   **OVEN** at 325°F

- 1   recipe Cherry and Wild Rice Stuffing
- 1   3-pound boneless pork top loin roast (single loin)
- 1   teaspoon snipped fresh thyme or ¼ teaspoon dried thyme, crushed
- ¼   teaspoon salt
- ¼   teaspoon black pepper
- 1   cup water
- ⅓   cup cold water
- 2   tablespoons flour
  Fresh whole tart red cherries (optional)
  Fresh thyme sprigs (optional)

① Prepare Cherry and Wild Rice Stuffing; set aside. Trim fat from pork. Butterfly the meat by making a lengthwise cut down the center of the meat, cutting to within ½ inch of the other side. Spread open. Place knife in the V of the first cut. Cut horizontally to the cut surface and away from the first cut to within ½ inch of the other side of the meat. Repeat on opposite side of the V. Spread these sections open. Cover the roast with plastic wrap. Working from center (thicker part) to edges, pound with flat side of a meat mallet until meat is ½ to ¾ inch thick. Make sure the meat is a uniform thickness. Remove plastic wrap. Set meat aside.

② Preheat oven to 325°F. Spread the stuffing on the butterflied roast. Roll loin into a spiral, beginning with a short side. Tie meat with clean 100%-cotton kitchen string. (Wrap several strands of string crosswise around the meat and tie securely.) Place on a rack in a shallow roasting pan. Sprinkle with thyme, salt, and pepper. Insert an ovenproof meat thermometer in center of roast. Roast, uncovered, for 1¾ to 2¼ hours or until thermometer registers 155°F, covering ends of meat after 45 minutes to keep stuffing moist. Transfer meat to a serving platter. Cover loosely with foil and let stand 15 minutes before carving. (The temperature of the roast after standing should be 160°F.)

③ For the pan gravy, add the 1 cup water to pan, scraping up browned bits. In a small saucepan whisk together the ⅓ cup cold water and the flour. Whisk in pan juices. Cook and stir over medium heat until thickened and bubbly. Cook and stir 1 minute more.

④ Remove string from pork roast; discard. Slice roast; serve with pan gravy. If desired, garnish with tart red cherries and fresh thyme sprigs.

Cherry and Wild Rice Stuffing: Rinse ⅓ cup wild rice in a strainer, lifting the rice with your fingers to thoroughly clean under cold running water about 1 minute; drain. In a small saucepan combine rice; 1¼ cups water; 2 teaspoons snipped fresh rosemary or ½ teaspoon dried rosemary, crushed; and ½ teaspoon salt. Bring to boiling; reduce heat. Cover and simmer for 40 to 45 minutes or until rice is tender. Remove from heat. Stir in ¾ cup coarsely chopped dried cherries; set aside. In a large skillet cook 6 ounces bulk pork sausage and ½ cup chopped onion until sausage is browned and onion is tender. Drain fat. Stir in 1 tablespoon snipped fresh parsley; 1 teaspoon snipped fresh thyme or ¼ teaspoon dried thyme, crushed; and ¼ teaspoon black pepper. If necessary, drain the cooked rice mixture to remove liquid. Stir cooked rice mixture into sausage mixture.

PER SERVING 353 calories; 10 g total fat (4 g sat. fat); 121 mg cholesterol; 392 mg sodium; 19 g carbohydrate; 1 g fiber; 43 g protein

Make it a happy and healthy holiday with this gorgeous and festive stuffed pork roast.

Greek Honey-Lemon Pork Chops

MAKES 4 servings **PREP** 15 minutes **MARINATE** 4 hours
GRILL 11 minutes

4	bone-in pork rib chops, cut ¾ inch thick (about 1¾ pounds)
¼	cup honey
4	teaspoons finely shredded lemon peel
¼	cup lemon juice
2	tablespoons snipped fresh mint or 1 teaspoon dried mint, crushed
2	tablespoons olive oil
1	teaspoon salt
½	teaspoon cayenne pepper

① Trim fat from chops. Place chops in a large resealable plastic bag set in a shallow dish. For marinade, in a small bowl stir together honey, lemon peel, lemon juice, mint, oil, salt, and cayenne pepper. Pour over chops in bag; seal bag. Turn to coat chops. Marinate in the refrigerate for 4 to 24 hours, turning bag occasionally. Drain chops, discarding marinade.

② For a charcoal grill, grill chops on the rack of an uncovered grill directly over medium coals for 11 to 14 minutes or until chops are slightly pink in center (160°F), turning once halfway through grilling. (For a gas grill, preheat grill. Reduce heat to medium. Place chops on grill rack over heat. Cover; grill as directed.)

PER SERVING 272 calories; 15 g total fat (3 g sat. fat); 75 mg cholesterol; 219 mg sodium; 5 g carbohydrate; 0 g fiber; 27 g protein

Greek Honey-Lemon Pork Chops

Mushroom-Sauced Pork Chops

MAKES 4 servings **PREP** 20 minutes
COOK 8 hours (low) to 9 hours (high)

4	pork loin chops, cut ¾ inch thick (about 1¾ pounds total)
1	tablespoon vegetable oil
1	small onion, thinly sliced
2	tablespoons quick-cooking tapioca
1	10¾-ounce can reduced-fat and reduced-sodium condensed cream of mushroom soup
½	cup apple juice or apple cider
1	teaspoon Worcestershire sauce
2	teaspoons snipped fresh thyme or ¾ teaspoon dried thyme, crushed
¼	teaspoon garlic powder
1½	cups sliced fresh mushrooms
	Cooked peas and carrots (optional)

① Trim fat from chops. In a large skillet heat oil over medium heat. Add chops; cook until browned, turning to brown evenly. Drain off fat. Place onion in a 3½- or 4-quart slow cooker; add chops. Using a mortar and pestle, crush tapioca. In a medium bowl combine tapioca, mushroom soup, apple juice, Worcestershire sauce, thyme, and garlic powder; stir in mushrooms. Pour over chops in slow cooker.

② Cover and cook on low-heat setting for 8 to 9 hours or on high-heat setting for 4 to 4½ hours. If desired, serve with cooked peas and carrots.

PER SERVING 330 calories; 10 g total fat (3 g sat. fat); 110 mg cholesterol; 381 mg sodium; 17 g carbohydrate; 1 g fiber; 39 g protein

Tapioca might seem an odd addition to a savory dish if you are used to eating it in pudding form—with sugar, butter, eggs, and milk. It has another use, though—as a thickener in slow-cooker dishes such as these mushroom-sauced chops.

Mushroom-Sauced Pork Chops

Pork and Potato Gratin

Pork and Potato Gratin

MAKES 4 servings **PREP** 45 minutes **BAKE** 25 minutes
STAND 10 minutes **OVEN** at 375°F

2   medium sweet potatoes, peeled and cut into quarters

3   medium turnips, peeled and halved

½   teaspoon salt

½   teaspoon paprika

¼   teaspoon ground cumin

⅛   teaspoon ground cinnamon

4   boneless pork loin chops, cut ½ inch thick (1 to 1¼ pounds total)

    Nonstick cooking spray

2   teaspoons canola oil

½   cup chopped onion

2   cloves garlic, minced

1½   cups fat-free milk

3   tablespoons flour

⅛   teaspoon black pepper

⅓   cup whole wheat panko (Japanese-style bread crumbs)

2   tablespoons snipped fresh parsley (optional)

① In a saucepan cook sweet potatoes and turnips in enough boiling water to cover for 15 to 20 minutes or just until tender. Drain; set aside until cool enough to handle.

② Preheat oven to 375°F. In a bowl combine ¼ teaspoon of the salt, paprika, cumin, and cinnamon. Sprinkle over the pork chops. Coat a nonstick skillet with cooking spray. Heat over medium-high heat; add pork chops. Cook for 3 to 4 minutes or until browned but not fully cooked, turning to brown both sides evenly. Remove from skillet; set aside.

③ For sauce, add oil to the same skillet. Add onion and cook for 3 to 5 minutes or just until tender, stirring occasionally. Stir in garlic. In a bowl whisk together milk and flour until smooth. Add all at once to onion mixture; add remaining ¼ teaspoon salt and the pepper. Cook and stir until thickened and bubbly. Remove from heat.

④ Thinly slice turnips and arrange in a 3-quart rectangular baking dish. Pour half of the sauce over turnips. Arrange pork chops in a single layer over turnips. Thinly slice sweet potatoes and place around chops. Pour remaining sauce over potatoes. Sprinkle with panko.

⑤ Bake, uncovered, for 25 to 30 minutes or until pork chops are cooked through. If desired, sprinkle with parsley.

PER SERVING 362 calories; 10 g total fat (3 g sat. fat); 64 mg cholesterol; 487 mg sodium; 35 g carbohydrate; 5 g fiber; 32 g protein

Asian Pork and Cabbage Salad ㉚

MAKES 4 servings **PREP** 20 minutes **COOK** 5 minutes

¼   cup low-sugar orange marmalade or low-sugar apricot preserves

2   tablespoons reduced-sodium soy sauce

2   tablespoons rice vinegar

1   tablespoon toasted sesame oil

1   clove garlic, minced

    Nonstick cooking spray

12   ounces boneless pork loin chops, cut into bite-size pieces

1   medium red or yellow sweet pepper, cut into thin bite-size strips

6   cups napa cabbage, shredded

1   cup chopped cucumber

4   green onions, bias-sliced into 1-inch pieces

¼   cup slivered almonds, toasted

① For dressing, in a small bowl stir together orange marmalade, soy sauce, vinegar, toasted sesame oil, and garlic. Set aside.

② Lightly coat an unheated wok or large nonstick skillet with cooking spray. Add pork and cook over medium-high heat for 2 minutes. Add sweet pepper to the pan and continue to cook for 3 minutes or until pork is no longer pink and sweet pepper is crisp-tender, stirring occasionally. Add one-fourth of the dressing to pan; stir until well coated. Remove pan from heat.

③ In a large bowl coat cabbage with remaining dressing. On a serving platter layer cabbage, pork mixture, and cucumber. Sprinkle with green onions and almonds. Serve immediately.

PER SERVING 242 calories; 10 g total fat (2 g sat. fat); 59 mg cholesterol; 352 mg sodium; 16 g carbohydrate; 3 g fiber; 23 g protein

Peppered Pork Burgers ③⓪

MAKES 4 burgers **PREP** 20 minutes **GRILL** 10 minutes

1	recipe Honey-Mustard Spread
12	ounces lean ground pork
½	teaspoon black pepper
½	teaspoon paprika
¼	teaspoon garlic powder
¼	teaspoon ground cumin
⅛	teaspoon salt
4	whole wheat hamburger buns, split and toasted
2	romaine lettuce leaves, halved
¾	cup bottled roasted red sweet peppers, drained and divided into large pieces

① Prepare Honey-Mustard Spread; cover and chill. In a medium bowl combine pork, black pepper, paprika, garlic powder, cumin, and salt. Shape into four ½-inch-thick patties.

② For a charcoal grill, place patties on the rack of an uncovered grill directly over medium coals. Grill for 10 to 12 minutes or until an instant-read thermometer inserted into side of each patty registers 160°F, turning patties once halfway through grilling. (For a gas grill, preheat grill. Reduce heat to medium. Place patties on the grill rack over heat. Cover and grill as above.)

③ To assemble, spread Honey-Mustard Spread on cut sides of bun tops. Place lettuce leaves, grilled patties, and roasted red peppers on bun bottoms. Add bun tops, spread sides down.

Honey-Mustard Spread: In a small bowl combine 3 tablespoons light mayonnaise, 1 tablespoon Dijon mustard, and 1 teaspoon honey. Makes ¼ cup.

PER SERVING 272 calories; 8 g total fat (2 g sat. fat); 63 mg cholesterol; 510 mg sodium; 26 g carbohydrate; 3 g fiber; 23 g protein

Jerk Pork Wraps with Lime Mayo

MAKES 6 wraps **PREP** 30 minutes **COOK** 8 hours (low) or 4 hours (high)

1	recipe Lime Mayo
1	1½- to 2-pound boneless pork shoulder roast
1	tablespoon Jamaican jerk seasoning
¼	teaspoon dried thyme, crushed
1	cup water
1	tablespoon lime juice
6	8-inch flour tortillas
6	lettuce leaves (optional)
½	cup chopped red or green sweet pepper
1	medium mango, peeled, seeded, and chopped, or 1 cup chopped pineapple

① Prepare Lime Mayo. Trim fat from meat. Sprinkle jerk seasoning evenly over pork; rub into meat with your fingers. Place meat in a 3½- or 4-quart slow cooker. Sprinkle with thyme. Pour the water over meat in cooker.

② Cover and cook on low-heat setting for 8 to 10 hours or on high-heat setting for 4 to 5 hours.

③ Remove meat from slow cooker; discard cooking liquid. When cool enough to handle, shred meat by pulling two forks through it in opposite directions; discard any fat. Place meat in a medium bowl. Stir lime juice into meat.

④ If desired, line tortillas with lettuce leaves. Spoon ½ cup meat mixture onto the center of each tortilla. Top with about 1 tablespoon sweet pepper, 2 to 3 tablespoons mango, and about 2 tablespoons Lime Mayo. Fold up bottom of each tortilla; fold in sides. Roll up and serve immediately.

Lime Mayo: In a small bowl stir together ½ cup light mayonnaise, ¼ cup finely chopped red onion, ¼ teaspoon finely shredded lime peel, 1 tablespoon lime juice, and 1 clove garlic, minced. Cover and refrigerate until ready to serve or up to 1 week. Makes about ¾ cup.

PER SERVING 319 calories; 13 g total fat (3 g sat. fat); 77 mg cholesterol; 539 mg sodium; 24 g carbohydrate; 2 g fiber; 25 g protein

Salmon with Cilantro-Pineapple Salsa, page 172

Fresh Fish & Seafood

Pan-Fried Fish ✪ ③⓪

MAKES 4 servings **PREP** 10 minutes **COOK** 6 minutes per batch
OVEN at 300°F

- 1 pound fresh or frozen fish fillets, ½ to ¾ inch thick
- 1 egg, lightly beaten
- 2 tablespoons water
- ⅔ cup cornmeal or fine dry bread crumbs
- ½ teaspoon salt
   Dash black pepper
   Vegetable oil or shortening for frying

① Thaw fish, if frozen. Rinse fish; pat dry with paper towels. Cut into four serving-size pieces, if necessary. In a shallow dish combine egg and the water. In another shallow dish stir together cornmeal, salt, and pepper. Dip fish into egg mixture; coat fish with cornmeal mixture.

② Preheat oven to 300°F. In a large skillet heat ¼ inch oil or melted shortening. Add half of the fish in a single layer; fry on one side until golden. (If fillets have skin, fry skin side last.) Turn carefully. Fry until second side is golden and fish begins to flake when tested with a fork. Allow 3 to 4 minutes per side. Drain on paper towels. Keep warm in the preheated oven while frying remaining fish.

PER SERVING 255 calories; 13 g total fat (2 g sat. fat); 101 mg cholesterol; 230 mg sodium; 12 g carbohydrate; 1 g fiber; 23 g protein

Potato Chip Pan-Fried Fish: Prepare as above, except substitute 1⅓ cups finely crushed potato chips (about 4 cups chips) or saltine crackers for the cornmeal and omit the salt.

PER SERVING FOR POTATO CHIP VARIATION 278 calories, 17 g total fat (3 g sat. fat), 101 mg cholesterol, 153 mg sodium, 7 g carbohydrate, 1 g fiber, 23 g protein

Wasabi-Glazed Whitefish

MAKES 4 servings **PREP** 25 minutes **CHILL** 2 hours
GRILL 4 to 6 minutes per ½-inch thickness

- 1⅓ cups coarsely shredded zucchini
- 1 cup sliced radishes
- 1 cup fresh pea pods, halved
- 2 tablespoons snipped fresh chives
- 3 tablespoons rice vinegar
- 1 teaspoon toasted sesame oil
- ½ teaspoon sugar
- 4 4-ounce fresh or frozen skinless whitefish, sea bass, or orange roughy fillets
- 2 tablespoons reduced-sodium soy sauce
- ¼ teaspoon wasabi powder or 1 tablespoon prepared horseradish

① For slaw, in a medium bowl combine zucchini, radishes, pea pods, and chives. For vinaigrette, in a small bowl combine vinegar, ½ teaspoon of the oil, and ¼ teaspoon of the sugar. Drizzle vinaigrette over slaw; toss gently to coat. Cover and chill for 2 to 4 hours. Let stand at room temperature while grilling fish.

② Thaw fish, if frozen. Rinse fish; pat dry with paper towels. Measure thickness of fish. In a small bowl combine the remaining ½ teaspoon oil, the remaining ¼ teaspoon sugar, soy sauce, and wasabi powder. Brush both sides of each fish fillet with soy mixture. Place fish in a greased grill basket, tucking under any thin edges.

③ For a charcoal grill, grill fish in basket on the rack of an uncovered grill directly over medium coals for 4 to 6 minutes per ½-inch thickness of fish or until fish flakes easily when tested with a fork, turning basket once halfway through grilling. (For a gas grill, preheat grill. Reduce heat to medium. Place fish in basket on grill rack over heat. Cover and grill as above.) Serve fish with slaw.

PER SERVING 198 calories; 8 g total fat (1 g sat. fat); 68 mg cholesterol; 367 mg sodium; 6 g carbohydrate; 0 g fiber; 24 g protein

Wasabi-Glazed Whitefish

Grilled Halibut Sarandeado

Grilled Halibut Sarandeado

MAKES 4 servings **PREP** 15 minutes **MARINATE** 30 minutes
GRILL 8 minutes

- 4 6-ounce fresh or frozen halibut or grouper fillets, about 1 inch thick
- ½ cup freshly squeezed lemon juice
- 1 medium fresh serrano chile, chopped
- 1 tablespoon Worcestershire sauce
- ½ teaspoon coarse salt
- ½ teaspoon black pepper
- ¼ cup coarsely chopped cilantro
-   Salt and black pepper
- 1 lemon, cut into wedges
-   Grilled green onions (optional)

① Thaw fish, if frozen. Rinse fish; pat dry with paper towels. Place fish in a large resealable plastic bag set in a shallow baking dish. In a blender combine lemon juice, chile, Worcestershire sauce, coarse salt, and the ½ teaspoon pepper. Cover and blend until smooth. Pour over fish in bag; seal bag. Marinate in the refrigerator for 30 minutes, turning bag once. (Do not marinate longer than 30 minutes.)

② Drain fish, reserving marinade. For a charcoal grill, grill fish on the greased rack of an uncovered grill directly over medium coals for 8 to 12 minutes or until fish begins to flake when tested with a fork, turning once and brushing with reserved marinade halfway through grilling. Discard remaining marinade. (For a gas grill, preheat grill. Reduce heat to medium. Place fish on greased grill rack over heat. Cover and grill as directed.)

③ Sprinkle fish with cilantro. Season to taste with salt and pepper. Serve with lemon wedges and, if desired, grilled green onions.

PER FILLET 176 calories; 2 g total fat (0 g sat. fat); 63 mg cholesterol; 481 mg sodium; 7 g carbohydrate; 2 g fiber; 34 g protein

Pescados sarandeado (sometimes spelled zarandeado) is simply fish that is cooked over charcoal—often outdoors on the beaches of Mexico, to which it is native. Serve it with warmed tortillas.

Oven-Roasted Fish with Peas and Tomatoes

MAKES 4 servings **PREP** 20 minutes **ROAST** 22 minutes
OVEN at 425°F

- 1¼ pounds fresh or frozen skinless ocean perch or cod fillets
- 2 cups frozen peas, thawed
- 1 cup fresh button mushrooms, halved
- ¾ cup grape tomatoes
- 1 small onion, cut into very thin wedges
- 4 teaspoons olive oil
- ¼ teaspoon salt
- ¼ teaspoon black pepper
-   Nonstick cooking spray
- 2 teaspoons snipped fresh dillweed or ½ teaspoon dried dillweed

① Thaw fish, if frozen. Rinse fish; pat dry with paper towels. If necessary, cut fish into four serving-size pieces.

② Preheat oven to 425°F. In a medium bowl combine peas, mushrooms, tomatoes, and onion. Drizzle with 3 teaspoons of the olive oil and sprinkle with ⅛ teaspoon of the salt and ⅛ teaspoon of the black pepper; toss to coat. Lightly coat a 15 x 10 x 1-inch baking pan with cooking spray. Spoon vegetables onto one side of the pan. Roast for 10 minutes.

③ Arrange fish fillets next to the vegetable mixture in pan, turning under any thin portions. Brush fish with the remaining 1 teaspoon olive oil and sprinkle with the remaining ⅛ teaspoon salt and ⅛ teaspoon black pepper. Stir vegetable mixture. Roast about 12 minutes more or until fish flakes easily when tested with a fork and vegetables are tender.

④ To serve, transfer fish and vegetables to four serving plates. Sprinkle with dillweed.

PER SERVING 228 calories; 6 g total fat (1 g sat. fat); 60 mg cholesterol; 306 mg sodium; 13 g carbohydrate; 4 g fiber; 30 g protein

Grilled Cod with Red Pepper Sauce ✪

MAKES 4 servings **PREP** 30 minutes
GRILL 4 minutes to 6 minutes per ½-inch thickness

- 4 4- to 6-ounce fresh or frozen skinless cod fillets
- 1¼ cups chopped red sweet pepper (1 large)
- 1 tablespoon olive oil
- 1 cup peeled, seeded, and chopped tomatoes (2 medium)
- 2 tablespoons white wine vinegar
- ¼ teaspoon salt
  Dash cayenne pepper
- 1 tablespoon olive oil
- 1 tablespoon snipped fresh basil or oregano or ½ teaspoon dried basil or oregano, crushed
  Red and/or yellow cherry tomatoes (optional)
  Fresh basil or oregano sprigs (optional)

① Thaw fish, if frozen. Rinse fish; pat dry with paper towels. Measure thickness of fish; set aside.

② For sauce, in a small skillet cook sweet pepper in 1 tablespoon hot oil over medium heat for 3 to 5 minutes or until tender, stirring occasionally. Stir in chopped tomatoes, 1 tablespoon of the vinegar, the salt, and cayenne pepper. Cook about 5 minutes or until tomatoes are softened, stirring occasionally. Cool slightly. Transfer mixture to a blender or food processor. Cover and blend until smooth. Return sauce to skillet; cover and keep warm.

③ In a small bowl stir together the remaining 1 tablespoon vinegar, 1 tablespoon oil, and snipped fresh or dried basil; brush over both sides of fish. Place fish in a greased grill basket, tucking under any thin edges.

④ For a charcoal grill, grill fish in basket on the rack of an uncovered grill directly over medium coals until fish begins to flake when tested with a fork, turning basket once halfway through grilling. Allow 4 to 6 minutes per ½-inch thickness of fish. (For a gas grill, preheat grill. Reduce heat to medium. Place fish in basket on grill rack over heat. Cover and grill as directed.)

⑤ Serve fish with sauce. If desired, garnish with cherry tomatoes and fresh basil sprigs.

PER SERVING 194 calories; 8 g total fat (1 g sat. fat); 41 mg cholesterol; 223 mg sodium; 4 g carbohydrate; 1 g fiber; 26 g protein

Tilapia Tacos with Jalapeño Slaw

MAKES 4 servings **PREP** 20 minutes **CHILL** 6 hours
GRILL 4 to 6 minutes per ½-inch thickness

- 1 pound fresh or frozen tilapia fillets
- 2½ cups purchased shredded cabbage with carrot (coleslaw mix)
- ¼ cup thinly sliced, halved red onion
- 1 small fresh jalapeño chile pepper, seeded and finely chopped (see tip, page 8)
- 2 tablespoons lime juice
- 2 tablespoons orange juice
- 2 tablespoons olive oil
- 1 teaspoon ground cumin
- ⅛ teaspoon salt
- ¼ teaspoon ancho chili powder or cayenne pepper
- 4 8-inch whole grain flour tortillas
  Peach or mango salsa (optional)
  Lime wedges

① Thaw fish, if frozen. Rinse fish; pat dry with paper towels. Measure thickness of fish fillets. Set aside. For Jalapeño Slaw, in a medium bowl combine coleslaw mix, red onion, and jalapeño pepper; set aside. In a small bowl whisk together lime juice, orange juice, oil, half of the cumin, and half of the salt. Pour lime juice mixture over the slaw. Toss to coat. Cover and chill for up to 6 hours.

② In a small bowl combine the remaining cumin, the remaining salt, and the ancho chili powder; sprinkle evenly on one side of each fish fillet.

③ Stack tortillas and wrap in heavy foil. Place fish and tortilla stack on the greased rack of an uncovered grill directly over medium coals. Grill just until fish flakes easily when tested with a fork and tortillas are heated through, turning fish and tortilla stack once halfway through grilling (allow 4 to 6 minutes per ½-inch thickness of fish). (For a gas grill, preheat grill. Reduce heat to medium. Place fish and tortilla stack on greased grill rack over heat. Cover and grill as above.)

④ Remove fish and tortillas from grill. Cut fish into four serving-size pieces and divide among tortillas. Top with slaw. If desired, serve with salsa. Pass lime wedges.

PER SERVING 324 calories; 12 g total fat (3 g sat. fat); 57 mg cholesterol; 466 mg sodium; 21 g carbohydrate; 12 g fiber; 32 g protein

Grilled Cod with Red Pepper Sauce

Thai Sole and Vegetables en Papillote

Thai Sole and Vegetables en Papillote ✪

MAKES 4 servings **PREP** 30 minutes **BAKE** 15 minutes
OVEN at 400°F

4   4- to 5-ounce fresh or frozen skinless sole or
    cod fillets
    Parchment paper
8   ounces fresh thin green beans, trimmed
2   medium red sweet peppers, seeded and
    thinly sliced
1   small onion, cut into thin wedges
¼   to ½ teaspoon crushed red pepper
4   cloves garlic, thinly sliced
2   teaspoons canola oil
1½ teaspoons finely shredded lemon peel
    Small fresh basil leaves (optional)

① Preheat oven to 400°F. Thaw fish, if frozen. Rinse fish;
pat dry with paper towels. Set aside.

② Tear off four 20 x 12-inch sheets of parchment paper;
fold each in half crosswise and crease. Unfold paper flat.
On half of each sheet, arrange beans, sweet peppers, and
onion. Sprinkle each with some of the crushed red pepper
and garlic. Top each with a piece of fish. Drizzle with
canola oil. Sprinkle with lemon peel. To make packets,
fold paper over fish and vegetables. To seal packets,
fold each of the open sides over ½ inch, then fold over
again ½ inch.

③ Place packets on a large baking sheet. Bake about
15 minutes or until fish flakes easily when tested with a
fork. (Carefully open the packets to test doneness.) If
desired, sprinkle with basil just before serving.

PER SERVING 157 calories; 4 g total fat (0 g sat. fat); 52 mg cholesterol;
95 mg sodium; 10 g carbohydrate; 4 g fiber; 21 g protein

Red Snapper with Sweet Peppers

MAKES 4 servings **PREP** 20 minutes **COOK** 12 minutes

1   pound fresh or frozen red snapper fillets, ½ to
    ¾ inch thick
2   tablespoons snipped fresh parsley
2   teaspoons finely shredded lemon peel
¼   teaspoon garlic salt
¼   teaspoon cracked black pepper
    Parchment paper
1   small red sweet pepper, cut into ½-inch
    wide strips
1   small green sweet pepper, cut into ½-inch
    wide strips

① Thaw fish, if frozen. Rinse fish; pat dry with paper
towels. Cut into 4 serving-size pieces; set aside. In a small
bowl combine parsley, lemon peel, garlic salt, and black
pepper; set aside.

② Tear four 20 x 12-inch pieces of parchment paper; fold
each in half crosswise and crease. Open. On half of each
parchment sheet, arrange one-fourth of the red and green
peppers. Top with one-fourth of the red snapper. Top with
one-fourth of the parsley mixture. To make packet, fold
parchment paper over fish. Crimp and fold edges to seal;
twist corners.

③ Fill a large Dutch oven* with water to a depth of
1 inch. Bring water to boiling. Place a steamer basket in
the Dutch oven. Arrange fish packets in a single layer in
the steamer basket, overlapping slightly if necessary.
Cover and steam for 12 to 14 minutes or until fish flakes
easily when tested with a fork. Serve immediately.

*Tip: Use a Dutch oven that is wide enough to allow the
steamer basket to lay fully open so there is enough room
for the fish.

PER SERVING 125 calories; 2 g total fat (0 g sat. fat); 42 mg cholesterol;
167 mg sodium; 3 g carbohydrate; 1 g fiber; 24 g protein

*Fish cooked "en papillote"—baked
in a parchment packet with
veggies—is super healthy.*

Mahi Mahi with Tropical Fruit Salsa ✪

MAKES 4 servings **PREP** 15 minutes **MARINATE** 30 minutes
GRILL 4 minutes to 6 minutes per ½-inch thickness

4	5- to 6-ounce fresh or frozen skinless mahi mahi or grouper fillets
½	cup reduced-sodium soy sauce
2	tablespoons honey
2	teaspoons toasted sesame oil or olive oil
1	teaspoon grated fresh ginger
1	cup peeled and chopped mango
1	cup chopped firm, ripe banana or sliced and quartered carambola (star fruit)
⅓	cup chopped macadamia nuts
2	tablespoons lime juice
2	tablespoons toasted coconut
	Lime wedges (optional)

① Thaw fish, if frozen. Rinse fish; pat dry with paper towels. Measure thickness of fish. Place fish in a shallow dish. For marinade, in a small bowl stir together soy sauce, honey, oil, and ginger. Pour marinade over fish; turn to coat. Cover and marinate in the refrigerator for 30 minutes, turning fish once or twice.

② Meanwhile, for salsa, in a medium bowl combine mango, banana, macadamia nuts, and lime juice. Cover and chill until ready to serve.

③ Drain fish, discarding marinade. Place fish in a greased grill basket, tucking under any thin edges.

④ For a charcoal grill, grill fish in basket on the rack of an uncovered grill directly over medium coals until fish begins to flake when tested with a fork, turning basket once halfway through grilling. Allow 4 to 6 minutes per ½-inch thickness of fish. (For a gas grill, preheat grill. Reduce heat to medium. Place fish in basket on grill rack over heat. Cover and grill as directed.)

⑤ Serve fish with salsa. Sprinkle each serving with toasted coconut. If desired, serve with lime wedges.

PER SERVING 286 calories; 11 g total fat (3 g sat. fat); 103 mg cholesterol; 368 mg sodium; 20 g carbohydrate; 3 g fiber; 28 g protein

Cuban-Style Swordfish

MAKES 4 servings **PREP** 25 minutes **MARINATE** 30 minutes
GRILL 8 minutes

1	recipe Fresh Tomato Salsa
1	pound fresh or frozen swordfish steaks, cut 1 inch thick
1	large clove garlic, halved
2	tablespoons lime juice
½	teaspoon ground cumin
¼	teaspoon black pepper
⅛	teaspoon salt

① Prepare Fresh Tomato Salsa. Thaw fish, if frozen. Rinse fish; pat dry with paper towels. Cut fish into 4 serving-size pieces. Rub fish on both sides with cut sides of halved garlic clove. Place fish in a shallow glass dish; drizzle with lime juice. Cover and marinate in the refrigerator for 30 minutes, turning once. Drain fish. In a small bowl combine cumin, black pepper, and salt; sprinkle over fish.

② Place fish on the greased rack of an uncovered grill directly over medium coals. Grill for 8 to 12 minutes or until fish flakes easily when tested with a fork, turning once halfway through grilling.

③ Serve swordfish with Fresh Tomato Salsa.

Fresh Tomato Salsa: In a medium bowl combine 1 cup chopped red and/or yellow tomato; ¼ cup chopped tomatillo; ¼ cup chopped avocado; 2 tablespoons snipped fresh cilantro; 1 medium fresh jalapeño chile pepper, seeded and finely chopped (see tip, page 8); 1 clove garlic, minced; 1 tablespoon lime juice; ⅛ teaspoon salt; and ⅛ teaspoon ground black pepper. Serve immediately or cover and chill up to 4 hours.

PER SERVING 181 calories; 7 g total fat (2 g sat. fat); 43 mg cholesterol; 253 mg sodium; 6 g carbohydrate; 2 g fiber; 24 g protein

Look for avocados that are not bruised or overly soft and that have no gouges or broken skin. Firm, ripe avocados that are ready to eat and good for chopping yield to gentle pressure when cradled in your hands. A very ripe avocado—the kind you need to make guacamole—feels soft but not mushy.

Thai Tuna Kabobs

Thai Tuna Kabobs

MAKES 4 servings **PREP** 30 minutes **MARINATE** 2 hours
GRILL 10 minutes

- 1 pound fresh or frozen tuna steaks, cut 1 inch thick
- ¼ cup snipped fresh cilantro
- 1 teaspoon finely shredded lemon peel or lime peel
- 3 tablespoons lemon juice or lime juice
- 3 tablespoons rice vinegar
- 1 to 2 fresh Thai, serrano, or jalapeño chile peppers, seeded and finely chopped (see tip, page 8)
- 1 teaspoon sesame seeds
- 1 teaspoon toasted sesame oil
- 2 medium zucchini, cut into 1-inch slices
- 1 medium red onion, cut into 8 wedges
   Lime wedges (optional)

① Thaw fish, if frozen. If using wooden skewers, soak skewers in water for at least 30 minutes. Rinse fish; pat dry with paper towels. Cut fish into 1-inch pieces; set aside. For marinade, in a small bowl combine 2 tablespoons of the cilantro, the lemon peel, lemon juice, vinegar, chile pepper, sesame seeds, and oil; set aside.

② On eight skewers, alternately thread fish,* zucchini, and red onion, leaving ¼ inch between pieces. Place kabobs on a platter or in a shallow dish. Brush ¼ cup of the marinade over kabobs. Cover and marinate in the refrigerator for 2 to 4 hours. Cover and chill the remaining marinade.

③ For a charcoal grill, grill kabobs on the greased rack of an uncovered grill directly over medium coals for 10 to 12 minutes or until fish begins to flake when tested with a fork but is still slightly pink inside, turning occasionally during grilling. (For a gas grill, preheat grill. Reduce heat to medium. Place kabobs on greased grill rack over heat. Cover and grill as directed.)

④ Transfer kabobs to a serving platter. Sprinkle with the remaining 2 tablespoons cilantro. Serve the remaining chilled marinade as a sauce. If desired, garnish with lime wedges.

*Note: Thread tuna onto skewers perpendicular to the grain of the fish.

PER 2 KABOBS 215 calories; 7 g total fat (2 g sat. fat); 43 mg cholesterol; 58 mg sodium; 8 g carbohydrate; 2 g fiber; 28 g protein

Tuna and Hummus Wrap

MAKES 4 servings **START TO FINISH** 20 minutes

- 1 6-ounce can very low sodium chunk white tuna (water pack), drained
- 1 small cucumber, peeled, seeded, and finely chopped
- 1 small tomato, seeded and chopped
- 2 tablespoons olive oil
- 1 tablespoon snipped fresh dill or 1 teaspoon dried dill, crushed
- ¼ teaspoon black pepper
- 4 8-inch whole wheat tortillas
- ⅓ cup refrigerated cucumber-dill hummus
- 4 cups torn packaged lettuce (such as hearts of romaine, European blend, or Mediterranean blend)

① In a medium bowl stir together tuna, cucumber, tomato, oil, dill, and pepper.

② Spread hummus on one side of each tortilla. Toss tuna mixture with lettuce. Divide evenly among the tortillas. Roll up.

PER SERVING 280 calories; 11 g total fat (1 g sat. fat); 19 mg cholesterol; 482 mg sodium; 32 g carbohydrate; 4 g fiber; 16 g protein

Tuna and Hummus Wrap

{

menu

Roasted Broccoli and
Tomatoes

Tuna and Noodles
[below]

Chocolate Whoopie
Pies

}

Tuna and Noodles

MAKES 4 servings **STAND** 35 minutes **PREP** 15 minutes

- 1   **6.5-ounce container light semisoft cheese with cucumber and dill or garlic and herb**
- 4   **ounces dried wide rice noodles, broken**
- 1½   **cups sliced fresh mushrooms**
- 1   **small onion, chopped**
- 1   **stalk celery, sliced**
- ¼   **cup water**
- ⅓   **cup fat-free milk**
- 3   **4.5-ounce cans very low-sodium chunk white tuna (water pack), drained and broken into chunks**
- ½   **cup cornflakes or crushed reduced-fat shredded wheat crackers**

① Let cheese stand at room temperature for 30 minutes. Place noodles in a large bowl. Add enough *boiling water* to cover noodles by several inches. Let stand for 5 minutes, stirring occasionally. Drain and set aside.

② Meanwhile, in a microwave-safe 2-quart casserole combine mushrooms, onion, celery, and the ¼ cup water. Microwave, covered, on high for 3 to 4 minutes or until vegetables are tender, stirring once halfway through cooking.

③ Add the cheese and milk to mushroom mixture. Stir until well mixed. Stir in drained noodles and tuna. Microwave, covered, on high for 3 to 4 minutes or until heated through, gently stirring once halfway through cooking. Sprinkle with cornflakes.

PER SERVING 331 calories; 9 g total fat (5 g sat. fat); 73 mg cholesterol; 454 mg sodium; 33 g carbohydrate; 1 g fiber; 31 g protein

Lime Salmon with Green Beans

MAKES 4 servings **PREP** 25 minutes **GRILL** 20 minutes

- 12   **ounces fresh green beans, trimmed**
- 1   **medium yellow summer squash, sliced**
- 4   **4-ounce skinless salmon fillets**
- 1   **tablespoon olive oil**
- 2   **tablespoons snipped fresh parsley**
- 1   **teaspoon finely shredded lime peel**
- 2   **cloves garlic, minced**
- ¼   **teaspoon seasoned salt**

① Tear off four 24 x 18-inch pieces of heavy-duty foil. Fold each in half to make an 18 x 12-inch rectangle. Divide green beans and summer squash among foil rectangles.

② Place fish on the vegetable mixture. Drizzle fish with oil; sprinkle with snipped parsley, lime peel, garlic, and seasoned salt. For each packet, bring up two opposite edges of the foil and seal with a double fold. Fold remaining ends to completely enclose the food, allowing space for steam to build.

③ For a charcoal grill, grill foil packets on the rack of an uncovered grill directly over medium coals about 20 minutes or until fish begins to flake when tested with a fork and vegetables are tender, carefully opening packets to check doneness. (For a gas grill, preheat grill. Reduce heat to medium. Place foil packets on grill rack over heat. Cover and grill as above.)

Oven Method: Preheat oven to 350°F. Prepare as directed through Step 2. Bake packets directly on the oven rack about 20 minutes or until fish begins to flake when tested with a fork and vegetables are tender, carefully opening packets to check doneness.

PER SERVING 301 calories; 19 g total fat (4 g sat. fat); 62 mg cholesterol; 169 mg sodium; 8 g carbohydrate; 4 g fiber; 25 g protein

Lime Salmon with Green Beans

Grilled Salmon Salad Niçoise

Grilled Salmon Salad Niçoise

MAKES 6 servings **PREP** 20 minutes **COOK** 15 minutes
GRILL 4 to 6 minutes per ½-inch thickness

- 2   4- to 5-ounce fresh or frozen skinless salmon fillets
- 8   tiny new potatoes
- 8   ounces fresh green beans, trimmed
- ¼   teaspoon lemon-pepper seasoning
      Nonstick cooking spray
- 6   cups torn mixed salad greens
- 8   grape tomatoes or cherry tomatoes, halved
- ½   cup snipped fresh chives
- 4   hard-cooked eggs, cut into wedges
- ¼   cup niçoise olives, pitted, and/or other pitted olives
- 1   recipe Lemon Vinaigrette

① Thaw salmon, if frozen. Rinse salmon; pat dry with paper towels. Set aside. Peel a strip around the center of each potato. In a covered large saucepan, cook potatoes in enough lightly salted boiling water to cover for 10 minutes. Add green beans. Return to boiling; reduce heat. Cover and simmer about 5 minutes more or until potatoes and beans are tender. Drain. Rinse with cold water to cool quickly; drain again. Set aside.

② Meanwhile, measure thickness of salmon fillets. Sprinkle salmon with lemon-pepper seasoning. Lightly coat both sides of salmon fillets with cooking spray.

③ For a charcoal grill, place salmon fillets on the rack of an uncovered grill directly over medium coals. Grill for 4 to 6 minutes per ½-inch thickness or until fish flakes easily when tested with a fork, turning once halfway through grilling if fish is more than ¾ inch thick. (For a gas grill, preheat grill. Reduce heat to medium. Place salmon fillets on grill rack over heat. Cover and grill as above.) Cut salmon into serving-size pieces.

④ Line six plates with salad greens. Arrange salmon, potatoes, green beans, tomatoes, chives, eggs, and olives on greens. Drizzle with Lemon Vinaigrette.

Lemon Vinaigrette: In a screw-top jar combine ½ teaspoon finely shredded lemon peel; ¼ cup lemon juice; 2 tablespoons olive oil; 1 clove garlic, minced; ⅛ teaspoon salt; and ⅛ teaspoon ground black pepper. Cover and shake well. Makes about ½ cup.

PER SERVING 242 calories; 16 g total fat (3 g sat. fat); 162 mg cholesterol; 221 mg sodium; 12 g carbohydrate; 4 g fiber; 14 g protein

Broiled Salmon Orzo ㉚

MAKES 4 servings **START TO FINISH** 25 minutes

- 4   4- to 5-ounce fresh or frozen skinless salmon fillets
- ¼   teaspoon salt
- ⅛   teaspoon ground black pepper
- ⅓   cup dried orzo pasta (rosamarina)
- 1   tablespoon chopped pitted ripe olives
- 1   tablespoon snipped fresh parsley
- 1   teaspoon olive oil
- ½   teaspoon finely shredded lemon peel
      Lemon wedges

① Preheat broiler. Thaw fish, if frozen. Rinse fish; pat dry with paper towels. Measure thickness of fish. Place fish on the greased unheated rack of a broiler pan, tucking under any thin edges. Sprinkle with ⅛ teaspoon of the salt and half of the pepper. Set aside.

② Cook orzo according to package directions; drain. Return to hot pan. Stir in olives, parsley, oil, lemon peel, the remaining ⅛ teaspoon salt, and the remaining pepper.

③ Meanwhile, broil fish about 4 inches from the heat for 4 to 6 minutes per ½-inch thickness or until fish flakes easily when tested with a fork. (If fillets are 1 inch or more thick, carefully turn once halfway through broiling.)

④ Serve fish with orzo and lemon wedges.

PER SERVING 304 calories; 17 g total fat (4 g sat. fat); 62 mg cholesterol; 220 mg sodium; 12 g carbohydrate; 1 g fiber; 25 g protein

Broiled Salmon Orzo

Salmon with Roasted Vegetables ③⓪

MAKES 4 servings **START TO FINISH** 30 minutes **OVEN** at 450°F

4   4- to 5-ounce fresh or frozen skinless salmon fillets, about 1 inch thick

Nonstick cooking spray

1   tablespoon snipped fresh dillweed or 1 teaspoon dried dillweed

½   teaspoon salt

¼   teaspoon black pepper

2   medium zucchini and/or yellow summer squash, cut crosswise into ¼-inch-thick slices (about 2½ cups)

1   cup grape or cherry tomatoes, halved

4   green onions, cut into 1-inch pieces

1   tablespoon Dijon mustard

① Preheat oven to 450°F. Thaw fish, if frozen. Rinse fish and pat dry with paper towels. Set aside. Line a 15 x 10 x 1-inch baking pan with foil; lightly coat foil with cooking spray. Set aside.

② In a small bowl combine dillweed, salt, and pepper; set aside. In a large bowl combine zucchini, tomatoes, and onions. Generously coat vegetables with cooking spray, tossing to coat evenly. Sprinkle with half of the dillweed mixture, tossing to coat evenly.

③ Spoon vegetable mixture into one side of the prepared baking pan. Place fish in other side of pan. Stir mustard into remaining dillweed mixture. Spread mustard mixture evenly over fish. Measure thickness of fish in the thickest part of the fillets.

④ Bake, uncovered, for 4 to 6 minutes per ½-inch thickness of fish or until fish begins to flake when tested with a fork and zucchini is crisp-tender.

PER SERVING 239 calories; 12 g total fat (3 g sat. fat); 66 mg cholesterol; 463 mg sodium; 6 g carbohydrate; 2 g fiber; 24 g protein

Salmon with Cilantro-Pineapple Salsa ③⓪

MAKES 4 servings **PREP** 20 minutes **GRILL** 8 minutes

1   1-pound fresh or frozen skinless salmon fillet, about 1 inch thick

2   cups coarsely chopped fresh pineapple

½   cup chopped red or green sweet pepper

¼   cup finely chopped red onion

1   small fresh jalapeño chile pepper, seeded and finely chopped (see tip, page 8)

2   tablespoons snipped fresh cilantro or parsley

½   teaspoon finely shredded lime peel

3   tablespoons lime juice

½   teaspoon chili powder

¼   teaspoon salt

Dash cayenne pepper

Lime wedges (optional)

Torn lettuce (optional)

① Thaw fish, if frozen. Rinse fish; pat dry with paper towels. For Cilantro Pineapple Salsa, in a medium bowl combine chopped pineapple, sweet pepper, red onion, 2 tablespoons of the lime juice, the chile pepper, and 1 tablespoon of the cilantro. Set aside. In a small bowl combine lime peel, the remaining 1 tablespoon lime juice, the remaining 1 tablespoon cilantro, the chili powder, salt, and cayenne pepper. Brush on both sides of fish.

② Spray wire grill basket with nonstick cooking spray. Place fish in grill basket, tucking under any thin edges for an even thickness. Place grill basket on the rack of an uncovered grill directly over medium coals. Grill for 8 to 12 minutes or just until fish flakes easily with a fork, carefully turning once halfway through grilling.

③ Serve with salsa, and, if desired, lime wedges and lettuce.

PER SERVING 257 calories; 12 g total fat (2 g sat. fat); 66 mg cholesterol; 219 mg sodium; 13 g carbohydrate; 2 g fiber; 23 g protein

To prepare a fresh pineapple, first cut off the crown and bottom. Working from top to bottom, cut the skin off with a knife, removing any remaining "eyes" with the tip of the knife. Cut the pineapple into wedges, then cut the core off the top of each wedge.

Salmon with Cilantro-Pineapple Salsa

Steamed Orange Salmon

Steamed Orange Salmon ③⓪

MAKES 4 servings   **PREP** 15 minutes   **COOK** 6 minutes

4   4- to 5-ounce fresh or frozen skinless
    salmon fillets
1   orange
2   teaspoons olive oil
1   teaspoon toasted sesame seeds
¼   teaspoon salt
¼   teaspoon ground white pepper
    Cooked fresh asparagus (optional)
    Orange slices and/or toasted sesame seeds
    (optional)

① Thaw fish, if frozen. Rinse fish; pat dry with paper
towels; set aside. Finely shred 2 teaspoons peel from the
orange; set aside. Thinly slice orange and lay slices
evenly in the bottom of a steamer basket. Place the fish in
a single layer on top of the orange slices. In a small bowl
combine orange peel, olive oil, sesame seeds, salt, and
pepper. Spoon evenly on salmon fillets.

② Fill a large Dutch oven* with water to a depth of
1 inch. Bring water to boiling. Carefully place steamer
basket over water. Cover and steam over gently boiling
water for 6 to 8 minutes or until fish flakes easily when
tested with a fork.

③ To serve, arrange salmon on a serving platter. Discard
orange slices. If desired, serve with asparagus, orange
slices, and/or sprinkle with additional sesame seeds.

***Tip:** Use a Dutch oven that is wide enough to allow the
steamer basket to lay fully open so there is enough room
for the fish.

PER SERVING 275 calories; 18 g total fat (4 g sat. fat); 62 mg cholesterol;
213 mg sodium; 4 g carbohydrate; 1 g fiber; 24 g protein

*To toast sesame seeds, spread in a single
layer in a small skillet. Place over medium-
low heat for 5 to 7 minutes or until seeds
are golden-brown, swirling the skillet
occasionally.*

Blackened Salmon with Vegetables ③⓪

MAKES 4 servings   **PREP** 20 minutes   **BROIL** 8 minutes

4   4-ounce fresh or frozen skinless, boneless
    salmon fillets, about 1 inch thick
6   cups cauliflower and/or broccoli florets
1   tablespoon smoked paprika or sweet paprika
1   tablespoon chili powder
1   teaspoon garlic powder
½   teaspoon salt
½   teaspoon ground cumin
½   teaspoon black pepper
    Nonstick cooking spray
    Lemon slices (optional)

① Thaw fish, if frozen. Preheat broiler. Rinse fish; pat dry
with paper towels. Set aside.

② Place cauliflower and/or broccoli in a large
microwave-safe bowl; add 2 tablespoons water. Cover with
vented plastic wrap. Microwave for 2 minutes; drain.

③ In a small bowl combine paprika, chili powder, garlic
powder, salt, cumin, and black pepper. Transfer half
(about 1½ tablespoons) of the spice mixture to a large
piece of waxed paper. Gently roll fish fillets in spice
mixture to coat. Toss drained vegetables with remaining
spice mixture in a large bowl.

④ Coat the bottom of a 15 x 10 x 1-inch baking pan with
nonstick cooking spray. Place fish fillets on one side of the
pan and vegetables on other side of the pan. Turn under
any thin portions of fish to make uniform thickness. Coat
tops of fish with nonstick cooking spray.

⑤ Broil fish and vegetables 4 inches from the heat for
8 to 12 minutes or until fish flakes easily when tested with
a fork and vegetables are crisp-tender, carefully turning
fish and stirring vegetables once halfway through broiling.

⑥ If desired, serve salmon with lemon slices.

PER SERVING 288 calories; 16 g total fat (4 g sat. fat); 62 mg
cholesterol; 424 mg sodium; 11 g carbohydrate; 5 g fiber; 27 g protein

Sautéed Shrimp and Bok Choy ⑳

MAKES 4 servings **PREP** 15 minutes **COOK** 5 minutes

1   pound fresh or frozen large shrimp in shells
3   cups bok choy, cut into 2-inch slices
2   cloves garlic, minced
1   tablespoon toasted sesame oil
1   cup snow pea pods
2   teaspoons reduced-sodium soy sauce
¼   teaspoon black pepper
1   tablespoon toasted sesame seeds
    Hot cooked udon noodles or whole grain spaghetti (optional)

① Thaw shrimp, if frozen. Peel and devein shrimp, leaving tails intact. Rinse shrimp; pat dry with paper towels.

② In an extra-large skillet cook and stir shrimp, bok choy, and garlic in hot oil over medium-high heat for 4 to 6 minutes or just until shrimp are opaque. Carefully add pea pods, soy sauce, and black pepper to skillet. Cook and stir 1 minute.

③ To serve, sprinkle each serving with sesame seeds. If desired, serve with hot cooked udon noodles or whole grain spaghetti.

PER SERVING 185 calories; 7 g total fat (1 g sat. fat); 172 mg cholesterol; 301 mg sodium; 6 g carbohydrate; 2 g fiber; 25 g protein

Sautéed Shrimp and Bok Choy

Asian Spring Rolls ⑳

MAKES 4 servings **START TO FINISH** 30 minutes

8   ounces fresh or frozen cooked, peeled, and deveined shrimp, coarsely chopped (1⅓ cups)
1   small head butterhead (Boston or bibb) lettuce, cored and shredded (2 cups)
1   cup shredded carrots (2 medium)
¼   cup sliced green onions (2)
2   tablespoons snipped fresh cilantro
1   recipe Peanut Sauce
1   tablespoon seasoned rice vinegar
    Hot water
8   8-inch round rice paper spring roll wrappers
    Fresh cilantro leaves (optional)

① For filling, in a bowl combine shrimp, lettuce, carrots, green onions, and snipped cilantro. Add 2 tablespoons of the Peanut Sauce and the vinegar. Toss to coat.

② For the dipping sauce, in a small bowl whisk together remaining Peanut Sauce and enough hot water to make dipping consistency; set aside.

③ Fill a very large skillet about half full with water. Bring just to simmering then remove from heat. Place 1 wrapper in the skillet at a time, pushing it down gently to cover with water. Allow to soften for about 10 to 15 seconds. Using two tongs, gently lift the wrapper from the water and place it on a dinner plate (ensure that it is laying flat on the plate, so rice paper doesn't stick to itself). Pull gently and carefully on the edges to straighten while warm.

④ Place about ⅓ cup of the filling about ½ inch from the bottom edge of one moistened wrapper. Fold the bottom edge over the filling. Fold in sides. Roll up. Repeat with remaining filling and wrappers. Cut rolls in half; serve with dipping sauce. If desired, garnish with fresh cilantro leaves.

Peanut Sauce: In a small saucepan combine 3 tablespoons creamy peanut butter; 2 tablespoons water; 1 tablespoon light soy sauce; 1 clove garlic, minced; and ¼ teaspoon ground ginger. Heat over very low heat until smooth, whisking constantly.

PER SERVING 231 calories; 7 g total fat (1 g sat. fat); 111 mg cholesterol; 396 mg sodium; 26 g carbohydrate; 3 g fiber; 17 g protein

Shrimp Boil-Style Dinner

Shrimp Boil-Style Dinner

MAKES 4 servings **PREP** 30 minutes **GRILL** 12 minutes

- 1 pound fresh or frozen large shrimp in shells
- 1 pound tiny new potatoes, quartered
- 2 small fresh ears of corn, husked and cut into 1½- to 3-inch-long pieces
- 3 ounces cooked kielbasa or andouille sausage, coarsely chopped
- ¾ teaspoon Old Bay Seasoning or 1½ teaspoons reduced-sodium Old Bay Seasoning
- 1 lemon, cut into wedges
- 2 tablespoons snipped fresh parsley

① Thaw shrimp, if frozen. Peel and devein shrimp, leaving tails intact. Rinse shrimp; pat dry with paper towels. Set aside. In a large covered saucepan cook potatoes in a small amount of boiling water for 6 minutes. Add corn; cook for 6 minutes more. Drain; set aside. Tear off four 24 x 18-inch pieces of heavy-duty foil. Fold each in half to make an 18 x 12-inch rectangle.

② Divide shrimp, potatoes, corn, and sausage among foil rectangles. Sprinkle with seasoning. For each packet, bring up two opposite edges of the foil and seal with a double fold. Fold remaining ends to completely enclose the food, allowing space for steam to build.

③ For a charcoal grill, grill foil packets on the rack of an uncovered grill directly over medium coals for 12 to 15 minutes or until shrimp turn opaque and vegetables are tender, carefully opening packets to check doneness. (For a gas grill, preheat grill. Reduce heat to medium. Place foil packets on grill rack over heat. Cover and grill as above.)

④ Serve with lemon wedges and sprinkle with parsley.

Oven Method: Preheat oven to 350°F. Prepare as directed through Step 2. Bake packets directly on the oven rack for 12 to 15 minutes or until shrimp turn opaque and vegetables are tender, carefully opening packets to check doneness. Serve as directed in Step 4.

PER SERVING 303 calories; 9 g total fat (3 g sat. fat); 187 mg cholesterol; 477 mg sodium; 28 g carbohydrate; 4 g fiber; 29 g protein

menu

Heirloom Tomato Salad

Spicy Shrimp Casserole [below]

Fruited Oatmeal Cookies

Spicy Shrimp Casserole

MAKES 6 servings **PREP** 20 minutes **BAKE** 52 minutes
STAND 10 minutes **OVEN** at 350°F

- 6 6-inch corn tortillas, cut into bite-size strips
- 1 cup bottled green salsa
- 1 cup shredded reduced-fat Monterey Jack cheese (4 ounces)
- ½ cup light sour cream
- 3 tablespoons flour
- ¼ cup snipped fresh cilantro
- 1 12-ounce package frozen cooked, peeled, and deveined shrimp, thawed
- 1 cup frozen gold and white whole kernel corn
- 1 medium tomato, coarsely chopped
- ¼ cup light sour cream (optional)

① Preheat oven to 350°F. Place half of the tortilla strips in the bottom of a lightly greased 2-quart baking dish; set aside. Arrange remaining tortilla strips on a baking sheet; bake for 12 to 14 minutes or until crisp.

② Meanwhile, in a large bowl stir together salsa, cheese, the ½ cup sour cream, the flour, and 2 tablespoons of the cilantro. Stir in shrimp and corn. Spoon shrimp mixture over tortilla strips in baking dish.

③ Bake, uncovered, for 40 to 45 minutes or until heated through. Let stand for 10 minutes before serving. Sprinkle with baked tortilla strips, tomato, and the remaining 2 tablespoons cilantro. If desired, serve with the ¼ cup sour cream.

PER SERVING 242 calories; 8 g total fat (4 g sat. fat); 129 mg cholesterol; 564 mg sodium; 25 g carbohydrate; 3 g fiber; 20 g protein

Pasta with Asparagus and Shrimp 30

MAKES 4 servings **START TO FINISH** 30 minutes

- 12 ounces fresh or frozen medium shrimp in shells
- 6 ounces dried whole wheat bow tie pasta
- 12 ounces fresh asparagus, trimmed and cut into 1-inch pieces
- 1 tablespoon olive oil
- 4 cloves garlic, minced
- 2 teaspoons snipped fresh lemon-thyme or thyme, or ½ teaspoon dried thyme, crushed
- ⅓ cup fat-free half-and-half

① Thaw shrimp, if frozen. Peel and devein shrimp, leaving tails intact if desired. Rinse shrimp; pat dry with paper towels. Set aside. In a large saucepan cook pasta according to package directions, adding the asparagus for the last 2 minutes of cooking. Drain pasta mixture and return to pan.

② Meanwhile, in a large skillet heat oil over medium-high heat. Add garlic and dried thyme (if using). Cook and stir for 10 seconds. Add shrimp; cook for 2 to 3 minutes or until shrimp turn opaque, stirring frequently. Stir in half-and-half; reduce heat. Heat through. Remove from heat.

③ Add shrimp mixture and fresh thyme (if using) to the pasta mixture in pan. Toss to coat. Serve warm.

PER SERVING 315 calories; 6 g total fat (1 g sat. fat); 130 mg cholesterol; 157 mg sodium; 38 g carbohydrate; 4 g fiber; 25 g protein

Shrimp and Mushroom Pasta

Shrimp and Mushroom Pasta 30

MAKES 4 servings **START TO FINISH** 30 minutes

- 12 ounces fresh or frozen medium shrimp in shells
- 8 ounces dried whole grain angel hair pasta or spaghetti
- 1 tablespoon olive oil
- 8 ounces fresh shiitake mushrooms, chopped
- 8 ounces fresh cremini or button mushrooms, sliced
- 2 cloves garlic, minced
- 1 14.5-ounce can no-salt-added diced tomatoes, undrained
- 2 teaspoons snipped fresh oregano
- ¼ teaspoon salt
- ¼ teaspoon freshly ground black pepper
  Fresh oregano sprigs or snipped fresh parsley

① Thaw shrimp, if frozen. Peel and devein shrimp; remove tails. Rinse shrimp; pat dry with paper towels. Set aside. Cook pasta according to package directions; drain. Return to hot pan; cover and keep warm.

② Meanwhile, for sauce, in a 12-inch nonstick skillet heat oil over medium-high heat. Add mushrooms and garlic; cook and stir for 4 minutes. Stir in undrained tomatoes, snipped oregano, salt, and pepper. Bring to boiling; reduce heat. Simmer, uncovered, for 5 to 10 minutes or until mixture is thickened. Stir in shrimp. Simmer, covered, about 2 minutes more or until shrimp are opaque.

③ Serve shrimp and mushrooms over hot cooked pasta. Garnish with oregano sprigs.

PER SERVING 371 calories; 6 g total fat (1 g sat. fat); 129 mg cholesterol; 343 mg sodium; 49 g carbohydrate; 7 g fiber; 31 g protein

The stems of shiitake mushrooms are woody and bitter. Be sure to cut off and discard them before chopping the mushrooms.

Coconut Shrimp with Mango Rice Pilaf

Coconut Shrimp with Mango Rice Pilaf

MAKES 4 servings **PREP** 25 minutes **BAKE** 8 minutes **OVEN** at 450°F

1	pound fresh or frozen extra-large shrimp in shells
	Nonstick cooking spray
¼	cup refrigerated or frozen egg product, thawed, or 2 egg whites, lightly beaten
¾	cup finely crushed reduced-fat or reduced-sodium shredded wheat crackers
⅓	cup shredded coconut
¼	teaspoon ground ginger
¼	teaspoon black pepper
1	8.8-ounce package cooked brown rice
⅓	cup chopped fresh mango or chopped jarred mango, rinsed and drained
⅓	cup sliced green onions
2	tablespoons snipped fresh cilantro

① Thaw shrimp, if frozen. Preheat oven to 450°F. Lightly coat a large baking sheet with nonstick cooking spray; set aside. Peel and devein shrimp, leaving tails intact. Rinse shrimp; pat dry with paper towels.

② Place egg in a shallow dish. In another shallow dish combine crushed crackers, coconut, ginger, and pepper. Dip shrimp into egg, turning to coat. Dip in coconut mixture, pressing to coat, leaving tails uncoated. Arrange shrimp in a single layer on the prepared baking sheet.

③ Bake for 8 to 10 minutes or until shrimp are opaque and coating is lightly browned. Meanwhile, heat rice according to package directions. Transfer to a serving bowl. Stir in mango and green onions. Serve rice with shrimp; sprinkle with cilantro.

PER SERVING 328 calories; 8 g total fat (3 g sat. fat); 172 mg cholesterol; 291 mg sodium; 35 g carbohydrate; 3 g fiber; 29 g protein

Seafood-Stuffed Shells

MAKES 6 servings **PREP** 45 minutes **BAKE** 30 minutes **STAND** 10 minutes **OVEN** at 350°F

1	pound fresh or frozen large shrimp in shells
12	dried jumbo shell macaroni
1	medium red sweet pepper, chopped
½	cup chopped sweet onion
1	tablespoon olive oil
3	cloves garlic, minced
⅓	cup dry white wine or reduced-sodium chicken broth
¾	cup reduced-sodium chicken broth
¼	cup flour
2	cups fat-free milk
8	ounces cooked crabmeat, coarsely chopped, or good quality canned lump crabmeat, drained
2	tablespoons snipped fresh basil
1	tablespoon snipped fresh chives

① Thaw shrimp, if frozen. Peel and devein shrimp; rinse with cold water and pat dry with paper towels. Coarsely chop shrimp and set aside. Meanwhile, cook pasta according to package directions; drain. Rinse with cold water; drain again.

② Preheat oven to 350°F. In a large nonstick skillet cook sweet pepper and onion in hot oil over medium heat for 5 minutes, stirring occasionally. Add shrimp. Cook for 2 to 3 minutes or until shrimp are opaque, stirring occasionally. Transfer shrimp mixture to a medium bowl.

③ For sauce, add garlic to the same skillet. Cook and stir for 30 seconds. Remove skillet from heat. Carefully add wine; return skillet to heat and cook for 1 to 2 minutes or until most of the wine is evaporated, stirring to scrape up browned bits from bottom of skillet. In a small bowl whisk together the ¾ cup broth and the flour. Add all at once to the skillet along with the milk. Cook and stir until thickened and bubbly.

④ Stir ⅔ cup of the sauce and the crab into the shrimp mixture. Spoon shrimp mixture evenly into the cooked shells. Arrange shells in a 2-quart square baking dish. Pour remaining sauce over the shells.

⑤ Cover and bake for 30 to 35 minutes or until heated through. Let stand for 10 minutes. Sprinkle with basil and chives just before serving. Serve in shallow bowls.

PER SERVING 317 calories; 5 g total fat (1 g sat. fat); 154 mg cholesterol; 325 mg sodium; 33 g carbohydrate; 1 g fiber; 31 g protein

Scallops and Pasta with Lemon-Caper Cream Sauce

MAKES 6 servings **START TO FINISH** 35 minutes

1½	pounds fresh or frozen sea scallops
4	ounces dried multigrain or whole grain penne or rotini pasta
3	cups trimmed, coarsely shredded Swiss chard or kale
1	medium zucchini, halved lengthwise and bias-sliced crosswise
	Nonstick cooking spray
½	teaspoon salt
⅛	teaspoon black pepper
2	teaspoons olive oil
2	medium leeks, trimmed and thinly sliced
2	cloves garlic, minced
2	cups fat-free milk
2	tablespoons cornstarch
2	teaspoons finely shredded lemon peel
1½	teaspoons snipped fresh rosemary or thyme or ½ teaspoon dried rosemary or thyme, crushed
2	tablespoons capers, drained

① Thaw scallops, if frozen. Rinse scallops; pat dry with paper towels and set aside. In a large saucepan cook pasta according to package directions, adding chard and zucchini for the last 4 minutes of cooking time. Drain and keep warm.

② Meanwhile, lightly coat an unheated large nonstick skillet with cooking spray. Preheat over medium-high heat. Sprinkle scallops with ¼ teaspoon of the salt and the pepper. Add scallops to hot skillet; cook for 4 to 6 minutes or until scallops are opaque, turning once. Remove scallops from skillet; keep warm.

③ Add oil to skillet; reduce heat to medium. Add leeks and garlic; cook for 3 to 5 minutes or until tender, stirring to scrape up any browned bits from bottom of skillet.

④ In a medium bowl whisk together milk and cornstarch until smooth. Add to leek mixture in skillet along with lemon peel, rosemary, and the remaining ¼ teaspoon salt. Cook and stir until thickened and bubbly. Cook and stir for 2 minutes more. Add to pasta mixture, tossing to coat.

⑤ Divide pasta mixture among six serving plates. Top with scallops and capers.

PER SERVING 247 calories; 3 g total fat (0 g sat. fat); 39 mg cholesterol; 525 mg sodium; 28 g carbohydrate; 3 g fiber; 26 g protein

Curried Sea Scallops ㉚

MAKES 4 servings **START TO FINISH** 25 minutes

1	pound fresh or frozen sea scallops
1	teaspoon curry powder
¼	teaspoon ground ginger
⅛	teaspoon cracked black pepper
⅛	teaspoon chili powder
2	cups cherry tomatoes or grape tomatoes, halved
1	tablespoon olive oil
	Fresh cilantro sprigs
	Lemon slices, halved (optional)

① Thaw scallops, if frozen. Rinse scallops; pat dry with paper towels. Sprinkle scallops with curry powder, ginger, pepper, and chili powder; set aside. Tear off four 24 x 18-inch pieces of heavy-duty foil. Fold each in half to make an 18 x 12-inch rectangle.

② Divide seasoned scallops and tomatoes among foil rectangles. Drizzle with oil. For each packet, bring up two opposite edges of the foil and seal with a double fold. Fold remaining ends to completely enclose the food, allowing space for steam to build.

③ For a charcoal grill, grill foil packets on the rack of an uncovered grill directly over medium coals for 8 to 10 minutes or until scallops turn opaque, carefully opening packets to check doneness. (For a gas grill, preheat grill. Reduce heat to medium. Place foil packets on grill rack over heat. Cover and grill as above.)

④ Sprinkle individual servings with cilantro. If desired, serve with lemon slices.

Oven Method: Preheat oven to 450°F. Prepare as directed through Step 2. Bake packets directly on the oven rack for 10 to 12 minutes or until scallops turn opaque, carefully opening packets to check doneness. Serve as directed in Step 4.

PER SERVING 149 calories; 5 g total fat (1 g sat. fat); 37 mg cholesterol; 189 mg sodium; 7 g carbohydrate; 1 g fiber; 20 g protein

Curried Sea Scallops

Pasta with Ricotta and Vegetables,
page 188

Make-'em-Meatless Main Dishes

Pasta with Ricotta and Vegetables 🕤 (photo page 186)

MAKES 4 servings **START TO FINISH** 25 minutes

8	ounces dried cut ziti or penne pasta
1½	cups 1-inch pieces fresh asparagus or green beans
2½	cups broccoli florets
1	cup ricotta cheese
¼	cup snipped fresh basil
1	tablespoon snipped fresh thyme
1	tablespoon balsamic vinegar
1	tablespoon olive oil
1	clove garlic, minced
½	teaspoon salt
½	teaspoon black pepper
1⅓	cups chopped, seeded red and/or yellow tomatoes
	Shaved Parmesan or Romano cheese (optional)
	Fresh basil leaves or thyme sprigs (optional)

① Cook pasta according to package directions, adding green beans (if using) with pasta for the whole cooking time or adding broccoli and asparagus (if using) for the last 3 minutes of cooking time. Drain well. Return to hot pan; cover and keep warm.

② Meanwhile, in a large bowl combine ricotta cheese, basil, snipped thyme, balsamic vinegar, oil, garlic, salt, and pepper. Gently stir in tomatoes.

③ Add drained pasta mixture to tomato mixture; toss gently to combine. Top with Parmesan cheese. If desired, garnish with basil leaves.

PER SERVING 361 calories; 9 g total fat (2 g sat. fat); 17 mg cholesterol; 408 mg sodium; 55 g carbohydrate; 7 g fiber; 16 g protein

Leeks can contain lots of grit and dirt between their many layers. To clean leeks for Vegetable Lasagna, slice thinly, then swirl in cool water. If you have a salad spinner, dry the sliced leek in the salad spinner. If not, blot the slices dry between layers of clean paper towels.

Vegetable Lasagna ✪

MAKES 12 servings **PREP** 45 minutes **BAKE** 50 minutes
STAND 10 minutes **OVEN** at 350°F

9	dried whole grain lasagna noodles
	Nonstick cooking spray
1	medium leek, sliced (about ½ cup)
3	medium zucchini, thinly sliced
2	cups sliced mushrooms
¾	cup bottled roasted red peppers, drained and cut into bite-size strips
¼	cup chopped fresh basil
1	24-ounce carton fat-free cottage cheese (scant 3 cups)
½	cup refrigerated or frozen egg product, thawed
2	cloves garlic, minced
1	10-ounce packed frozen chopped spinach, thawed and well drained
1	cup shredded low-fat mozzarella cheese (about 4 ounces)
¼	teaspoon black pepper
½	cup shredded fresh spinach

① Cook lasagna noodles according to package directions. Preheat oven to 350°F. Lightly coat a 3-quart rectangular baking dish with nonstick cooking spray; set aside.

② Lightly coat a large skillet with nonstick cooking spray. Cook leek over medium heat for 4 minutes or just until tender. Stir in sliced zucchini, mushrooms, and roasted red peppers. Cook and stir for 8 to 10 minutes until vegetables are tender. Remove from heat and stir in chopped basil.

③ Meanwhile, in a food processor or blender combine cottage cheese, egg product, and garlic. Cover and process or blend until smooth. Stir in thawed spinach.

④ Layer 3 lasagna noodles in prepared baking dish then top with half the zucchini mixture. Spread one-third of the cottage cheese mixture on top. Repeat, ending with a layer of noodles. Spread remaining cottage cheese mixture. Sprinkle mozzarella cheese on top. Spray a piece of cooking foil with nonstick cooking spray and place over the cheese. Bake 45 minutes; uncover and bake 5 minutes more. Let stand 10 minutes before serving.

⑤ Sprinkle with black pepper to serve. Garnish with fresh spinach.

PER ABOUT ¾ CUP 156 calories; 2 g total fat (1 g sat. fat); 7 mg cholesterol; 300 mg sodium; 21 g carbohydrate; 4 g fiber; 14 g protein

Vegetable Lasagna

Pasta and Pepper Primavera

Pasta and Pepper Primavera 🕒

MAKES 4 servings **START TO FINISH** 20 minutes

- 4 ounces dried multigrain spaghetti
- 1 tablespoon olive oil or canola oil
- 2 teaspoons bottled minced garlic or 4 cloves garlic, minced
- 1 16-ounce package frozen (yellow, green, and red) peppers and onion stir-fry vegetables
- 1 15-ounce can cannellini beans (white kidney beans), rinsed and drained
- ¼ cup dry white wine or reduced-sodium chicken broth
- 1 tablespoon fresh lemon juice
- ½ teaspoon dried thyme, crushed
- ¼ teaspoon salt
- ¼ teaspoon freshly ground black pepper
- ¼ teaspoon crushed red pepper
- 1 tablespoon butter
- 1 ounce Parmesan cheese, shaved
- ½ teaspoon finely shredded lemon peel

① Cook pasta according to package directions.

② Meanwhile, in a large skillet heat oil over medium heat. Add garlic; cook and stir for 30 seconds. Add frozen vegetables. Cook and stir for 2 minutes. Add beans, white wine, lemon juice, thyme, salt, black pepper, and crushed red pepper. Bring to boiling; reduce heat. Cook, uncovered, about 4 minutes or until vegetables are crisp-tender, stirring occasionally. Remove from heat. Stir in butter.

③ Drain pasta. Add pasta to vegetable mixture in skillet. Toss gently to combine.

④ To serve, divide pasta mixture among four shallow bowls. Sprinkle with Parmesan shavings and lemon peel.

PER SERVING 272 calories; 9 g total fat (3 g sat. fat); 12 mg cholesterol; 410 mg sodium; 37 g carbohydrate; 7 g fiber; 13 g protein

Pasta with Mushrooms and Spinach 🕒

MAKES 4 (1¾-cup) servings **START TO FINISH** 25 minutes

- 8 ounces dried multigrain or whole grain penne, rotini, or bow tie pasta
- 1 tablespoon olive oil
- 2 cups sliced portobello or other fresh mushrooms
- 1 large onion, chopped
- 4 cloves garlic, minced
- 2 teaspoons snipped fresh thyme or ½ teaspoon dried thyme, crushed
- 8 cups thinly sliced fresh spinach
- ⅓ cup shredded Parmesan cheese

① Cook pasta according to package directions. Drain well.

② Meanwhile, in a very large skillet heat oil over medium heat. Add mushrooms, onion, and garlic; cook for 2 to 3 minutes or until mushrooms are nearly tender, stirring occasionally. Stir in thyme. Gradually add spinach, cooking and tossing about 1 minute or until heated through and spinach is slightly wilted.

③ Stir cooked pasta into spinach mixture; toss gently to combine. Sprinkle with cheese to serve.

PER SERVING 303 calories; 7 g total fat (2 g sat. fat); 5 mg cholesterol; 189 mg sodium; 47 g carbohydrate; 6 g fiber; 16 g protein

Pasta with Mushrooms and Spinach

Tomato and Cheese Ravioli ⭐ 🕧

MAKES 4 servings **START TO FINISH** 20 minutes

1	9-ounce package refrigerated light four cheese ravioli or 100% whole wheat four cheese ravioli
2	pints grape tomatoes or cherry tomatoes, halved (4 cups)
1	8-ounce package sliced fresh mushrooms
1	tablespoon olive oil
¼	cup refrigerated reduced fat pesto with basil
¼	cup shredded fresh basil

① In a large saucepan cook ravioli according to package directions, except do not add oil or salt to the water. Meanwhile, in a large skillet cook tomatoes and mushrooms in hot oil over medium heat for 5 to 7 minutes or just until mushrooms are tender and tomatoes are softened, stirring occasionally.

② Drain cooked pasta and return to the hot saucepan; add pesto and toss until coated. Stir in tomato mixture and basil. Divide among four serving plates. Serve immediately.

PER SERVING 314 calories; 12 g total fat (3 g sat. fat); 35 mg cholesterol; 463 mg sodium; 39 g carbohydrate; 5 g fiber; 14 g protein

Tomato and Cheese Ravioli

Grilled Summer Vegetables Sandwich

MAKES 4 sandwiches **START TO FINISH** 35 minutes

2	Japanese eggplant, trimmed and halved lengthwise
1	large red onion, cut into ¼-inch-thick slices
1	large tomato, cut into 4 slices
1	medium yellow summer squash, trimmed and cut lengthwise into 4 slices
1	tablespoon olive oil
¼	teaspoon ground black pepper
⅛	teaspoon salt
2	ounces soft goat cheese (chèvre), softened
1	tablespoon purchased basil pesto
8	slices crusty whole grain bread

① Brush eggplant, onion, tomato, and squash slices with oil. Sprinkle with pepper and salt. For a charcoal grill, grill vegetables on the rack of an uncovered grill directly over medium coals just until tender, turning once halfway through grilling. Allow 5 to 7 minutes for the squash and tomato and 7 to 9 minutes for the eggplant and onion. (For a gas grill, preheat grill. Reduce heat to medium. Add vegetables to grill rack over heat. Cover and grill as above.) Remove vegetables from grill.

② Cut squash slices in half crosswise. In a small bowl stir together goat cheese and pesto.

③ To assemble, spread goat cheese mixture evenly onto bread slices. Top half of the bread slices with the grilled vegetables, cutting vegetables to fit as needed. Top with the remaining bread slices, spread sides down.

PER SANDWICH 305 calories; 11 g total fat (3 g sat. fat); 8 mg cholesterol; 383 mg sodium; 39 g carbohydrate; 11 g fiber; 14 g protein

Find pesto in jars on grocery store shelves and in containers in the refrigerated section. If you can find it, buy the refrigerated variety—its flavor and color is superior. The best option, of course, is to make your own—when you have the time and fresh basil.

Asparagus Pesto Pasta

Asparagus Pesto Pasta 🕥

MAKES 6 servings **START TO FINISH** 25 minutes

1	pound fresh asparagus spears
1	cup frozen peas, thawed
1	ounce Parmesan cheese, finely shredded
2	tablespoons pine nuts, toasted
1	teaspoon finely shredded lemon peel
2	cloves garlic, quartered
¼	teaspoon salt
¼	teaspoon black pepper
3	tablespoons olive oil
10	ounces dried fettuccine

① Snap off and discard woody bases from asparagus. Cut into 2-inch pieces. Cook asparagus and peas in a large saucepan of boiling water for 3 to 5 minutes or until tender. Drain.

② For pesto, in a blender container or food processor bowl combine half of the asparagus and peas, the cheese, half of the nuts, the lemon peel, garlic, salt, and black pepper. Cover and blend or process with several on-off turns until a paste forms, stopping the machine several times and scraping the sides.

③ With the machine running slowly, gradually add olive oil and blend or process to the consistency of soft butter.

④ Cook fettuccine according to package directions. Drain well. Return fettuccine to pan. Toss fettuccine with pesto.

⑤ Serve fettuccine topped with remaining cooked asparagus and peas, and remaining pine nuts.

PER SERVING 304 calories; 11 g total fat (2 g sat. fat); 3 mg cholesterol; 203 mg sodium; 41 g carbohydrate; 4 g fiber; 10 g protein

To remove the woody stem end of asparagus, starting at the base of the spear, bend the spear several times, working toward the tip, until you find a place where it breaks easily. Break off the woody base and discard it.

menu

Goat Cheese and
Onion Scones

Heirloom Tomato
Salad

Quick Vegetable Pasta
with Provolone
[below]

Banana Cream Pie
Squares

Quick Vegetable Pasta with Provolone ✪ 🕥

MAKES 4 servings **START TO FINISH** 30 minutes

1	cup dried small alphabet-shape pasta, acini de pepe, or large couscous
1½	cups assorted vegetables, such as finely chopped carrots, red sweet pepper, and broccoli and/or frozen baby peas, edamame, and whole kernel corn
1	tablespoon olive oil
⅛	teaspoon black pepper
⅓	cup finely chopped provolone or cheddar cheese

① In a large saucepan cook pasta according to package directions, adding vegetables for the last 5 minutes of cooking; drain. Return pasta mixture to hot saucepan.

② Add oil and pepper to pasta mixture; toss gently to coat. Cool slightly. Add cheese; toss gently to combine.

PER SERVING 314 calories; 8 g total fat (3 g sat. fat); 11 mg cholesterol; 159 mg sodium; 47 g carbohydrate; 3 g fiber; 12 g protein

Stuffed Peppers ㉚

MAKES 4 servings   **START TO FINISH** 30 minutes

- 4   large yellow, red, or green sweet peppers
- 3   tablespoons water
- 1   15-ounce can no-salt-added black beans, rinsed and drained
- 1   15-ounce can no-salt-added whole kernel corn, drained
- 1   14.5-ounce can diced tomatoes, undrained
- 1   8.8-ounce pouch precooked whole grain brown rice, heated according to package directions
- ½   cup salsa
- ½   teaspoon cumin or chili powder

① Cut off the top of each sweet pepper; remove cores and stems, hollowing out the peppers. Arrange peppers in a 2-quart square microwave-safe baking dish. Pour the water around peppers.

② Microwave peppers on high about 8 minutes or just until peppers are starting to soften.

③ Meanwhile, in a medium bowl stir together black beans, corn, diced tomatoes, rice, salsa, and cumin.

④ Divide bean mixture evenly among the peppers. Microwave on high about 4 minutes or until filling is heated through and peppers are tender.

PER SERVING 362 calories; 3 g total fat (0 g sat. fat); 0 mg cholesterol; 327 mg sodium; 76 g carbohydrate; 12 g fiber; 13 g protein

Stuffed Peppers

Lentil and Veggie Shepherd's Pie

MAKES 8 servings   **PREP** 45 minutes   **BAKE** 35 minutes
OVEN at 350°F

- 1   14-ounce can vegetable broth
- 1   cup water
- 1   cup dry brown lentils, rinsed and drained
- 3   cloves garlic, minced
- 4   medium carrots, peeled and bias sliced into ½-inch slices (2 cups)
- 3   small parsnips, peeled and bias sliced into ½-inch slices (1½ cups)
- 6   white boiling onions (8 ounces), quartered, or 1 medium onion, cut into thin wedges
- 4   cups coarsely shredded trimmed fresh chard or kale
- 1   14.5-ounce can no-salt-added diced tomatoes, undrained
- 2   tablespoons no-salt-added tomato paste
- 2   tablespoons snipped fresh basil or 2 teaspoons dried basil, crushed
- 4   medium potatoes, peeled and cut up
- 4   cloves garlic, peeled
- 1   tablespoon butter
- 3   to 4 tablespoons fat-free milk
- ½   cup finely shredded Parmesan cheese (2 ounces)
- 1   tablespoon snipped fresh basil or ½ teaspoon dried basil, crushed

① In a saucepan combine broth, the water, lentils, and garlic. Bring to boiling; reduce heat. Cover; simmer 20 minutes. Add carrots, parsnips, and onions. Return to boiling; reduce heat. Cover; simmer 10 to 15 minutes or until vegetables and lentils are tender. Stir in chard; remove from heat. Stir in undrained tomatoes, tomato paste, and the 2 tablespoons fresh basil dried basil.

② Preheat oven to 350°F. In a covered saucepan cook potatoes and whole garlic cloves in enough boiling lightly salted water to cover for 20 to 25 minutes or until tender; drain. Mash with a potato masher or beat with an electric mixer on low. Add butter. Gradually beat in enough milk to make potatoes light and fluffy. Fold in cheese and the 1 tablespoon fresh basil or ½ teaspoon dried basil.

③ Spread lentil mixture in a 2- to 2½-quart casserole or gratin dish. Spoon potato mixture over lentil mixture, spreading evenly. Bake, uncovered, about 35 minutes or until heated through.

PER SERVING 234 calories; 3 g total fat (2 g sat. fat); 8 mg cholesterol; 386 mg sodium; 41 g carbohydrate; 13 g fiber; 12 g protein

Lentil and Veggie Shepherd's Pie

Tex-Mex Bean Tostadas

menu

Fruit Salad with a Crunch

Spanish Rice

Tex-Mex Bean Tostadas [below]

Tiramisu Shots

Lemon Iced Tea

Pumpkin, Rice, and Bean Enchiladas

MAKES 4 servings **PREP** 30 minutes **BAKE** 20 minutes **OVEN** at 400°F

Nonstick cooking spray
2   teaspoons olive oil
½   cup chopped onion
1   fresh jalapeño seeded and finely chopped (see tip, page 8)
1   15-ounce can pumpkin
1½   to 1¾ cups water
1   teaspoon chili powder
½   teaspoon ground cumin
¼   teaspoon salt
1   15-ounce can no-salt-added red kidney beans, rinsed and drained
1½   cups cooked brown rice
½   cup shredded reduced-fat Monterey Jack cheese with jalapeño peppers (2 ounces)
8   6-inch corn tortillas, softened*
Pico de gallo or salsa (optional)

① Preheat oven to 400°F. Coat a 2-quart rectangular baking dish with cooking spray; set aside. In a medium saucepan heat oil over medium-high heat. Add onion and chile pepper; cook and stir until onion is tender. Stir in pumpkin, 1½ cups of the water, the chili powder, cumin, and salt. Cook and stir until heated through. If necessary, stir in enough of the additional ¼ cup water to reach desired consistency.

② In a large bowl slightly mash beans. Stir in half of the pumpkin mixture, the cooked rice, and ¼ cup of the cheese.

③ For enchiladas, spoon a generous ⅓ cup bean mixture onto each tortilla. Roll up tortillas; place, seam sides down, in the prepared baking dish. Pour the remaining pumpkin mixture over enchiladas.

④ Bake, covered, for 15 minutes. Sprinkle with the remaining ¼ cup cheese. Bake, uncovered, for 5 to 10 minutes more or until heated through. If desired, serve with pico de gallo.

*Tip: To soften tortillas, place tortillas between paper towels. Microwave on high for 30 to 40 seconds.

PER SERVING 383 calories; 7 g total fat (2 g sat. fat): 8 mg cholesterol; 286 mg sodium; 67 g carbohydrate; 17 g fiber; 17 g protein

Tex-Mex Bean Tostadas

MAKES 4 servings **PREP** 15 minutes **BAKE** 8 minutes **OVEN** at 350°F

4   packaged tostada shells
1   15-ounce can no-salt-added pinto beans, rinsed and drained
½   cup purchased salsa
½   teaspoon salt-free Southwest chipotle seasoning blend
½   cup shredded reduced-fat cheddar cheese (2 ounces)
1½   cups packaged shredded iceberg lettuce
1   cup chopped tomato
¼   cup shredded reduced-fat cheddar cheese (1 ounce) (optional)
Lime wedges (optional)

① Preheat oven to 350°F. Place tostada shells on a baking sheet. Heat for 3 to 5 minutes or until warm. Meanwhile, in a medium bowl combine beans, salsa, and seasoning blend. Use a potato masher or fork to coarsely mash the mixture. Divide bean mixture among tostada shells, spreading evenly. Top with the ½ cup cheese.

② Bake about 5 minutes or until cheese is melted. Top tostadas with shredded lettuce, chopped tomato, and, if desired, the ¼ cup cheese. If desired, serve with lime wedges.

PER SERVING 211 calories; 7 g total fat (2 g sat. fat); 8 mg cholesterol; 294 mg sodium; 27 g carbohydrate; 7 g fiber; 10 g protein

Healthy Home-Style Cooking **199**

Sweet Potato Hash 🕧

MAKES 4 servings **START TO FINISH** 30 minutes

- 1 tablespoon olive oil
- 1 medium onion, halved and thinly sliced
- 1 large sweet potato, peeled and cut into ½-inch pieces
- 12 ounces refrigerated or frozen uncooked ground meat substitute (soy protein), thawed
- 1 medium zucchini, coarsely chopped
- 1 teaspoon snipped fresh rosemary or ½ teaspoon dried rosemary, crushed
- 1 tablespoon Dijon mustard
- 1 tablespoon fat-free milk
- 2 teaspoons honey
  Snipped fresh rosemary (optional)

① In a very large nonstick skillet heat oil over medium heat. Add onion to skillet; cook for 3 minutes, stirring occasionally. Add sweet potato. Cook for 8 to 10 minutes or until potato is tender and browned, stirring often.

② Add meat substitute, zucchini, and 1 teaspoon snipped rosemary. Cook for 3 to 5 minutes or until zucchini is tender, stirring often.

③ In a small bowl combine mustard, milk, and honey. Stir mustard mixture into potato mixture; heat through. If desired, garnish with additional snipped rosemary.

PER SERVING 216 calories; 7 g total fat (1 g sat. fat); 0 mg cholesterol; 487 mg sodium; 20 g carbohydrate; 7 g fiber; 17 g protein

Sweet Potato Hash

Marinated Tofu with Edamame Stir-Fry

MAKES 4 servings **PREP** 30 minutes **COOK** 6 minutes
MARINATE 30 minutes

- ¼ cup rice vinegar
- 2 tablespoons reduced-sodium soy sauce
- 1 tablespoon toasted sesame oil
- 1 tablespoon honey
- 1 tablespoon finely chopped, peeled fresh ginger
- 2 cloves garlic, minced
- 1 16- to 18-ounce package firm or extra-firm tofu (fresh bean curd), drained and cut into 4 slices
  Nonstick cooking spray
- 3 cups sliced, stemmed shiitake mushrooms and/or button mushrooms
- 2 medium red, yellow, and/or orange sweet peppers, seeded and cut into bite-size strips
- ½ cup chopped red onion
- 4 cups coarsely shredded bok choy
- 1 cup frozen shelled sweet soybeans (edamame), thawed
- ½ teaspoon cornstarch
- 1 tablespoon sesame seeds, toasted
- ¼ teaspoon crushed red pepper (optional)

① For marinade, in a 2-quart rectangular baking dish, combine vinegar, soy sauce, ½ tablespoon of the sesame oil, honey, ginger, and garlic. Add tofu slices, turning to coat. Marinate at room temperature for 30 minutes, turning tofu once halfway through marinating time.

② Coat an unheated nonstick grill pan with nonstick spray. Preheat over medium-high heat. Transfer tofu slices to grill pan, reserving marinade in the baking dish. Cook tofu for 4 to 6 minutes or until heated through and starting to brown, turning once halfway through cooking.

③ Meanwhile, in a nonstick skillet heat the remaining ½ tablespoon sesame oil over medium-high heat. Add mushrooms, sweet peppers, and red onion. Cook and stir for 3 to 5 minutes or until crisp-tender. Add bok choy and edamame. Cook and stir for 2 to 3 minutes more or until bok choy is wilted. Whisk cornstarch into the reserved marinade; add to vegetable mixture. Cook and stir until thickened and bubbly. Cook and stir for 1 minute more.

④ Divide vegetable mixture among four serving bowls or plates. Place tofu on top of vegetable mixture. Sprinkle with sesame seeds and, if desired, crushed red pepper.

PER SERVING 293 calories; 12 g total fat (1 g sat. fat); 0 mg cholesterol; 323 mg sodium; 25 g carbohydrate; 6 g fiber; 21 g protein

Marinated Tofu with Edamame Stir-Fry

Roasted Tofu and Veggie Pockets

Roasted Tofu and Veggie Pockets

MAKES 6 servings **PREP** 25 minutes **ROAST** 10 minutes
OVEN at 450°F

- ½ of a 16- to 18-ounce package extra-firm water-packed tofu (fresh bean curd)
- 1 small zucchini (6 ounces), thinly sliced
- 1 medium onion, halved and thinly sliced
- 1 red or yellow sweet pepper, seeded and cut into thin strips
- 1 tablespoon olive oil
- ¼ teaspoon salt
- ¼ teaspoon black pepper
- Nonstick cooking spray
- 3 large whole wheat pita bread rounds, halved
- 2 tablespoons bottled light balsamic vinaigrette or reduced-calorie Italian salad dressing
- ⅓ cup shredded mozzarella-flavor soy cheese

① Preheat oven to 450°F. Drain tofu; pat tofu with paper towels until well dried. Using a sharp knife, cut tofu into ¼-inch-thick slices; then cut into ½-inch-wide strips. In a large bowl combine tofu strips, zucchini, onion, and sweet pepper. Add oil, salt, and pepper; toss to coat.

② Lightly coat a 15 x 10 x 1-inch baking pan with nonstick cooking spray. Spread tofu mixture evenly in prepared pan. Roast, uncovered, for 10 to 12 minutes or until vegetables are tender, gently stirring once.

③ Open pita halves to create pockets. Divide roasted tofu and vegetables among pita pockets; drizzle with vinaigrette. Top with shredded soy cheese. Place the filled pitas, filled sides up, in a 2-quart square baking dish. Bake for 1 to 2 minutes or until cheese melts.

PER SERVING 189 calories; 7 g total fat (1 g sat. fat); 0 mg cholesterol; 433 mg sodium; 23 g carbohydrate; 4 g fiber; 9 g protein

Vegetable Sandwich with Feta-Yogurt Spread ③⓪

MAKES 4 sandwiches **START TO FINISH** 15 minutes

- 1 recipe Feta-Yogurt Spread
- 4 whole wheat bagel thins or multigrain sandwich rounds, split
- 1 cup lightly packed packaged fresh baby spinach
- 1 cup thinly sliced English cucumber
- ½ cup halved and thinly sliced red onion
- ½ cup thinly sliced radishes
- 1 roma tomato, thinly sliced

① Prepare Feta-Yogurt Spread. To assemble sandwiches, evenly spread cut sides of bagel halves with yogurt mixture. Layer spinach, cucumber slices, red onion, radishes, and tomato slices on half. Top with remaining bagel halves, spread sides down.

Feta-Yogurt Spread: In a small bowl stir together ½ cup thick nonfat plain Greek yogurt, ½ cup crumbled nonfat or reduced-fat feta cheese, 1 teaspoon snipped fresh mint, 1 teaspoon snipped fresh oregano, and ⅛ teaspoon black pepper.

PER SERVING 157 calories; 1 g total fat (0 g sat. fat); 1 mg cholesterol; 397 mg sodium; 29 g carbohydrate; 6 g fiber; 10 g protein

English cucumbers are longer and thinner than regular cucumbers, and they have thinner skin. The seeds are so small that English cucumbers are often labeled "seedless." You'll find them with the regular cucumbers, but they are often wrapped in plastic.

With vegetarian food this good, no one will miss the meat.

Poblano-Portobello Panini

MAKES 4 sandwiches **PREP** 25 minutes **BAKE** 20 minutes
STAND 15 minutes **GRILL** 10 minutes **OVEN** at 425°F

- 2 fresh poblano chile peppers (see tip, page 8)
- 2 4-ounce fresh portobello mushrooms
  Nonstick cooking spray
- ½ of a 16-ounce Italian flat bread (focaccia)
- 2 1-ounce slices reduced-fat mozzarella cheese, halved
- 1 recipe Mashed Avocado Spread

① Preheat oven to 425°F. To roast chile peppers, cut peppers in half lengthwise; remove stems, seeds, and membranes. Place pepper halves, cut sides down, on a foil-lined baking sheet. Bake for 20 to 25 minutes or until peppers are charred and very tender. Bring the foil up around peppers and fold edges together to enclose. Let stand about 15 minutes or until cool enough to handle. Use a sharp knife to loosen edges of the skins; gently pull off skins in strips; discard. Set peppers aside.

② Preheat a covered indoor grill or grill pan over medium heat. Remove stems and, if desired, gills from mushrooms. Lightly coat mushrooms with nonstick spray. Place mushrooms in grill or on grill pan. Grill for 4 to 5 minutes if using a covered grill or 8 to 10 minutes if using a grill pan or until mushrooms are tender, turning once halfway through grilling if using a grill pan.

③ Meanwhile, cut flat bread into four wedges. Split wedges in half horizontally. Halve the grilled mushrooms; place a half on bottom half of each wedge. Top with cheese, roasted peppers, and tops of focaccia wedges.

④ Place sandwiches (half at a time, if necessary) in the covered indoor grill, if using; cover and cook about 6 minutes or until cheese melts and bread is toasted. (If using a grill pan, place sandwiches on grill pan. Weight sandwiches with a heavy skillet; grill about 2 minutes or until bread is toasted. Carefully remove weight. Turn sandwiches over, weight, and grill until remaining side is toasted.) Serve sandwiches with Mashed Avocado Spread.

Mashed Avocado Spread: Cut 1 medium avocado in half. Remove the seed and peel the avocado. In a medium bowl mash avocado. Stir in ½ teaspoon finely shredded lemon peel; 2 teaspoons lemon juice; 1 small clove garlic, minced; ⅛ to ¼ teaspoon crushed red pepper; and ⅛ teaspoon salt. Makes about ¾ cup.

PER SANDWICH 257 calories; 10 g total fat (2 g sat. fat); 14 mg cholesterol; 390 mg sodium; 35 g carbohydrate; 4 g fiber; 11 g protein

menu

Gingered Lemon
Broccoli Salad

Tomato-Mozarella
Open-Face
Sandwiches
[below]

Peanut Butter
Blossom Mini Cakes

Iced Tea

Tomato-Mozzarella Open-Face Sandwiches

MAKES 4 sandwiches **PREP** 15 minutes **BROIL** 2 minutes

- 2 medium tomatoes, seeded and chopped
- ¼ cup finely chopped red onion
- 2 tablespoons shredded fresh basil
- 2 teaspoons olive oil
- 1 teaspoon balsamic vinegar
- ¼ teaspoon salt
- ¼ teaspoon black pepper
- 4 diagonally cut slices whole grain French bread
- ⅓ cup part-skim mozzarella cheese cut into bite-size strips
  Fresh basil sprigs (optional)

① Preheat broiler. In a medium bowl combine tomatoes, red onion, shredded basil, oil, balsamic vinegar, salt, and pepper; set aside.

② Place bread on the unheated rack of a broiler pan. Broil 4 to 5 inches from heat for 1 to 2 minutes or until toasted, turning once. Top with tomato mixture. Broil for 1 to 2 minutes more or until heated through. Top with cheese. If desired, garnish with basil sprigs.

PER SANDWICH 134 calories; 5 g total fat (1 g sat. fat); 6 mg cholesterol; 332 mg sodium; 17 g carbohydrate; 2 g fiber; 5 g protein

Tomato-Mozzarella Open-Face Sandwiches

Open-Face Egg Sandwiches

Open-Face Egg Sandwiches 30

MAKES 4 sandwiches **START TO FINISH** 15 minutes

- 1 cup frozen shelled sweet soybeans (edamame), thawed
- 1 small avocado, halved, seeded, and peeled
- 2 tablespoons lemon juice
- 2 cloves garlic, minced
- ¼ teaspoon salt
- ½ cup chopped red sweet pepper
- 4 very thin slices firm-texture whole wheat bread, toasted, or 2 whole wheat pita bread rounds, split in half horizontally
- 4 hard-cooked eggs, thinly sliced*

  Freshly ground black pepper

① In a medium bowl combine edamame, avocado, lemon juice, garlic, and salt; use a fork or potato masher to mash ingredients together until avocado is smooth and edamame is coarsely mashed. Stir in sweet pepper.

② Spread edamame mixture on bread slices. Arrange egg slices on edamame mixture. Sprinkle with black pepper.

***Tip:** Look for hard-cooked eggs in the deli section or salad bar area of your supermarket.

PER SANDWICH 221 calories; 12 g total fat (3 g sat. fat); 212 mg cholesterol; 292 mg sodium; 16 g carbohydrate; 5 g fiber; 13 g protein

Quick Rice and Red Beans 30

MAKES 8 servings **START TO FINISH** 25 minutes

- ½ cup chopped onion (1 medium)
- 1 tablespoon olive oil or canola oil
- 1 14-ounce package instant brown rice (2 cups)
- 1 cup water
- 2 15-ounce cans kidney beans or black beans, rinsed and drained
- 2 14.5-ounce cans Italian-style stewed tomatoes, cut up
- ¼ teaspoon crushed red pepper (optional)
- 1 cup shredded Monterey Jack cheese or cheddar cheese (4 ounces)
- ¼ cup snipped fresh cilantro

① In a large saucepan cook onion in hot oil until tender. Add rice and the water. Stir in beans, tomatoes, and, if desired, crushed red pepper. Bring to boiling; reduce heat. Simmer, covered, for 10 minutes. Remove from heat.

② Stir in half of the cheese and the cilantro. Let stand, covered, for 5 minutes. Top with the remaining cheese.

PER SERVING 376 calories; 8 g total fat (3 g sat. fat); 13 mg cholesterol; 479 mg sodium; 67 g carbohydrate; 10 g fiber; 17 g protein

Going meatless, for even a few days a week, is good for your health—and for your grocery budget.

Roasted Vegetable and Quinoa Salad

MAKES 4 servings **PREP** 25 minutes **ROAST** 35 minutes
COOK 15 minutes **OVEN** at 400°F

    Nonstick cooking spray
3   medium beets, trimmed, peeled, and cut into thin wedges
1   small zucchini, trimmed and cut into 1-inch pieces
1   cup small fresh cremini or button mushrooms, halved
¼   teaspoon salt
¼   teaspoon black pepper
2   cups water
1   cup quinoa or red quinoa, rinsed and drained
⅛   teaspoon salt
1   recipe Herb Vinaigrette
1   ounce semisoft goat cheese (chèvre) or reduced-fat feta cheese, crumbled

① Preheat oven to 400°F. Lightly coat a shallow baking dish with cooking spray. Add beet wedges to the dish. Coat lightly with cooking spray. Cover and roast for 25 minutes. Uncover and add zucchini and mushrooms. Lightly coat with cooking spray and sprinkle with the ¼ teaspoon salt and the pepper. Cover and roast for 10 to 15 minutes more or just until vegetables are tender. Place baking dish on a wire rack to cool.

② Meanwhile, in a medium saucepan combine the water, quinoa, and ⅛ teaspoon salt. Bring to boiling; reduce heat. Simmer, covered, for 15 minutes or until quinoa is tender. Drain if necessary. Cool completely.

③ Add Herb Vinaigrette to cooled vegetable mixture and toss to coat. Divide quinoa among four serving plates. Top with vegetable mixture and goat cheese.

Herb Vinaigrette: In a screw-top jar combine ¼ cup white wine vinegar, 2 tablespoons olive oil, 1 tablespoon snipped fresh parsley, 1 teaspoon snipped fresh rosemary, 1 teaspoon snipped fresh oregano, 1 teaspoon Dijon mustard, and 1 clove garlic, minced. Cover and shake well. Makes ½ cup.

PER SERVING 286 calories; 12 g total fat (3 g sat. fat); 6 mg cholesterol; 343 mg sodium; 36 g carbohydrate; 5 g fiber; 10 g protein

Asian Tofu Salad

MAKES 6 servings **PREP** 20 minutes **MARINATE** 30 minutes
COOK 5 minutes

¼   cup reduced-sodium soy sauce
¼   cup sweet chili sauce
1   tablespoon creamy peanut butter
1   clove garlic, minced
1   teaspoon grated fresh ginger
1   16- to 18-ounce package firm water-packed tofu (fresh bean curd)
1   teaspoon toasted sesame oil
4   cups shredded romaine lettuce
1½ cups chopped, peeled jicama
1   medium red sweet pepper, seeded and thinly sliced
1   cup coarsely shredded carrot
2   tablespoons unsalted dry-roasted peanuts
2   tablespoons snipped fresh cilantro

① In a bowl whisk together soy sauce, chili sauce, peanut butter, garlic, and ginger. Pat tofu dry with paper towels. Cut tofu crosswise into 12 slices. Place slices in a 2-quart rectangular baking dish. Drizzle tofu with 3 tablespoons of the soy sauce mixture, turning to coat tofu. Marinate for 30 minutes, turning tofu occasionally. Set aside the remaining soy sauce mixture for dressing.

② In a very large nonstick skillet heat sesame oil over medium-high heat. Remove tofu slices from the marinade. Add remaining marinade to the skillet. Add tofu slices to the hot skillet. Cook for 5 to 6 minutes or until lightly browned, turning once halfway through cooking.

③ In a large bowl combine lettuce, jicama, sweet pepper, and carrot. Divide among six serving plates. Top with tofu, peanuts, and cilantro. Serve with reserved dressing mixture.

PER SERVING 179 calories; 7 g total fat (1 g sat. fat); 0 mg cholesterol; 515 mg sodium; 18 g carbohydrate; 3 g fiber; 11 g protein

Caribbean Pork Chili,
page 215

Satisfying Soups & Stews

Beer Brat Soup

MAKES 4 servings **PREP** 20 minutes **COOK** 20 minutes

- 12 ounces lean ground pork
- 1 medium onion, chopped
- 1 teaspoon fennel seeds, crushed
- ½ teaspoon dried sage, crushed
- ¼ teaspoon black pepper
- 2 14-ounce cans lower-sodium beef broth
- 1 12-ounce can light beer or nonalcoholic beer
- 2 medium carrots, thinly sliced
- 2 cups shredded green cabbage
- 4 ½-inch-thick slices whole grain baguette-style French bread, toasted
- 1 tablespoon country Dijon mustard

① In a large saucepan cook pork, onion, fennel seeds, sage, and pepper about 10 minutes or until pork is browned and onion is tender, stirring to break up pork as it cooks. Drain off fat if necessary.

② Add broth, beer, and carrots. Bring to boiling; reduce heat. Simmer, covered, for 5 minutes. Add cabbage. Cook, covered, about 5 minutes more or until carrots and cabbage are tender.

③ To serve, ladle soup into bowls. Spread tops of bread slices with mustard. Float a bread slice on top of each bowl of soup.

PER SERVING 215 calories; 4 g total fat (1 g sat. fat); 59 mg cholesterol; 579 mg sodium; 15 g carbohydrate; 4 g fiber; 24 g protein

Country Dijon mustard is the coarse-ground variety. Even if the label doesn't say "country," if it's coarse-ground, it's the kind you want to use in this soup.

Posole (Pork and Hominy Soup)

MAKES 4 servings **PREP** 35 minutes **COOK** 20 minutes

- 12 ounces pork tenderloin, trimmed of fat and cut in bite-size pieces
- 1 medium poblano or Anaheim pepper, seeded and chopped (see tip, page 8)
- 1 large onion, cut in thin wedges
- 3 cloves garlic, minced
- 2 teaspoons vegetable oil
- 1 15.5-ounce can golden or white hominy, rinsed and drained
- 1 14.5-ounce can no-salt-added diced tomatoes, undrained
- 1 14-ounce can reduced-sodium chicken broth
- 1¾ cups water
- 1 tablespoon lime juice
- 2 teaspoons snipped fresh oregano or 1 teaspoon dried oregano, crushed
- 1 teaspoon ground cumin
- 1 teaspoon ground pasilla, ancho, or chipotle chile pepper*
- ¼ teaspoon black pepper
- ¼ cup sliced radishes, shredded cabbage, and/or sliced green onions

① In a Dutch oven cook pork, poblano, onion, and garlic in hot oil over medium heat for 5 minutes or until tender. Stir in hominy, tomatoes, broth, the water, lime juice, oregano, cumin, pasilla pepper, and black pepper. Bring to boiling. Reduce heat and simmer, covered, for 15 minutes. Top servings with radishes, cabbage, and/or green onions.

*Tip: For mild flavor, choose pasilla or ancho chile pepper. For spicy smoky flavor, choose chipotle chile pepper.

PER SERVING 258 calories; 6 g total fat (1 g sat. fat); 55 mg cholesterol; 569 mg sodium; 29 g carbohydrate; 6 g fiber; 23 g protein

Every country and culture loves soup. The world over, it's the ultimate comfort food.

Posole (Pork and Hominy Soup)

Chicken Cassoulet with Gremolata

MAKES 6 servings **PREP** 20 minutes **COOK** 25 minutes

Nonstick cooking spray

6   skinless, boneless chicken thighs, trimmed of fat (about 1¼ pounds total)

2   teaspoons olive oil

2   medium leeks, trimmed and thinly sliced

1   medium red sweet pepper, cut into thin bite-size strips

⅓   cup dry white wine (optional)

2   15-ounce cans no-salt-added cannellini beans (white kidney beans), rinsed and drained

1   14-ounce can reduced-sodium chicken broth

½   teaspoon dried thyme, crushed

¼   teaspoon salt

¼   teaspoon black pepper

1   recipe Gremolata

① Lightly coat an unheated 4-quart nonstick saucepan or Dutch oven with cooking spray. Preheat over medium-high heat. Add chicken thighs to hot pan and cook until browned on both sides. Remove from pan; set aside.

② Add oil to pan. Add leeks and sweet pepper. Cook for 5 minutes or until tender, stirring occasionally. If desired, add wine. Bring to boiling and cook until wine is nearly evaporated. Stir in beans, broth, thyme, salt, and black pepper. Bring to boiling; reduce heat. Place chicken thighs on top of bean mixture. Simmer, covered, for 20 minutes or until chicken thighs are no longer pink (180°F).

③ Prepare Gremolata. To serve, divide beans and chicken among six shallow serving bowls. Sprinkle with Gremolata just before serving.

Gremolata: In a small bowl combine ⅓ cup snipped fresh parsley, 1 tablespoon finely shredded lemon peel, and 3 cloves garlic, minced.

PER SERVING 268 calories; 6 g total fat (1 g sat. fat); 78 mg cholesterol; 388 mg sodium; 25 g carbohydrate; 7 g fiber; 27 g protein

Caribbean Pork Chili

MAKES 6 servings **PREP** 20 minutes
COOK 4 hours (low) or 2 hours (high)

1½   pounds boneless pork loin roast, cut into 1-inch pieces

1   tablespoon chili powder

½   teaspoon ground chipotle chile pepper (optional)

½   teaspoon ground cumin

¼   teaspoon salt

2   cloves garlic, minced

1   tablespoon canola oil

2   14.5-ounce cans no-salt-added diced tomatoes, undrained

1   15-ounce can no-salt-added black beans, rinsed and drained

1   8-ounce can no-salt-added tomato sauce

1   cup frozen whole kernel corn

¼   cup snipped fresh cilantro

1   medium mango, halved, seeded, peeled, and chopped

Fresh cilantro sprigs (optional)

① In a medium bowl combine pork, chili powder, chile pepper (if using), cumin, salt, and garlic; toss to coat. In a large nonstick skillet heat oil over medium-high heat. Cook pork, half at a time, in hot skillet until browned on all sides, stirring occasionally.

② Place pork in a 3½- or 4-quart slow cooker. Add tomatoes, beans, tomato sauce, and corn. Cover and cook on low-heat setting for 4 to 5 hours or on high-heat setting for 2 to 2½ hours.

③ Stir in ¼ cup cilantro. Garnish individual servings with mango and cilantro sprigs.

PER SERVING 315 calories; 7 g total fat (2 g sat. fat); 78 mg cholesterol; 246 mg sodium; 32 g carbohydrate; 8 g fiber; 32 g protein

The best way to dice a mango is to stand it upright and cut down along the seed on four sides of the fruit. Discard the seed, then cut the fruit in a cross-hatch pattern. Run a knife close to the skin to remove the diced or cubed fruit.

{
menu

Whole wheat corn bread

Cut-up fresh vegetables

Chicken Fajita Chili [below]

Sorbet
}

Chicken Fajita Chili

MAKES 6 servings **PREP** 20 minutes
COOK 4 hours (low) or 2 hours (high)

- 2 pounds skinless, boneless chicken breast halves, cut into 1-inch pieces
- 1 tablespoon chili powder
- 1 teaspoon fajita seasoning
- ½ teaspoon ground cumin
- 2 cloves garlic, minced
  Nonstick cooking spray
- 2 14½-ounce cans no-salt-added diced tomatoes
- 1 16-ounce package frozen pepper (yellow, green, and red) and onion stir-fry vegetables
- 1 15-ounce can cannellini beans (white kidney beans), rinsed and drained
- 3 tablespoons shredded reduced-fat cheddar cheese

① In a medium bowl combine chicken, chili powder, fajita seasoning, cumin, and garlic; toss to coat. Coat an unheated large skillet with nonstick cooking spray. Preheat skillet over medium-high heat. Cook chicken, half at a time, in hot skillet until browned on all sides, stirring occasionally.

② Place chicken in a 3½- or 4-quart slow cooker. Add undrained tomatoes, frozen vegetables, and cannellini beans. Cover and cook on low-heat setting for 4 to 5 hours or on high-heat setting for 2 to 2½ hours.

③ Top individual servings with shredded cheese.

PER SERVING 271 calories; 3 g total fat (1 g sat. fat); 90 mg cholesterol; 320 mg sodium; 22 g carbohydrate; 7 g fiber; 42 g protein

Cream of Chicken and Rice Florentine

MAKES 6 servings **PREP** 25 minutes **COOK** 40 minutes

- 2 tablespoons olive oil
- 1 pound skinless, boneless chicken breast halves
- 1½ cups finely chopped onions (3 medium)
- 1 8-ounce package fresh mushrooms, sliced
- ½ cup shredded carrot (1 medium)
- 1 tablespoon bottled minced garlic
- ⅓ cup long grain rice, uncooked
- 1 14-ounce can reduced-sodium chicken broth
- 1 cup water
- ¼ teaspoon ground nutmeg
- ½ teaspoon black pepper
- 2 12-ounce cans evaporated fat-free milk
- 2 tablespoons all-purpose flour
- 4 cups packed fresh spinach
- 2 teaspoons finely shredded lemon peel
- 2 tablespoons lemon juice
  Black pepper (optional)

① In a Dutch oven heat oil over medium-high heat; reduce heat to medium. Add chicken; cook for 12 to 15 minutes or until no longer pink (170°F), turning once halfway through cooking. Remove chicken to a plate to cool. When cool enough to handle, use two forks to pull chicken apart into coarse shreds.

② Meanwhile, add onions, mushrooms, carrot, and garlic to the Dutch oven; cook for 5 minutes, stirring occasionally. Stir in rice; cook for 1 minute more. Add broth, the water, nutmeg, and black pepper. Bring to boiling; reduce heat. Simmer, covered, for 15 minutes.

③ In a small bowl stir together 1 can of the evaporated milk and the flour; stir into mixture in Dutch oven. Stir in the remaining can of milk. Cook and stir until bubbly.

④ Stir in spinach and the shredded chicken. Simmer for 5 minutes. Stir in lemon peel and lemon juice. If desired, sprinkle with additional black pepper.

PER SERVING 300 calories; 6 g total fat (1 g sat. fat); 48 mg cholesterol; 365 mg sodium; 31 g carbohydrate; 2 g fiber; 30 g protein

Cream of Chicken and Rice Florentine

Mexican Chicken Soup

Mexican Chicken Soup

MAKES 6 servings **PREP** 30 minutes **BAKE** 20 minutes
COOK 1 hour **STAND** 15 minutes **OVEN** at 425°F

- 2 to 2½ pounds chicken breast halves, skin removed
- 6 cups water
- 2 cups coarsely chopped onions (2 large)
- 2 cups coarsely chopped celery (4 stalks)
- 1 cup coarsely chopped tomato (1 large)
- ½ cup snipped fresh cilantro
- 1 teaspoon salt
- 1 teaspoon ground cumin
- ¼ to ½ teaspoon cayenne pepper
- ¼ to ½ teaspoon black pepper
- 1½ cups chopped carrots (3 medium)
- 1 or 2 fresh poblano chile peppers (see tip, page 8)
- 1 avocado, halved, seeded, peeled, and diced
- 3 tablespoons fresh cilantro sprigs

① In a 4½-quart Dutch oven combine chicken breast halves, the water, 1 cup of the onions, 1 cup of the celery, the tomato, the snipped cilantro, salt, cumin, cayenne pepper, and black pepper. Bring to boiling; reduce heat. Cover and simmer for 40 to 50 minutes or until chicken is tender. Remove chicken pieces and set aside to cool slightly. Strain the broth mixture, reserving broth and discarding the vegetables.

② Return the broth to the Dutch oven. Add the remaining 1 cup onion, the remaining 1 cup celery, and the carrots. Bring to boiling; reduce heat. Cover and simmer for about 20 minutes or until vegetables are tender.

③ Meanwhile, preheat oven to 425°F. Line a baking sheet with foil; set aside. Cut chile peppers in half lengthwise and remove seeds, stems, and veins. Place pepper halves, cut sides down, on prepared baking sheet. Bake for 20 to 25 minutes or until skins are blistered and dark. Wrap peppers in the foil; let stand about 15 minutes or until cool enough to handle. Use a sharp knife to loosen the edges of the skins from the pepper halves; gently and slowly pull off the skin in strips. Discard skin. Chop peppers.

④ Remove chicken from bones; discard bones. Chop the chicken. Stir chicken and poblano peppers into broth mixture. Heat through. Garnish with avocado and cilantro sprigs.

PER SERVING 203 calories; 5 g total fat (1 g sat. fat); 57 mg cholesterol; 518 mg sodium; 14 g carbohydrate; 5 g fiber; 25 g protein

Thai Chicken Soup

MAKES 5 servings **START TO FINISH** 30 minutes

- Nonstick cooking spray
- 1 medium onion, chopped
- 1 tablespoon grated fresh ginger
- 3 cloves garlic, minced
- 2 14-ounce cans reduced-sodium chicken broth
- 1 14-ounce can unsweetened light coconut milk
- 1 tablespoon lime juice
- 2 teaspoons Thai seasoning
- 2 medium carrots, thinly bias-sliced
- ½ of a jalapeño, julienned or finely chopped (see tip, page 8)
- 1½ cups shredded cooked chicken breast
- 1 cup fresh shiitake, straw, or button mushrooms, sliced
- ⅔ cup snow peas, trimmed and halved diagonally
- 1 tablespoon chopped fresh basil

① Lightly coat a 4-quart Dutch oven with nonstick cooking spray. Heat over medium heat. Add onion, ginger, and garlic to Dutch oven. Cook and stir 2 to 3 minutes or until tender. Stir in broth, coconut milk, lime juice, and Thai seasoning. Bring to boiling. Reduce heat. Add carrots and jalapeño. Simmer, covered, 5 minutes. Add chicken, mushrooms, snow peas, and basil. Cook 3 minutes more or until heated through.

PER SERVING 159 calories; 6 g total fat (3 g sat. fat); 36 mg cholesterol; 566 mg sodium; 10 g carbohydrate; 2 g fiber; 16 g protein

Thai Chicken Soup

Moroccan-Spiced Chicken Lentil Stew

MAKES 8 servings **PREP** 30 minutes
COOK 7 hours (low) or 3½ hours (high) + 15 minutes (high)

- 2 pounds skinless, boneless chicken thighs, trimmed of fat and cut into 2- to 3-inch chunks
- 2 cloves garlic, minced
- ½ teaspoon ground cumin
- ½ teaspoon ground coriander
- ¼ teaspoon black pepper
- ¼ teaspoon ground cinnamon
  Nonstick cooking spray
- 1¼ cups dry brown lentils, rinsed and drained
- 1 medium onion, cut into thin wedges
- 2 14-ounce cans reduced-sodium chicken broth
- 1 cup water
- 1 large yellow summer squash, quartered lengthwise and cut into 1-inch-thick pieces
- ½ cup snipped dried apricots or golden raisins
- 2 tablespoons sliced green onions (optional)

① In a large bowl combine chicken, garlic, cumin, coriander, pepper, and cinnamon; toss to coat. Coat an unheated very large nonstick skillet with nonstick cooking spray. Preheat over medium heat. Add chicken to hot skillet; cook until browned, turning to brown all sides.

② Transfer chicken to a 4- to 5-quart slow cooker. Add lentils and onion to slow cooker. Pour chicken broth and the water over all.

③ Cover and cook on low-heat setting for 7 to 8 hours or on high-heat setting for 3½ to 4 hours. If using low-heat setting, turn to high-heat setting. Add squash and apricots to slow cooker. Cover and cook about 15 minutes more or just until squash is tender. If desired, garnish individual servings with sliced green onions.

PER SERVING 274 calories; 5 g total fat (1 g sat. fat); 94 mg cholesterol; 318 mg sodium; 26 g carbohydrate; 10 g fiber; 32 g protein

Turkey Wild Rice Soup ✪

MAKES 6 servings **PREP** 30 minutes **ROAST** 35 minutes
COOK 50 minutes **OVEN** at 400°F

- 1 pound turkey breast tenderloin
- 12 ounces Brussels sprouts, trimmed and halved
- 2 teaspoons olive oil
- ¼ teaspoon salt
- 2 cups water
- 1 14-ounce can reduced-sodium chicken broth
- ½ cup wild rice, rinsed and drained
- 1 medium onion, chopped
- 2 cloves garlic, minced
- 1 medium sweet potato, peeled and cut into 1-inch pieces (1½ cups)
- 1½ cups fat-free milk
- 2 tablespoons all-purpose flour
- 1 tablespoon snipped fresh sage
- 1 teaspoon finely shredded lemon peel
- ¼ teaspoon black pepper
  Small fresh sage leaves

① Preheat oven to 400°F. On one side of a 15 x 10 x 1-inch baking pan place the turkey tenderloin. On the other side of the pan place the Brussels sprouts. Brush the turkey with 1 teaspoon of the oil. Drizzle remaining oil over Brussels sprouts. Sprinkle turkey and sprouts with the salt. Roast, uncovered, for 35 minutes or until turkey is done (170°F) and sprouts are tender, turning turkey once. Remove from oven. When cool enough to handle, cut turkey into 1-inch pieces. Set turkey and Brussels sprouts aside.

② Meanwhile, in a large saucepan combine the water, broth, rice, onion, and garlic. Bring to boiling; reduce heat. Simmer, covered, for 35 minutes. Add sweet potato and return to boiling; reduce heat. Simmer, covered, for 10 minutes more or until rice and potato are tender. Stir in Brussels sprouts and turkey.

③ In a medium bowl whisk together milk and flour until smooth. Add to soup. Cook and stir until bubbly. Cook and stir 1 minute more. Stir in 1 tablespoon sage, lemon peel, and black pepper. To serve, ladle soup into bowls. Garnish with additional sage.

PER SERVING 232 calories; 2 g total fat (0 g sat. fat); 48 mg cholesterol; 348 mg sodium; 27 g carbohydrate; 4 g fiber; 26 g protein

Moroccan-Spiced Chicken Lentil Stew

Beefy Italian Vegetable Soup

Beefy Italian Vegetable Soup ✪

MAKES 4 servings **PREP** 25 minutes **COOK** 15 minutes

12	ounces beef sirloin, trimmed of fat and cut in bite-size pieces
1	teaspoon vegetable oil
8	ounces mushrooms, quartered
1	medium onion, chopped
3	cloves garlic, minced
1	tablespoon balsamic vinegar
2	14-ounce cans lower-sodium beef broth
1	14.5-ounce can no-salt-added diced tomatoes, undrained
¼	cup dry red wine (optional)
½	teaspoon dried Italian seasoning, crushed
¼	teaspoon fennel seeds, crushed
¼	teaspoon black pepper
3	cups escarole or kale, chopped
1	cup fresh green beans, trimmed and bias-sliced in bite-size pieces
1	medium yellow sweet pepper, chopped

① In a Dutch oven brown beef in hot oil over medium-high heat. Remove from Dutch oven with a slotted spoon.

② Add mushrooms, onion, and garlic to Dutch oven. Cook and stir 6 minutes or until tender and mushrooms are browned. Add vinegar and stir to remove browned bits on the bottom of the pan.

③ Add broth, undrained tomatoes, wine (if desired), Italian seasoning, fennel seeds, and pepper. Bring to boiling. Add beef, escarole, green beans, and sweet pepper to Dutch oven. Reduce heat and simmer, covered, for 15 minutes or until vegetables and beef are tender.

PER SERVING 209 calories; 5 g total fat (1 g sat. fat); 36 mg cholesterol; 469 mg sodium; 17 g carbohydrate; 5 g fiber; 25 g protein

BBQ Bean Chili ✪

MAKES 6 servings **PREP** 15 minutes **COOK** 30 minutes

	Nonstick cooking spray
1	medium onion, cut into thin wedges
1	medium green sweet pepper, chopped
2	large ripe tomatoes, chopped (2 cups)
2	15-ounce cans no-salt-added red kidney beans, rinsed and drained
1	15-ounce can no-salt-added navy beans, rinsed and drained
1	14-ounce can reduced-sodium chicken broth
1	8-ounce can no-salt-added tomato sauce
8	ounces smoked turkey sausage, chopped
1	tablespoon chili powder
1	tablespoon molasses or sugar-free or light pancake syrup
6	tablespoons low-fat plain Greek yogurt
	Fresh cilantro sprigs (optional)

① Coat an unheated 4-quart nonstick saucepan or Dutch oven with cooking spray. Heat over medium heat. Add onion and sweet pepper. Cook for 5 to 10 minutes or until tender, stirring occasionally.

② Stir in tomatoes, beans, broth, tomato sauce, sausage, chili powder, and molasses. Bring to boiling; reduce heat. Simmer, covered, for 30 minutes, stirring occasionally. To serve, ladle soup into bowls. Top with a dollop of yogurt. If desired, garnish with cilantro.

PER SERVING 293 calories; 4 g total fat (1 g sat. fat); 26 mg cholesterol; 572 mg sodium; 43 g carbohydrate; 19 g fiber; 23 g protein

Vegetarian Bean Chili: Prepare as directed above except use vegetable broth and omit the turkey sausage.

The melange of meat and vegetables in flavorful broth makes a one-dish meal.

Burgundy Beef Stew

MAKES 8 servings **PREP** 20 minutes
COOK 10 hours (low) or 5 hours (high)

- 2 pounds boneless beef chuck pot roast
- ½ teaspoon salt
- ¼ teaspoon black pepper
- 1 tablespoon cooking oil (optional)
- 2 tablespoons quick-cooking tapioca
- 6 medium carrots, cut into 1½-inch pieces
- 1 9-ounce package frozen cut green beans
- ½ of a 16-ounce package frozen small whole onions (2 cups)
- 2 cloves garlic, minced
- 1 14-ounce can reduced-sodium beef broth
- 1 cup Burgundy wine
- 3 cups cooked wide noodles
- 4 slices turkey bacon, cooked according to package directions and chopped

① Trim fat from meat. Cut meat into 1-inch pieces. Sprinkle meat with salt and pepper. If desired, in a large skillet cook meat, half at a time, in hot oil over medium heat until brown. Drain off fat.

② Place meat in a 3½- or 4-quart slow cooker. Sprinkle with tapioca. Stir in carrots, green beans, onions, and garlic. Pour broth and Burgundy wine over meat mixture in cooker.

③ Cover and cook on low-heat setting for 10 to 12 hours or on high-heat setting for 5 to 6 hours. Serve over noodles and sprinkle with bacon.

PER SERVING 318 calories; 7 g total fat (2 g sat. fat); 92 mg cholesterol; 451 mg sodium; 27 g carbohydrate; 3 g fiber; 30 g protein

This is a vegetable-rich, slow-cooker version of that famous French dish, Boeuf Bourguignon. Although it calls for Burgundy wine, you could use any hearty red, such as Cabernet Sauvignon, Merlot, or Zinfandel.

Mediterranean Meatball Soup

MAKES 6 servings **PREP** 25 minutes **BAKE** 15 minutes
COOK 20 minutes **OVEN** at 350°F

- ¾ cup soft whole wheat bread crumbs
- ¼ cup refrigerated or frozen egg product, thawed, or 1 egg, lightly beaten
- 4 cloves garlic, minced
- 2 teaspoons snipped fresh rosemary or ½ teaspoon dried rosemary, crushed
- ¼ teaspoon black pepper
- 1 pound 90% or higher lean ground beef
- 1 tablespoon olive oil
- 3 medium carrots, peeled and coarsely chopped
- 2 medium yellow and/or red sweet peppers, seeded and cut into bite-size strips
- 1 medium onion, chopped
- 2 cups lower-sodium beef broth
- 2 cups water
- 1 15-ounce can Great Northern beans, rinsed and drained
- ½ cup quick-cooking barley
- 4 cups packaged fresh baby spinach leaves

① Preheat oven to 350°F. In a large bowl combine bread crumbs, egg, half the garlic, half the rosemary, and the black pepper. Add ground beef; mix well. Shape meat mixture into 1½-inch meatballs. Place meatballs in a foil-lined 15 x 10 x 1-inch baking pan. Bake about 15 minutes or until done in centers (160°F). Set aside.

② In a 5- to 6-quart Dutch oven heat oil over medium heat. Add carrots, sweet peppers, onion, and the remaining garlic; cook for 5 minutes, stirring occasionally. Add beef broth, the water, Great Northern beans, barley, and the remaining rosemary. Bring to boiling; reduce heat. Cover and simmer about 15 minutes or until barley is tender.

③ Add meatballs to barley mixture; heat through. Stir in spinach just before serving.

PER SERVING 301 calories; 10 g total fat (3 g sat. fat); 49 mg cholesterol; 400 mg sodium; 31 g carbohydrate; 7 g fiber; 25 g protein

Adobo Black Bean Chili

menu

Warm whole wheat
tortillas

Cut-up fresh fruit

Adobo Black Bean
Chili
[below]

Adobo Black Bean Chili

MAKES 4 servings **PREP** 20 minutes **COOK** 20 minutes

12	ounces 95%-lean ground beef
1	medium onion, chopped (½ cup)
1	medium green sweet pepper, chopped (¾ cup)
2	cloves garlic, minced
1	15-ounce can no-salt-added black beans, rinsed and drained or 1¾ cups cooked black beans
1	14.5-ounce can no-salt-added diced tomatoes, undrained
1	8-ounce can no-salt-added tomato sauce
½	cup frozen whole kernel corn
1	tablespoon canned chipotle chile peppers in adobo sauce, finely chopped
2	teaspoons chili powder
1	teaspoon dried oregano, crushed
1	teaspoon ground cumin
¼	teaspoon black pepper
¼	cup light sour cream
2	tablespoons shredded reduced-fat cheddar cheese

① In a 4-quart Dutch oven cook ground beef, onion, sweet pepper, and garlic until meat is brown and onion is tender; drain fat. Stir in beans, diced tomatoes, tomato sauce, corn, chile peppers, chili powder, oregano, cumin, and black pepper. Bring to boiling; reduce heat. Simmer, covered, for 20 minutes, stirring occasionally.

② Top each serving with sour cream and cheddar cheese.

PER SERVING 317 calories; 7 g total fat (3 g sat. fat); 59 mg cholesterol; 184 mg sodium; 35 g carbohydrate; 10 g fiber; 28 g protein

Southwestern Steak and Potato Soup ✪

MAKES 14 servings **PREP** 30 minutes
COOK 8 hours (low) or 4 hours (high)

2	pounds boneless beef sirloin steak, cut ¾ inch thick
3	medium potatoes, cut into ¾-inch pieces (3 cups)
1	16-ounce package frozen cut green beans
1	medium onion, sliced and separated into rings
2	teaspoons dried basil, crushed
4	cloves garlic, minced
2	16-ounce jars thick and chunky salsa
2	14-ounce cans lower sodium beef broth

① Trim fat from meat. Cut meat into ¾-inch pieces. Set aside.

② In a 6-quart slow cooker combine potatoes, green beans, and onion. Add meat. Sprinkle with basil and garlic. Pour salsa and broth over meat and vegetables in cooker.

③ Cover; cook on low-heat setting for 8 to 10 hours or on high-heat setting for 4 to 5 hours. Stir before serving. If desired, sprinkle individual servings with cheese.

PER SERVING 142 calories; 3 g total fat (1 g sat. fat); 27 mg cholesterol; 532 mg sodium; 12 g carbohydrate; 3 g fiber; 17 g protein

Southwestern Steak and Potato Soup

Beef Fajita Soup ✪

MAKES 4 servings **START TO FINISH** 40 minutes

- ½ teaspoon garlic powder
- ½ teaspoon ground cumin
- ½ teaspoon paprika
- ⅛ teaspoon cayenne pepper
- 12 ounces boneless beef sirloin steak, trimmed and cut into very thin bite-size strips*
- Nonstick cooking spray
- 2 teaspoons canola oil
- 2 medium yellow or green sweet peppers, cut into thin bite-size strips
- 1 medium onion, halved and thinly sliced
- 2 14-ounce cans lower-sodium beef broth
- 1 14.5-ounce can no-salt-added diced tomatoes, undrained
- ¼ cup light sour cream
- ½ teaspoon finely shredded lime peel
- 1 ounce baked tortilla chips, coarsely crushed (⅔ cup)
- ½ of an avocado, seeded, peeled, and chopped (optional)
- ¼ cup snipped fresh cilantro (optional)

① In a medium bowl combine garlic powder, cumin, paprika, and cayenne pepper. Add steak strips and toss to coat. Coat an unheated 4-quart nonstick Dutch oven with cooking spray. Heat over medium-high heat. Add half of the steak strips. Cook for 2 to 4 minutes or until browned, stirring occasionally. Remove meat from the pan and repeat with remaining steak strips. Remove from pan.

② Add oil to the Dutch oven. Add sweet peppers and onion. Cook over medium heat for 5 minutes or just until lightly browned and tender, stirring occasionally. Add broth and undrained tomatoes. Bring to boiling. Stir in steak strips and heat through.

③ To serve, ladle soup into bowls; add a dollop of sour cream and sprinkle with lime peel and tortilla chips. If desired, top with avocado and cilantro.

*Tip: Partially freeze beef about 30 minutes for easier slicing into strips.

PER SERVING 244 calories; 8 g total fat (2 g sat. fat); 40 mg cholesterol; 515 mg sodium; 21 g carbohydrate; 4 g fiber; 24 g protein

Italian-Style Lentil Soup

MAKES 6 servings **PREP** 25 minutes **COOK** 45 minutes

- 1 tablespoon olive oil or canola oil
- ½ cup chopped onion
- 1 tablespoon bottled minced garlic or 6 cloves garlic, minced
- 1 32-ounce box reduced-sodium chicken broth (4 cups)
- 2 cups water
- 1 cup dry brown lentils
- 1½ teaspoons dried Italian seasoning, crushed
- ½ teaspoon black pepper
- 1 14.5-ounce can no-salt-added diced tomatoes, undrained
- 1 6-ounce can no-salt-added tomato paste
- 2 cups frozen peas and carrots
- 2 ounces dried multigrain penne pasta or multigrain elbow macaroni
- ¼ cup finely shredded Parmesan cheese (optional)

① In a large saucepan or 4-quart Dutch oven heat oil over medium heat. Add onion and garlic to saucepan; cook about 5 minutes or until onion is tender, stirring occasionally.

② Add broth, the water, lentils, Italian seasoning, and pepper to onion mixture. Bring to boiling; reduce heat. Simmer, covered, for 30 minutes.

③ Stir in undrained tomatoes and tomato paste. Stir in peas and carrots and uncooked pasta. Return to boiling; reduce heat. Simmer, uncovered, about 10 minutes or until pasta is tender.

④ To serve, ladle soup into bowls. If desired, sprinkle with Parmesan cheese.

PER SERVING 251 calories; 3 g total fat (0 g sat. fat); 0 mg cholesterol; 467 mg sodium; 42 g carbohydrate; 15 g fiber; 15 g protein

French Onion Soup

French Onion Soup

MAKES 6 servings **START TO FINISH** 40 minutes

3	medium onions, halved and thinly sliced
1	tablespoon olive oil
2	cloves garlic, minced
2½	cups lower-sodium beef broth
2½	cups water
2	teaspoons snipped fresh sage or ½ teaspoon dried sage, crushed
⅛	teaspoon black pepper
6	½-inch-thick slices whole grain baguette-style bread
¼	cup shredded reduced-fat Italian blend cheeses (1 ounce)
1	tablespoon balsamic vinegar

① In a large skillet cook onions, covered, in hot oil over medium-low heat for 15 minutes, stirring occasionally. Uncover and add garlic. Increase heat to medium. Cook for 3 to 5 minutes or until onions are lightly browned, stirring occasionally.

② Carefully add broth, the water, sage, and pepper to skillet. Bring to boiling; reduce heat. Simmer, covered, for 10 minutes to blend flavors.

③ Meanwhile, preheat broiler. Place bread slices on a baking sheet. Broil 3 to 4 inches from the heat for 2 to 3 minutes or until lightly toasted, turning once. Sprinkle bread slices evenly with cheese. Broil about 1 minute more or until cheese is melted. Stir vinegar into soup and ladle into six serving bowls. Top each serving with a piece of bread, cheese side up.

PER SERVING 99 calories; 4 g total fat (1 g sat. fat); 3 mg cholesterol; 270 mg sodium; 12 g carbohydrate; 3 g fiber; 5 g protein

Although white and yellow onions are similar in quality, they have different uses. White onions are stronger and the onion of choice for Mexican salsas, such as pico de gallo. Yellow onions are milder and have a higher sugar content—ideal for giving this soup a rich, sweet flavor.

Creamy Pumpkin Soup ✪

MAKES 4 servings **PREP** 15 minutes **COOK** 20 minutes

1	teaspoon canola oil
2	medium leeks, sliced (⅔ cup)
2	14-ounce cans low-sodium chicken broth
1	15-ounce can pumpkin
2	teaspoons snipped fresh thyme or 1 teaspoon dried thyme, crushed
¼	teaspoon black pepper
1	8-ounce carton light sour cream
	Small fresh thyme sprigs (optional)

① In a large saucepan heat oil over medium-high heat. Add leeks; cook and stir until tender. Stir in broth, pumpkin, dried thyme (if using), and pepper. Bring to boiling; reduce heat. Simmer, covered, for 20 minutes. Cool slightly. Stir in fresh snipped thyme, if using.

② Transfer soup to a blender or food processor. Cover and blend or process until smooth. Return to saucepan; heat through. Stir in half of the sour cream.

③ Ladle into soup bowls. Swirl in the remaining sour cream. If desired, garnish with thyme sprigs.

PER SERVING 165 calories; 9 g total fat (4 g sat. fat); 20 mg cholesterol; 108 mg sodium; 17 g carbohydrate; 3 g fiber; 7 g protein

Creamy Pumpkin Soup

Spiced Apple and Sweet Potato Soup

MAKES 4 side-dish servings **PREP** 20 minutes **COOK** 20 minutes

- 1 tablespoon chopped shallots
- 2 teaspoons olive oil
- ¼ teaspoon ground cumin
- ⅛ teaspoon ground cinnamon
  Dash crushed red pepper
- 6 ounces sweet potatoes, peeled and cut into 1-inch pieces
- 1 medium red-skin cooking apple, cored and cut into 1-inch pieces
- ½ cup reduced-sodium chicken broth
- ½ cup water
- ½ of a small green-skin apple, cored and thinly sliced

① In a medium saucepan cook shallots in hot oil over medium heat for 5 minutes, stirring occasionally. Add cumin, cinnamon, and crushed red pepper; cook and stir for 30 seconds. Add sweet potatoes, red-skin apple, broth, and the water. Bring to boiling; reduce heat. Simmer, covered, for 15 minutes or until potatoes and apple are very tender. Cool slightly.

② Transfer the soup to a blender or food processor; cover and blend or process until smooth. Return pureed soup to saucepan. Heat through. Ladle into four serving bowls. Top each serving with green-skinned apple slices.

PER SERVING 93 calories; 2 g total fat (0 g sat. fat); 0 mg cholesterol; 97 mg sodium; 18 g carbohydrate; 3 g fiber; 1 g protein

Roasted Root Vegetable Soup

MAKES 4 servings **PREP** 30 minutes **ROAST** 35 minutes **OVEN** at 425°F

- 2 medium carrots, peeled and cut into 1-inch-thick pieces
- 1 medium sweet potato, peeled and cut into 1-inch cubes
- 1 medium parsnip, peeled and cut into 1-inch-thick pieces
- ½ of a medium red onion, cut into thin wedges
- 3 cloves garlic, thinly sliced
- 1 tablespoon olive oil
- 1 teaspoon dried thyme, crushed
- ⅛ teaspoon black pepper
- 3 cups fat-free milk
- 1 cup reduced-sodium chicken broth
- ¼ cup all-purpose flour

① Preheat oven to 425°F. In a 13 x 9 x 2-inch baking pan combine carrots, sweet potato, parsnip, red onion, and garlic. Drizzle with oil; sprinkle with half the thyme and all the pepper. Toss to coat. Cover with foil.

② Roast for 20 minutes. Remove foil; stir vegetables. Roast, uncovered, for 15 to 20 minutes more or until vegetables are tender.

③ Meanwhile, in a large saucepan whisk together milk, chicken broth, flour, and the remaining thyme until smooth. Cook and stir over medium heat until thickened and bubbly. Add roasted vegetables. Cook and stir about 1 minute or until heated through.

PER SERVING 191 calories; 4 g total fat (1 g sat. fat); 4 mg cholesterol; 359 mg sodium; 31 g carbohydrate; 3 g fiber; 9 g protein

Fall vegetables and fruits—carrots, sweet potatoes, parsnips, and apples—add sweetness to soups.

Tomato-Basil Soup with Toasted Cheese Croutons

Tomato-Basil Soup with Toasted Cheese Croutons ✪

MAKES 4 servings **PREP** 25 minutes **COOK** 10 minutes

- 1 medium onion, chopped
- 2 cloves garlic, minced
- 2 teaspoons olive oil
- 2 14½-ounce cans no-salt-added diced tomatoes
- 1½ cups ⅓-less sodium vegetable broth or reduced-sodium chicken broth
- ¾ cup jarred roasted red sweet peppers, drained and chopped
- 2 tablespoons snipped fresh basil or 2 teaspoons dried basil, crushed
- 2 teaspoons balsamic vinegar
- 1 recipe Toasted Cheese Croutons

① In medium nonstick saucepan cook onion and garlic in hot oil about 5 minutes or until tender, stirring occasionally. Add undrained tomatoes, vegetable broth, roasted peppers, and dried basil (if using). Bring to boiling; reduce heat. Cover and simmer for 10 minutes to blend flavors. Cool slightly.

② Transfer half the soup to a blender or food processor. Cover and blend or process until smooth; add to remaining soup in saucepan. Heat through. Stir in fresh basil (if using) and vinegar just before serving. Top each serving with a few Toasted Cheese Croutons.

Toasted Cheese Croutons: Place four ¾-inch-thick slices whole grain baguette-style bread on a small baking sheet. Broil 4 to 5 inches from the heat for 1 to 2 minutes or until lightly toasted. Turn bread slices over; sprinkle tops with ¼ cup shredded reduced-fat Italian blend cheeses. Broil about 1 minute more or until cheese is melted. Cool bread slices slightly. Cut into irregular-shape bite-size pieces.

PER SERVING 146 calories; 4 g total fat (1 g sat. fat); 4 mg cholesterol; 406 mg sodium; 23 g carbohydrate; 5 g fiber; 5 g protein

Savory Bean and Spinach Soup

MAKES 6 servings **PREP** 15 minutes
COOK 5 hours (low) to 2½ hours (high)

- 3½ cups water
- 1 15-ounce can tomato puree
- 1 15-ounce can small white beans or Great Northern beans, rinsed and drained
- 1 14-ounce can vegetable broth
- 2 small onions, finely chopped (⅔ cup)
- ½ cup uncooked converted rice
- 1½ teaspoons dried basil, crushed
- ¼ teaspoon black pepper
- 2 cloves garlic, minced
- 8 cups coarsely chopped fresh spinach
- 2 tablespoons finely shredded Parmesan cheese

① In a 3½- or 4-quart slow cooker combine the water, tomato puree, drained beans, broth, onions, rice, basil, pepper, and garlic.

② Cover and cook on low-heat setting for 5 to 7 hours or on high-heat setting for 2½ to 3½ hours.

③ Before serving, stir in spinach. Sprinkle individual servings with Parmesan cheese.

PER SERVING 148 calories; 1 g total fat (0 g sat. fat); 1 mg cholesterol; 451 mg sodium; 31 g carbohydrate; 5 g fiber; 8 g protein

The rice in this vegetarian soup serves two purposes. It adds texture, and—as the soup cooks—the starch in the rice helps to slightly thicken the soup and give it body.

Creamy Broccoli Soup ✪ 🉐

MAKES 4 side-dish servings **START TO FINISH** 30 minutes

- ½ cup chopped onion
- 2 teaspoons canola oil
- 2 cloves garlic, minced
- 1 cup reduced-sodium vegetable broth
- 3 cups small broccoli florets
- 2 tablespoons flour
- 2 cups fat-free milk
- ¼ cup shredded reduced-fat Swiss cheese (1 ounce)
- ¼ teaspoon black pepper
- 2 tablespoons snipped fresh parsley
- 1 teaspoon finely shredded lemon peel

  Thin strips lemon peel and/or Italian (flat-leaf) parsley sprigs (optional)

① In a large saucepan cook onion in hot oil over medium heat for 5 minutes or until tender, stirring occasionally. Add garlic; cook and stir for 30 seconds. Add vegetable broth; bring to boiling. Add broccoli; cook, uncovered, for 3 to 5 minutes or until tender.

② Remove about half the broccoli florets with a slotted spoon and set aside. Transfer remaining broccoli soup to a blender or food processor. Cover and blend or process until smooth. Return to saucepan.

③ In a small screw-top jar combine the flour and ½ cup of the milk. Cover and shake until well combined. Add pureed soup and remaining milk to the saucepan. Cook and stir over medium heat until soup is slightly thickened, about 10 minutes; do not boil. Stir in cheese and pepper. Cook and stir until cheese is melted. Stir in reserved broccoli florets, the snipped parsley, and finely shredded lemon peel. Ladle into four serving bowls. If desired, garnish with lemon peel strips and/or parsley sprigs.

PER SERVING 137 calories; 4 g total fat (1 g sat. fat); 8 mg cholesterol; 243 mg sodium; 17 g carbohydrate; 2 g fiber; 9 g protein

Watermelon Soup with Fresh Mint

MAKES 4 servings **PREP** 20 minutes **CHILL** 2 hours

- 4 cups cut-up seedless watermelon
- 2 tablespoons lemon juice
- 2 tablespoons lime juice
- 1 tablespoon snipped fresh mint
- 1 tablespoon honey
- ¼ teaspoon ground ginger
- 1 tablespoon fresh mint leaves (optional)

① In a blender or food processor combine watermelon, lemon juice, lime juice, snipped mint, honey, and ginger. Cover and blend or process until nearly smooth. Cover and chill for 2 to 4 hours.

② To serve, ladle soup into bowls. If desired, garnish each serving with fresh mint leaves.

PER SERVING 75 calories; 0 g total fat (0 g sat. fat); 0 mg cholesterol; 8 mg sodium; 18 g carbohydrate; 1 g fiber; 2 g protein

Watermelon Soup with Fresh Mint

Creamy Broccoli Soup

New England Clam Chowder

New England Clam Chowder

MAKES 6 servings **START TO FINISH** 45 minutes

- 2 10-ounce cans whole baby clams, undrained
   Water
   Nonstick cooking spray
- 2 slices turkey bacon, halved
- 1 medium onion, chopped
- 1 stalk celery, thinly sliced
- 2 medium potatoes, cut into ½-inch pieces
- 2 cups small cauliflower florets (about 1-inch pieces)
- ¼ teaspoon dried thyme, crushed
- ⅛ teaspoon black pepper
- 2½ cups fat-free milk
- ½ cup fat-free half-and-half
- 2 tablespoons flour
- ¾ cup coarsely shredded carrots

① Drain clams, reserving liquid. Chop half the clams; set aside chopped and whole clams. Add enough water to the reserved clam liquid to measure 1½ cups; set clam liquid aside.

② Coat an unheated large saucepan with cooking spray; heat saucepan over medium heat. Add bacon, onion, and celery to saucepan. Cook for 5 to 8 minutes or until onion is tender and bacon is cooked through, stirring occasionally. Remove bacon from pan; drain on paper towels. Chop bacon; set aside.

③ Stir potatoes, cauliflower, thyme, pepper, and reserved clam liquid into onion mixture. Bring to boiling; reduce heat. Simmer, covered, for 10 to 12 minutes or until potatoes are tender. Remove from heat; cool slightly. Transfer half the chowder (about 2 cups) to a blender or food processor. Cover and blend or process until smooth. Return to the remaining chowder in saucepan.

④ In a medium bowl whisk together milk, half-and-half, and flour until smooth. Add all at once to chowder. Cook and stir just until boiling. Stir in chopped and whole clams and carrots. Return to boiling; reduce heat. Cook for 1 minute more. To serve, ladle chowder into bowls. Sprinkle each serving with chopped bacon.

PER SERVING 208 calories; 3 g total fat (1 g sat. fat); 77 mg cholesterol; 642 mg sodium; 25 g carbohydrate; 3 g fiber; 22 g protein

Crab Bisque

MAKES 4 servings **PREP** 20 minutes **COOK** 25 minutes

- ½ of a medium red onion, cut into very thin wedges
- 1 tablespoon olive oil
- 1 medium yellow sweet pepper, chopped
- 2 cloves garlic, minced
- 3 cups fat-free milk
- ¼ teaspoon black pepper
- ⅛ teaspoon cayenne pepper (optional)
- 1 14.5-ounce can reduced-sodium chicken broth
- ¼ cup flour
- 8 ounces cooked lump crabmeat
- 2 tablespoons snipped fresh chives
- 1 recipe Avocado-Cucumber Salsa

① In a large saucepan cook onion in hot oil over medium heat for 5 minutes, stirring occasionally. Turn heat to medium-low if onion starts to brown too quickly. Add sweet pepper and garlic. Cook 5 minutes or until tender, stirring occasionally. Carefully stir in milk, black pepper, and cayenne pepper (if using). Bring to boiling over medium heat.

② In a small bowl whisk together broth and flour until smooth. Add all at once to milk mixture. Cook and stir until thickened and bubbly. Cook and stir for 1 minute more. Stir in crabmeat and chives. Heat through. Ladle into four serving bowls. Top each serving with one-fourth of the Avocado-Cucumber Salsa.

Avocado-Cucumber Salsa: In a small bowl combine ⅓ cup chopped, peeled avocado; ⅓ cup chopped, seeded cucumber; ⅓ cup chopped, seeded tomato; 1 tablespoon snipped fresh parsley; and ½ teaspoon finely shredded lemon peel. Makes 1 cup.

PER SERVING 243 calories; 8 g total fat (1 g sat. fat); 60 mg cholesterol; 484 mg sodium; 23 g carbohydrate; 3 g fiber; 21 g protein

Asian Shrimp and Vegetable Soup

MAKES 6 servings **START TO FINISH** 45 minutes

12	ounces fresh or frozen large shrimp in shells
4	green onions
2	teaspoons canola oil
2	medium carrots, peeled and thinly sliced
8	ounces fresh shiitake or oyster mushrooms, stemmed and coarsely chopped
1	tablespoon grated fresh ginger or 1 teaspoon ground ginger
2	cloves garlic, minced
2	14-ounce cans reduced-sodium chicken broth
2	cups water
1	cup frozen shelled sweet soybeans (edamame)
1	tablespoon reduced-sodium soy sauce
¼	teaspoon crushed red pepper (optional)
1	cup trimmed sugar snap peas and/or coarsely shredded bok choy
2	tablespoons slivered green onions (optional)

① Thaw shrimp, if frozen. Peel and devein shrimp. Rinse shrimp; pat dry with paper towels. Set aside. Diagonally slice the whole green onions into 1-inch-long pieces, keeping white parts separate from green tops. Set green tops aside. In a large nonstick saucepan heat oil over medium heat. Add white parts of the green onions, the carrots, and mushrooms; cook for 5 minutes, stirring occasionally. Add ginger and garlic; cook and stir for 1 minute more.

② Add chicken broth, the water, soybeans, soy sauce, and, if desired, crushed red pepper to mushroom mixture. Bring to boiling; reduce heat. Cover and simmer about 5 minutes or just until carrots are tender.

③ Add shrimp and pea pods and/or bok choy. Return to boiling; reduce heat. Simmer, uncovered, for 2 to 3 minutes or until shrimp are opaque. Stir in green onion tops just before serving. If desired, garnish with slivered green onions.

PER SERVING 136 calories; 4 g total fat (0 g sat. fat); 65 mg cholesterol; 489 mg sodium; 10 g carbohydrate; 3 g fiber; 16 g protein

Caribbean Fish Stew

MAKES 6 servings **PREP** 30 minutes
COOK 6 hours (low) or 3 hours (high) + 15 minutes (high)

1	pound fresh or frozen firm white fish
2	pounds sweet potatoes, peeled and coarsely chopped
1¼	cups chopped red sweet pepper (1 large)
½	cup chopped onion (1 medium)
1	tablespoon grated fresh ginger
½	teaspoon finely shredded lime peel
1	tablespoon lime juice
1	teaspoon Jamaican jerk seasoning
2	cloves garlic, minced
2	14-ounce cans reduced-sodium chicken broth
1	14.5-ounce can no-salt-added diced tomatoes, undrained
	2 tablespoons snipped fresh cilantro

① Thaw fish, if frozen. In a 4- or 5-quart slow cooker combine sweet potatoes, sweet pepper, onion, ginger, lime peel, lime juice, jerk seasoning, and garlic. Pour broth and undrained tomatoes over vegetables.

② Cover and cook on low-heat setting for 6 to 8 hours or on high-heat setting for 3 to 4 hours.

③ Cut fish into 1-inch pieces. If using low-heat setting, turn to high-heat setting. Stir in fish. Cover and cook about 15 minutes more or until fish flakes easily when tested with a fork. Sprinkle each serving with cilantro.

PER SERVING 231 calories; 2 g total fat (0 g sat. fat); 24 mg cholesterol; 522 mg sodium; 33 g carbohydrate; 6 g fiber; 21 g protein

Use a sturdy white fish in this Caribbean-style stew so that the fish doesn't break apart after cooking. Good choices include cod, halibut, or pollock.

Caribbean Fish Stew

Simply Sides

Cranberry-Pear Chutney

MAKES 32 servings **PREP** 25 minutes **COOK** 30 minutes
CHILL 4 hours

1	12-ounce package fresh cranberries
1½	cups chopped Asian pears or chopped, peeled jicama
1½	cups finely chopped onion
1	cup sugar-free peach preserves
⅓	cup packed brown sugar
¼	cup balsamic vinegar
1	teaspoon dry mustard
1	teaspoon finely shredded lemon peel
½	teaspoon crushed red pepper

① In a large saucepan combine cranberries, Asian pears, onion, preserves, brown sugar, vinegar, mustard, lemon peel, and red pepper. Bring to boiling; reduce heat. Simmer, covered, for 30 minutes, stirring occasionally. Cool to room temperature.

② Transfer chutney to a glass serving dish. Cover and chill for at least 4 hours. If desired, store in an airtight container in the refrigerator for up to 5 days.

PER SERVING 29 calories; 0 g total fat; 0 mg cholesterol; 2 mg sodium; 8 g carbohydrate; 1 g fiber; 0 g protein

Cranberry-Pear Chutney

Fruit Salad with a Crunch

MAKES 4 servings **PREP** 20 minutes **CHILL** 1 hour

1	recipe Lime-Honey Dressing
2	cups cubed fresh pineapple
1	medium red pear, cored, quartered, and thinly sliced
2	kiwifruit, peeled, halved, and thinly sliced
¼	cup chopped, peeled jicama
1	tablespoon shredded coconut, toasted

① Prepare Lime-Honey Dressing. To dressing in the bowl add pineapple, pear, kiwifruit, and jicama. Toss to coat. Serve immediately or cover and chill for up to 1 hour to blend flavors. Sprinkle with coconut just before serving.

Lime-Honey Dressing: In a medium bowl whisk together 2 tablespoons lime juice, 1 tablespoon honey, ½ teaspoon grated fresh ginger, and, if desired, ⅛ teaspoon ground cardamom. Makes 3 tablespoons.

PER SERVING 116 calories; 1 g total fat (1 g sat. fat); 0 mg cholesterol; 8 mg sodium; 29 g carbohydrate; 4 g fiber; 1 g protein

To toast coconut, spread it in a single layer on a rimmed baking sheet. Bake in a 350° oven for 7 to 9 minutes, stirring occasionally, until golden brown. Watch carefully so that it doesn't burn. You can do this step ahead of time; just be sure to let the coconut cool completely before storing it at room temperature in a tightly sealed container.

Orange, Fennel, and Olive Salad
with Cranberry Vinaigrette

Orange, Fennel, and Olive Salad with Cranberry Vinaigrette 🟢

MAKES 12 servings **START TO FINISH** 25 minutes

1 small fennel bulb, thinly sliced (4 ounces)

6 cups torn mixed salad greens

4 medium navel oranges, peeled and sliced; 6 tangerines, peeled and sliced; and/or 8 kumquats, sliced

1 medium red onion, thinly sliced and separated into rings

½ cup pitted kalamata olives

1 recipe Cranberry Vinaigrette

① Place sliced fennel in a medium bowl and pour enough boiling water over fennel to cover. Let stand for 5 minutes; drain. Place greens in a large salad bowl. Arrange fennel, orange slices, onion, and olives on top of the greens. Drizzle Cranberry Vinaigrette over salad. Toss lightly before serving.

Cranberry Vinaigrette: In a medium saucepan combine 1 cup cranberry juice cocktail, ½ cup dry red wine, and ¼ cup dried cranberries. Bring to boiling; reduce heat. Simmer, uncovered, for 15 minutes or until mixture is reduced to about ⅓ cup; cool slightly. Meanwhile, in a small saucepan cook 2 tablespoons finely chopped shallots in 1 tablespoon hot olive oil until tender but not brown. In a food processor or blender combine cranberry mixture, shallots, 1 tablespoon olive oil, 2 tablespoons orange juice, 1 tablespoon red wine vinegar, 1 tablespoon honey, 1 teaspoon snipped fresh dillweed, ¼ teaspoon salt, and ¼ teaspoon black pepper. Cover; process or blend until smooth. Makes about ¾ cup.

PER SERVING 96 calories; 3 g total fat (0 g sat. fat); 0 mg cholesterol; 123 mg sodium; 15 g carbohydrate; 2 g fiber; 1 g protein

Spiced Apples and Raisins ⭐

MAKES 4 servings **PREP** 15 minutes **GRILL** 12 minutes

2 medium cooking apples (such as Granny Smith), cored and cut into wedges

½ cup golden raisins

1 tablespoon butter, cut into 4 pieces, or 1 tablespoon 60% to 70% tub-style vegetable oil spread

¼ cup orange juice

1 teaspoon apple pie spice

① Tear off four 24 x 18-inch pieces of heavy-duty foil. Fold each piece in half to make four 18 x 12-inch rectangles. Divide apples, raisins, and butter among foil pieces. Drizzle with orange juice and sprinkle with apple pie spice. For each packet, bring up two opposite edges of the foil and seal with a double fold. Fold remaining ends to completely enclose the food, allowing space for steam to build.

② For a charcoal grill, grill foil packets on the rack of an uncovered grill directly over medium coals for 12 to 14 minutes or until apples are tender, turning packets occasionally and carefully opening packets to check doneness. (For a gas grill, preheat grill. Reduce heat to medium. Place foil packets on grill rack over heat. Cover and grill as above.)

Oven Method: Preheat oven to 400°F. Prepare as directed in Step 1. Bake packets directly on the oven rack for 12 to 14 minutes or until apples are tender, carefully opening packets to check doneness.

PER SERVING 133 calories; 3 g total fat (2 g sat. fat); 8 mg cholesterol; 24 mg sodium; 28 g carbohydrate; 3 g fiber; 1 g protein

Salty, tangy olives and sweet oranges make a delicious combination in this salad.

Black Bean Slaw with Soy Ginger Dressing

MAKES 4 servings **PREP** 25 minutes **CHILL** overnight

1	15-ounce can black beans, rinsed and drained
6	cups shredded cabbage with carrots (coleslaw mix)
1⅓	cups chopped green apples (2 medium)
1	cup chopped red sweet pepper (1 large)
¼	cup cider vinegar
2	tablespoons reduced-sodium soy sauce
2	tablespoons peanut oil
2	teaspoons grated fresh ginger
2	teaspoons honey
¼	teaspoon black pepper

① In a large bowl combine black beans, shredded cabbage with carrots, apples, and sweet pepper.

② For dressing, in a screw-top jar combine vinegar, soy sauce, oil, ginger, honey, and black pepper; cover and shake well. Pour dressing over cabbage mixture; toss to coat. Cover and chill overnight.

PER SERVING 217 calories; 7 g total fat (1 g sat. fat); 0 mg cholesterol; 577 mg sodium; 36 g carbohydrate; 9 g fiber; 9 g protein

Cucumber-Radish Salad

MAKES 4 servings **PREP** 15 minutes **CHILL** 4 hours

½	cup plain low-fat yogurt
⅛	teaspoon salt
1	clove garlic, minced
	Dash black pepper
3	cups thinly sliced cucumber (1 large)
½	cup thinly sliced red onion (1 medium)
½	cup thinly sliced radishes

① In a medium bowl stir together yogurt, salt, garlic, and black pepper. Add cucumber, onion, and radishes. Toss to coat. Cover and chill for 4 to 24 hours, stirring often. Stir before serving.

PER SERVING 43 calories; 1 g total fat (0 g sat. fat); 2 mg cholesterol; 102 mg sodium; 8 g carbohydrate; 1 g fiber; 2 g protein

menu

Cheese and Date Stuffed Chicken Breasts

Goat Cheese and Onion Scones

Zucchini and Tomato [below]

Brown Sugar Peaches

Zucchini and Tomato

MAKES 4 servings **START TO FINISH** 15 minutes

1	medium zucchini, trimmed and cut lengthwise into 4 slices
	Nonstick cooking spray
1	large tomato, cut into 4 slices
¼	teaspoon dried Italian seasoning, crushed
¼	teaspoon black pepper
⅓	cup panko (Japanese-style bread crumbs)
¼	cup finely shredded Parmesan cheese (1 ounce)
1	clove garlic, minced

① Preheat broiler. Coat both sides of zucchini slices with cooking spray. Sprinkle zucchini and tomato slices with Italian seasoning and pepper.

② Place zucchini slices on the unheated rack of a broiler pan. Broil 4 to 5 inches from the heat about 8 minutes or until crisp-tender, turning once halfway through broiling.

③ Meanwhile, in a small bowl combine bread crumbs, cheese, and garlic. Place tomato slices on broiler pan next to zucchini slices. Sprinkle tops of vegetable slices with bread crumb mixture. Broil for 1 to 2 minutes more or until topping is golden.

PER SERVING 54 calories; 2 g total fat (1 g sat. fat); 4 mg cholesterol; 105 mg sodium; 7 g carbohydrate; 1 g fiber; 3 g protein

Heirloom Tomato Salad

Heirloom Tomato Salad

MAKES 8 servings **PREP** 30 minutes **CHILL** 2 hours

8	ounces fresh green beans, trimmed and cut into 2-inch pieces (about 2 cups)
1⅓	cups dried multigrain penne pasta (about 4 ounces)
¼	cup shredded fresh basil
¼	cup balsamic vinegar
2	tablespoons olive oil
2	teaspoons sugar
2	teaspoons Dijon mustard
1	clove garlic, minced
⅛	teaspoon salt
⅛	teaspoon black pepper
2	medium heirloom tomatoes, seeded and cut into bite-size wedges
½	cup finely shredded Parmesan cheese (2 ounces)
1	cup shredded fresh baby spinach
	Fresh basil sprigs (optional)

① Cook green beans and pasta according to the pasta package directions; drain. Rinse with cold water; drain again.

② Meanwhile, for dressing, in a screw-top jar combine shredded basil, vinegar, oil, sugar, mustard, garlic, salt, and pepper. Cover and shake well.

③ In a large bowl combine green beans and pasta, tomatoes, and cheese. Shake dressing. Pour dressing over pasta mixture; toss gently to coat. Cover and chill for 2 to 6 hours.

④ Before serving, add spinach to pasta mixture; toss gently to combine. If desired, garnish with basil sprigs. Use a slotted spoon to serve.

PER SERVING 131 calories; 5 g total fat (1 g sat. fat); 4 mg cholesterol; 166 mg sodium; 16 g carbohydrate; 3 g fiber; 5 g protein

Increasingly, grocery stores are carrying locally grown heirloom tomatoes during the summer tomato season. If you can't find them at your supermarket and don't grow them yourself, you'll find them at farmers' markets.

Roasted Broccoli and Tomatoes

MAKES 6 servings **PREP** 20 minutes
ROAST 15 minutes **OVEN** at 450°F

6	cups broccoli florets (12 ounces)
¼	cup coarsely chopped shallots
2	tablespoons olive oil
2	teaspoons snipped fresh thyme
¼	teaspoon salt
¼	teaspoon black pepper
2	cups cherry or grape tomatoes, halved
2	cloves garlic, minced
¼	cup shaved Asiago cheese (1 ounce)

① Preheat oven to 450°F. Lightly grease a 15 x 10 x 1-inch baking pan. In the prepared pan combine broccoli and shallots. In a small bowl combine oil, thyme, salt, and pepper. Drizzle oil mixture over broccoli and shallots; toss gently to coat.

② Roast, uncovered, for 10 minutes, stirring once. Stir in tomatoes and garlic. Roast, uncovered, for 5 to 10 minutes more or until broccoli is crisp-tender and tomatoes are soft. Sprinkle each serving with cheese.

PER SERVING 107 calories; 6 g total fat (2 g sat. fat); 5 mg cholesterol; 183 mg sodium; 10 g carbohydrate; 3 g fiber; 5 g protein

Roasted Broccoli and Tomatoes

Panzanella Salad with a Twist ③⓪

MAKES 6 servings **START TO FINISH** 25 minutes

4	ounces whole grain baguette-style French bread, cut into ½-inch slices
1	clove garlic, halved
6	cups packaged fresh baby spinach or torn romaine lettuce
⅓	cup torn fresh basil
½	of a small red onion, cut into thin wedges
1½	cups halved seedless red grapes
¼	cup reduced-calorie balsamic vinaigrette salad dressing

① Preheat broiler. Place bread slices on a baking sheet. Broil 2 to 3 inches from the heat for about 3 minutes or until lightly toasted, turning once to toast both sides. Cool on a wire rack. Lightly rub bread slices with cut sides of garlic clove. Cut bread into cubes.

② In a large glass salad bowl combine spinach and basil. Top with red onion, the bread cubes, and grapes. Drizzle with salad dressing and toss to coat. Serve immediately.

Make-Ahead Directions: Prepare bread cubes; set aside. In a salad bowl layer spinach, red onion, and grapes. Cover and chill salad for up to 4 hours. Top with basil and bread cubes and drizzle with vinaigrette; toss to coat.

PER SERVING 99 calories; 2 g total fat (0 g sat. fat); 0 mg cholesterol; 237 mg sodium; 17 g carbohydrate; 3 g fiber; 4 g protein

Panzanella Salad with a Twist

Green Beans with Peppers and Pineapple

MAKES 12 servings **PREP** 20 minutes **COOK** 12 minutes

2	pounds thin green beans
4	to 8 cloves garlic, thinly sliced
½	teaspoon crushed red pepper
2	tablespoons olive oil
¼	teaspoon salt
1	small red sweet pepper, cut into thin strips
½	of a peeled, quartered, and cored pineapple, thinly sliced
1	teaspoon finely shredded lime peel
2	tablespoons lime juice

① In a large Dutch oven bring salted water to boiling. Add beans. Return to boiling. Reduce heat; simmer, covered, for 6 minutes. Drain and rinse under cold water to stop cooking; drain again. (Beans may be covered and refrigerated for up to 24 hours.)

② In a very large skillet cook half the garlic and half the crushed red pepper in 1 tablespoon of the hot olive oil over medium-high heat for 15 seconds. Add half the green beans and cook, stirring frequently, for 2 to 3 minutes or until heated through. Sprinkle with half of the salt. Remove from skillet; repeat with remaining garlic, crushed red pepper, olive oil, salt, and green beans. Place all beans in a serving dish.

③ Add sweet pepper strips to the hot skillet and cook for 2 to 3 minutes. Remove pepper strips from skillet. Add pineapple slices to hot skillet. Cook for 4 minutes, turning once halfway through cooking time.

④ Toss beans with lime peel and juice. Top with pepper strips and pineapple slices.

PER SERVING 57 calories; 2 g total fat (0 g sat. fat); 0 mg cholesterol; 54 mg sodium; 9 g carbohydrate; 3 g fiber; 2 g protein

Green Beans with Peppers and Pineapple

Gingered Lemon Broccoli Salad

Gingered Lemon Broccoli Salad

MAKES 8 servings **PREP** 20 minutes **CHILL** 1 hour

- 3 tablespoons light mayonnaise or salad dressing
- 2 tablespoons plain soy yogurt
- ¼ teaspoon finely shredded lemon peel
- 2 teaspoons lemon juice
- ¼ teaspoon grated fresh ginger
- 4 cups small broccoli and/or cauliflower florets
- ⅓ cup finely chopped red onion
- ¼ cup dried cranberries
- 3 tablespoons roasted soy nuts

① In a large bowl stir together mayonnaise, soy yogurt, lemon peel, lemon juice, and ginger. Add broccoli, red onion, and cranberries. Toss to coat. Cover and chill for 1 to 24 hours. Just before serving, sprinkle with soy nuts.

PER SERVING 59 calories; 3 g total fat (0 g sat. fat); 2 mg cholesterol; 54 mg sodium; 8 g carbohydrate; 2 g fiber; 2 g protein

Brussels Sprouts with Shallot Sauce

MAKES 4 servings **PREP** 15 minutes **COOK** 10 minutes

- 12 ounces fresh Brussels sprouts
- 2 tablespoons finely chopped shallot
- 2 tablespoons chopped walnuts
- 1 tablespoon butter
- ⅓ cup light sour cream
- 1 teaspoon snipped fresh thyme or ¼ teaspoon dried thyme, crushed
- ⅛ teaspoon salt
  Milk (optional)

① Trim stems and remove any wilted outer leaves from fresh Brussels sprouts; wash. Cut any large sprouts in half lengthwise.

② Fill a large Dutch oven with water to a depth of 1 inch. Bring water to boiling. Place a steamer basket in the Dutch oven. Place Brussels sprouts in the steamer basket. Cover and steam for 10 minutes or until sprouts are tender. Remove sprouts from steamer basket and place in a large colander to drain.

③ Meanwhile, in a medium skillet cook shallot and walnuts in hot butter for 5 minutes or until shallot is tender and walnuts are toasted. Stir in sour cream, thyme, and salt; heat through. Toss steamed Brussels sprouts with shallot mixture. If desired, stir in milk, 1 tablespoon at a time, to reach desired consistency.

PER SERVING 111 calories; 7 g total fat (3 g sat. fat); 13 mg cholesterol; 126 mg sodium; 10 g carbohydrate; 4 g fiber; 4 g protein

Asparagus and Wild Mushrooms

MAKES 4 servings **PREP** 20 minutes **ROAST** 15 minutes **OVEN** at 400°F

- 3 cups halved cremini, shiitake, and/or button mushrooms
- 2 tablespoons white wine
- 2 teaspoons snipped fresh tarragon
- 1 pound asparagus spears
- 1 tablespoon olive oil
- ¼ teaspoon salt
- ¼ teaspoon black pepper
  Snipped fresh tarragon (optional)

① In a medium bowl toss together mushrooms, wine, and 2 teaspoons tarragon; set aside.

② Snap off and discard woody bases from asparagus. Place asparagus in a 15 x 10 x 1-inch baking pan. Drizzle with oil and sprinkle with salt and pepper. Toss to coat.

③ Roast, uncovered, in a 400°F oven for 5 minutes. Add mushroom mixture to the pan; toss gently to combine. Return to oven; roast about 10 minutes more or until asparagus is crisp tender. If desired, garnish with additional fresh tarragon.

PER SERVING 64 calories; 4 g total fat (1 g sat. fat); 0 mg cholesterol; 151 mg sodium; 5 g carbohydrate; 2 g fiber; 4 g protein

The licoricey flavor of tarragon is an acquired taste for some people. If you don't care for it or don't have it, fresh basil is a good substitute.

Mustard-Glazed Brussels Sprouts and Oranges 🕒

MAKES 6 servings **START TO FINISH** 25 minutes

- 3 medium blood oranges and/or oranges
- 1 pound Brussels sprouts (about 4 cups)
- 1 tablespoon butter
- 2 teaspoons cornstarch
- ¼ teaspoon five-spice powder or dried dill
- 2 tablespoons honey mustard

① Finely shred enough peel from one of the oranges to equal ½ teaspoon peel; set peel aside. Halve the orange; squeeze juice. Working over a bowl to catch the juices, peel and section the remaining two oranges; set orange sections aside. Combine the juices to equal ⅓ cup, adding water if necessary. Set juice aside.

② Trim stems and remove any wilted outer leaves from Brussels sprouts; wash. Halve any large sprouts. In a medium saucepan cook sprouts, uncovered, in a small amount of boiling water for 10 to 12 minutes or until tender. Drain; transfer to a serving bowl. Gently stir in the orange sections; cover and keep warm.

③ In the same saucepan melt butter. Stir in cornstarch and five-spice powder. Stir in reserved orange peel, orange juice, and mustard. Cook and stir until thickened and bubbly. Cook and stir for 1 minute more. Spoon over Brussels sprouts and orange sections; toss gently to coat.

PER SERVING 90 calories; 2 g total fat (1 g sat. fat); 5 mg cholesterol; 61 mg sodium; 16 g carbohydrate; 4 g fiber; 3 g protein

Mustard-Glazed Brussels Sprouts and Oranges

Lemon-Dill Cauliflower and Broccoli

MAKES 4 servings **PREP** 25 minutes **GRILL** 20 minutes

- 2 cups cauliflower florets
- 2 cups broccoli florets
- 1 tablespoon olive oil
- 2 teaspoons snipped fresh dill or ½ teaspoon dried dill
- ¼ teaspoon finely shredded lemon peel
- 2 teaspoons lemon juice
- 1 small clove garlic, minced
- ⅛ teaspoon salt
- ⅛ teaspoon sugar
- ⅛ teaspoon dry mustard
- ⅛ teaspoon black pepper
  Fresh dill sprigs (optional)

① Fold a 36 x 18-inch piece of heavy-duty foil in half to make an 18-inch square. Place cauliflower and broccoli in center of the foil square.

② In a small bowl combine oil, the snipped or dried dill, lemon peel, lemon juice, garlic, salt, sugar, mustard, and pepper; drizzle over vegetables. Bring up two opposite edges of the foil and seal with a double fold. Fold remaining ends to completely enclose the food, allowing space for steam to build.

③ For a charcoal grill, grill foil packet on the rack of an uncovered grill directly over medium coals about 20 minutes or until vegetables are tender, turning packet once halfway through cooking and carefully opening packet to check doneness. (For a gas grill, preheat grill. Reduce heat to medium. Place foil packet on grill rack over heat. Cover and grill as above.)

④ If desired, garnish with fresh dill sprigs.

Oven Method: Preheat oven to 350°F. Prepare as directed through Step 2. Bake packet directly on the oven rack about 35 minutes or until tender, carefully opening packet to check doneness.

PER SERVING 61 calories; 4 g total fat (0 g sat. fat); 0 mg cholesterol; 103 mg sodium; 6 g carbohydrate; 2 g fiber; 2 g protein

Lemon-Dill Cauliflower and Broccoli

Vegetable Gratin

Vegetable Gratin

MAKES 12 servings **START TO FINISH** 40 minutes

 1   slice whole grain bread
 ¼   cup slivered almonds
     Nonstick cooking spray
 4   medium carrots, peeled and cut crosswise into 1-inch-thick pieces
 3   cups broccoli florets
 3   cups cauliflower florets
 ¾   cup chopped sweet onion (such as Vidalia or Walla Walla)
 2   cloves garlic, minced
 ¼   teaspoon salt
 ¼   teaspoon black pepper
 1¼ cups fat-free milk
 3   tablespoons all-purpose flour
 2   tablespoons dry white wine or fat-free milk

① Place bread in a blender or small food processor; cover and blend or process to make coarse crumbs. In a small bowl combine bread crumbs and almonds; coat with cooking spray. Toss mixture; coat again with cooking spray. Coat an unheated large nonstick skillet with cooking spray. Preheat skillet over medium heat for 2 minutes; add crumb mixture. Cook about 5 minutes or until nuts are toasted, stirring frequently. Remove from skillet; set aside.

② In a Dutch oven cook carrots, uncovered, in a large amount of boiling water for 3 minutes. Add broccoli and cauliflower; cook for 3 to 5 minutes more or just until vegetables are tender. Drain well. Set aside.

③ Coat the large nonstick skillet with cooking spray again; preheat over medium heat. Add onion; cook about 5 minutes or until tender, stirring occasionally. Stir in garlic, salt, and pepper. In a small bowl whisk together milk and flour until smooth. Add to onion mixture. Cook and stir until thickened and bubbly. Stir in wine and vegetables; heat through. Place vegetables in serving dish; sprinkle with toasted crumb mixture.

PER SERVING 65 calories; 1 g total fat (0 g sat. fat); 1 mg cholesterol; 98 mg sodium; 10 g carbohydrate; 3 g fiber; 3 g protein

Green Beans with Bacon and Walnuts 30

MAKES 6 servings **START TO FINISH** 25 minutes

 12 ounces fresh haricot verts or thin green beans, trimmed
 1   small red sweet pepper, seeded and cut into strips
 2   slices bacon
 ¼   cup chopped walnuts
 2   cloves garlic, minced
 ¼   teaspoon salt
 ⅛   teaspoon crushed red pepper

① In a large saucepan cook green beans and sweet pepper in enough boiling water to cover for 3 minutes; drain.

② In a large skillet cook bacon over medium heat until crisp. Remove bacon and drain on paper towels, reserving drippings in skillet. Crumble bacon; set aside. Add green beans and sweet pepper, walnuts, garlic, salt, and crushed red pepper to the reserved drippings. Cook and stir about 5 minutes or until beans are tender and walnuts are lightly toasted. Sprinkle each serving with crumbled bacon.

PER SERVING 106 calories; 9 g total fat (2 g sat. fat); 7 mg cholesterol; 156 mg sodium; 6 g carbohydrate; 3 g fiber; 3 g protein

Pea Pod and Carrot Stir-Fry 30

MAKES 4 servings **START TO FINISH** 15 minutes

 2   teaspoons toasted sesame oil
 2   teaspoons bottled minced ginger
 1   teaspoon bottled minced garlic or 2 cloves garlic, minced
 2   cups fresh sugar snap pea pods, trimmed
 1   cup purchased shredded carrots
 2   teaspoons reduced-sodium soy sauce

① In a large skillet heat oil over medium-high heat. Add ginger and garlic to skillet; stir-fry for 15 seconds.

② Add pea pods and carrots. Stir-fry for 3 to 4 minutes or until pea pods are crisp-tender. Remove from heat. Drizzle with soy sauce; toss gently to coat.

PER SERVING 50 calories; 2 g total fat (0 g sat. fat); 0 mg cholesterol; 109 mg sodium; 6 g carbohydrate; 2 g fiber; 2 g protein

Two-Toned Potato Salad

MAKES 6 servings **PREP** 25 minutes **CHILL** 4 hours

- 6   small (about 2 inch) Yukon Gold potatoes, cut into ½-inch-thick wedges
- 1   6-ounce sweet potato, peeled and cut into 1-inch cubes
- ⅓   cup light mayonnaise
- 1   tablespoon Dijon mustard
- 1   tablespoon fat-free milk
- 2   teaspoons snipped fresh thyme or ½ teaspoon dried thyme, crushed
- ¼   teaspoon black pepper
- 1   stalk celery, thinly sliced
- 2   green onions, thinly sliced
- 2   slices turkey bacon, cooked and chopped

① In a large saucepan cook potatoes, covered, in enough boiling water to cover for 10 to 12 minutes or just until tender. Drain well; cool to room temperature.

② Meanwhile, for dressing, in a large bowl combine mayonnaise, mustard, milk, thyme, and pepper. Add potatoes, celery, and green onions. Toss to coat. Cover and chill at least 4 hours or up to 24 hours. Gently stir in bacon just before serving.

PER SERVING 106 calories; 5 g total fat (1 g sat. fat); 10 mg cholesterol; 248 mg sodium; 13 g carbohydrate; 2 g fiber; 2 g protein

Farmer's Market Salad Platter

MAKES 10 servings **PREP** 25 minutes **COOK** 20 minutes

- 1¼   pounds tiny new potatoes, halved or quartered
- 12   ounces fresh green beans and/or yellow wax beans, trimmed
- ¼   cup white wine vinegar or champagne vinegar
- 3   tablespoons olive oil
- 1   medium shallot, finely chopped (2 tablespoons)
- 1   tablespoon capers, rinsed and drained
- 1   teaspoon Dijon mustard
- ¼   teaspoon freshly ground black pepper
- 5   cups fresh baby arugula or baby spinach
- 4   medium roma tomatoes, coarsely chopped

① In a large covered saucepan cook potatoes in enough boiling water to cover about 10 minutes or just until tender; drain. Rinse with cold water and drain again. If desired, cover and chill for up to 24 hours.

② In a medium covered saucepan cook beans in enough boiling water to cover about 10 minutes or just until crisp-tender; drain. Submerse beans in a bowl of ice water to cool quickly; drain again. If desired, cover and chill for up to 24 hours.

③ For dressing, in a screw-top jar combine vinegar, olive oil, shallot, capers, mustard, and black pepper. Cover and shake well. If desired, chill for up to 24 hours.

④ To serve, if dressing is chilled, let it stand at room temperature for 30 minutes. Arrange arugula on a platter. Arrange potatoes, beans, and tomatoes on arugula. Shake the dressing well. Drizzle dressing over vegetables.

PER SERVING 106 calories; 4 g total fat (1 g sat. fat); 0 mg cholesterol; 49 mg sodium; 15 g carbohydrate; 3 g fiber; 3 g protein

Bright and colorful summer salads are a treat for the eyes and the taste buds.

Pumpkin Mashed Potatoes

Pumpkin Mashed Potatoes

MAKES 4 servings **PREP** 15 minutes **COOK** 20 minutes

- 1 pound medium baking potatoes, peeled and quartered
- 2 cloves garlic, peeled
- 1 cup canned pumpkin
- 2 tablespoons reduced-fat cream cheese (Neufchâtel)
- 1 tablespoon butter or tub-style vegetable oil spread
- ¼ teaspoon salt
- ¼ teaspoon black pepper
- ⅛ teaspoon ground sage
- ¼ cup fat-free milk
  Miniature Pumpkin Bowls (optional)
  Fresh sage leaves (optional)

① In a covered large saucepan cook potatoes and garlic in enough boiling water to cover for 20 to 25 minutes or until potatoes are tender; drain. Mash with a potato masher or beat with an electric mixer on low. Beat in pumpkin, cream cheese, butter, salt, pepper, and ground sage. Gradually beat in milk until light and fluffy. Return to saucepan; heat through.

② If desired, spoon mashed potatoes into Miniature Pumpkin Bowls and garnish with sage leaves.

PER SERVING 159 calories; 5 g total fat (3 g sat. fat); 13 mg cholesterol; 206 mg sodium; 26 g carbohydrate; 4 g fiber; 4 g protein

Miniature Pumpkin Bowls: Preheat oven to 325°F. Cut off ½ inch from the tops of 4 miniature pumpkins (6 to 8 ounces each); discard tops. Using a spoon, scoop out and discard seeds and membranes. Place pumpkins, cut sides down, on a baking sheet. Bake for 20 to 25 minutes or just until pumpkins are easily pierced with a fork.

Although real maple syrup is pricey, if you can afford it, use it in the Maple-Orange Sweet Potatoes. The intense flavor and aroma is worth it—especially if you're serving this dish for a holiday dinner.

Maple-Orange Sweet Potatoes

MAKES 4 servings **PREP** 20 minutes **COOK** 10 minutes
GRILL 10 minutes

- 2 medium sweet potatoes (about 1 pound total)
- ¼ cup pure maple syrup or maple-flavor syrup
- 2 tablespoons orange juice
- ¼ teaspoon salt
- ¼ teaspoon freshly ground black pepper
- ¼ cup dried cranberries

① Peel sweet potatoes. Cut sweet potatoes into ¼-inch-thick slices. In a medium covered saucepan cook sweet potato slices in enough boiling water to cover for 10 minutes. Drain; set aside. Tear off four 24 x 18-inch pieces of heavy-duty foil. Fold each in half to make an 18 x 12-inch rectangle.

② In a small bowl combine maple syrup, orange juice, salt, and pepper. Stir in cranberries. Divide sweet potatoes among foil rectangles; drizzle with maple syrup mixture.

③ For each packet bring up two opposite edges of the foil and seal with a double fold. Fold remaining ends to completely enclose the food, allowing space for steam to build.

④ For a charcoal grill, grill foil packets on the rack of an uncovered grill directly over medium coals for 10 to 15 minutes or until sweet potatoes are tender, turning packets once halfway through cooking and carefully opening packets to check doneness. (For a gas grill, preheat grill. Reduce heat to medium. Place foil packets on grill rack over heat. Cover and grill as above.)

Oven Method: Preheat oven to 350°F. Prepare as directed through Step 3. Bake packets directly on the oven rack for 10 to 15 minutes or until sweet potatoes are tender, carefully opening packets to check doneness.

PER SERVING 135 calories; 0 g total fat; 0 mg cholesterol; 183 mg sodium; 34 g carbohydrate; 2 g fiber; 1 g protein

Skillet Corn

MAKES 6 servings **START TO FINISH** 35 minutes

- 4 slices bacon
- 2 cups fresh or frozen corn kernels
- 1 cup frozen shelled sweet soybeans (edamame)
- 1 cup grape or cherry tomatoes, halved
- ½ of a small red onion, thinly sliced
- 2 tablespoons snipped fresh cilantro
- 1 small fresh jalapeño, seeded and finely chopped (see tip, page 8)
- 1 tablespoon olive oil
- ½ teaspoon finely shredded lime peel
- 1 tablespoon lime juice
- 2 cloves garlic, minced
- ¼ teaspoon ground cumin
- ⅛ teaspoon salt
- ⅛ teaspoon chili powder

① In a large skillet cook bacon over medium heat until crisp. Remove bacon and drain on paper towels, reserving 2 tablespoons of the drippings in skillet. Discard the remaining drippings. Crumble bacon; set aside. Add corn and soybeans to the reserved drippings. Cook and stir for 3 to 4 minutes or just until vegetables are crisp-tender.

② In a large bowl stir together crumbled bacon, corn and soybeans, tomatoes, red onion, cilantro, and jalapeño.

③ For dressing, in a screw-top jar combine oil, lime peel, lime juice, garlic, cumin, salt, and chili powder. Cover and shake well. Pour dressing over corn mixture; toss gently to coat.

PER SERVING 182 calories; 11 g total fat (3 g sat. fat); 9 mg cholesterol; 160 mg sodium; 17 g carbohydrate; 3 g fiber; 7 g protein

Smoky Baked Beans

MAKES 8 servings **PREP** 25 minutes **BAKE** 1 hour **OVEN** at 375°F

- 6 slices bacon, chopped
- ½ cup chopped green sweet pepper
- ½ cup chopped onion
- 2 cloves garlic, minced
- 1 15-ounce can no-salt-added black beans, rinsed and drained
- 1 15-ounce can no-salt-added butter beans, rinsed and drained
- 1 15-ounce can no-salt-added red kidney beans, rinsed and drained
- 1 8-ounce can no-salt-added tomato sauce
- ¼ cup orange juice
- 2 tablespoons packed brown sugar
- 1 tablespoon Worcestershire sauce
- 1 fresh jalapeño, seeded and finely chopped (see tip, page 8)
- Crisp-cooked bacon, crumbled (optional)

① Preheat oven to 375°F. In a large skillet cook chopped bacon, sweet pepper, onion, and garlic over medium heat about 10 minutes or until bacon is crisp and onion is tender; drain.

② In a large bowl combine bacon mixture, black beans, butter beans, kidney beans, tomato sauce, orange juice, brown sugar, Worcestershire sauce, and jalapeño. Transfer bean mixture to a 1½-quart casserole.

③ Bake, covered, for 1 hour, stirring once halfway through baking. If desired, garnish with crumbled bacon.

PER SERVING 218 calories; 6 g total fat (2 g sat. fat); 9 mg cholesterol; 168 mg sodium; 31 g carbohydrate; 10 g fiber; 11 g protein

Corn and beans—two American classics—make perfect sides for a summer barbecue.

Moroccan-Style Simmered Beans

Moroccan-Style Simmered Beans

MAKES 8 servings **PREP** 15 minutes **COOK** 30 minutes

2	teaspoons canola oil
½	cup chopped sweet onion
1	medium carrot, chopped
1	clove garlic, minced
¼	teaspoon ground cumin
¼	teaspoon ground coriander
⅛	teaspoon crushed red pepper
⅛	teaspoon ground cinnamon
1	15-ounce can garbanzo beans (chickpeas), rinsed and drained
1	15-ounce can Great Northern beans, rinsed and drained
½	cup frozen baby lima beans
½	cup chopped tomatoes
⅓	cup water
1	tablespoon lemon juice
	Ground cumin, cinnamon, and/or crushed red pepper (optional)

① In a large saucepan heat oil. Add onion and carrot to skillet; cook over medium heat for 8 to 10 minutes or until very tender, stirring occasionally. Stir in garlic, ¼ teaspoon cumin, the coriander, ⅛ teaspoon crushed red pepper, and the cinnamon. Cook and stir for 1 minute.

② Add beans, tomatoes, and the water. Bring to boiling; reduce heat. Cover and cook for 20 minutes to blend flavors, stirring occasionally. Stir in lemon juice just before serving. If desired, sprinkle with additional cumin, cinnamon, and/or crushed red pepper.

PER SERVING 127 calories; 2 g total fat (0 g sat. fat); 0 mg cholesterol; 202 mg sodium; 24 g carbohydrate; 6 g fiber; 8 g protein

A quartet of Moroccan spices—cumin, coriander, red pepper, and cinnamon—gives this bean dish exotic flavor.

Cilantro Tabbouleh with Cranberries

MAKES 4 servings **PREP** 25 minutes **COOK** 15 minutes **CHILL** 3 hours

	Nonstick cooking spray
1	tablespoon finely chopped shallot or onion
1¼	cups reduced-sodium chicken broth
½	cup bulgur
½	cup chopped seeded cucumber
2	tablespoons snipped fresh cilantro
2	tablespoons dried cranberries
¼	teaspoon finely shredded lime peel
1	tablespoon lime juice
	Dash black pepper

① Coat a small unheated nonstick saucepan with nonstick cooking spray. Preheat saucepan over medium heat. Add shallot to hot saucepan; cook and stir about 3 minutes or just until tender. Add chicken broth; bring to boiling. Stir in uncooked bulgur. Return to boiling; reduce heat. Cover and simmer about 15 minutes or until tender. Remove from heat; cool slightly. Transfer cooked bulgur to a large bowl. Cover and chill about 3 hours or until completely cool.

② Add cucumber, cilantro, cranberries, lime peel, lime juice, and pepper to cooled bulgur; mix well.

Make-Ahead Directions: Prepare as above. Cover and chill for up to 24 hours.

PER SERVING 82 calories; 0 g total fat (0 g sat. fat); 0 mg cholesterol; 184 mg sodium; 18 g carbohydrate; 4 g fiber; 3 g protein

Although traditionally tabbouleh is made with bulgur, you can substitute cracked wheat in this recipe, if you like. With dried cranberries, lime, and cilantro, it's not terribly traditional to start with!

Herbed Orzo

MAKES 4 servings **PREP** 10 minutes **COOK** 8 minutes

- ¾ cup whole wheat or regular orzo
- ½ cup halved red and yellow cherry or grape tomatoes
- ¼ cup crumbled reduced-fat feta cheese
- 2 tablespoons orange juice or reserved pasta cooking water
- 1 tablespoon snipped fresh basil or fresh parsley
- ½ teaspoon snipped fresh thyme

① In a medium saucepan cook orzo according to package directions, omitting any salt or oil. Drain orzo, reserving 2 tablespoons pasta cooking water if not using orange juice. Return orzo to the pan. Stir in tomatoes, feta cheese, orange juice, basil, and thyme.

PER SERVING 94 calories; 1 g total fat (1 g sat. fat); 3 mg cholesterol; 120 mg sodium; 17 g carbohydrate; 2 g fiber; 5 g protein

Herbed Orzo

Indian Basmati Rice

MAKES 6 servings **PREP** 30 minutes **COOK** 18 minutes

- 1 medium onion, chopped
- 1 tablespoon butter
- 1 cup basmati rice
- ⅔ cup snipped dried apricots
- 1 medium carrot, bias-sliced
- 1 teaspoon ground turmeric
- ½ teaspoon ground cumin
- ⅛ teaspoon crushed red pepper
- 1 14-ounce can reduced-sodium chicken broth
- ¼ cup water
- 1 6-ounce package frozen snow pea pods, thawed
- 2 tablespoons snipped fresh parsley
- 2 tablespoons slivered almonds, toasted

① In a medium saucepan cook onion in hot butter over medium heat about 5 minutes or until onion is tender. Stir in uncooked rice. Cook and stir for 4 minutes. Stir in apricots, carrot, turmeric, cumin, and crushed red pepper.

② Carefully stir broth and the water into rice mixture in saucepan. Bring to boiling; reduce heat. Cover and simmer for 18 to 20 minutes or until liquid is absorbed and rice is tender. Stir in pea pods and parsley. Sprinkle individual servings with almonds.

PER SERVING 200 calories; 3 g total fat (1 g sat. fat); 5 mg cholesterol; 184 mg sodium; 40 g carbohydrate; 3 g fiber; 5 g protein

Basmati rice has a wonderfully nutty flavor and aroma. You can use Texmati rice as well—it has similar qualities.

Spanish-Style Rice

Spanish-Style Rice

MAKES 5 servings **PREP** 20 minutes **COOK** 6 minutes

- 2 teaspoons olive oil
- ½ cup chopped green sweet pepper
- ¼ cup chopped onion
- ½ to 1 whole medium fresh serrano chile pepper, chopped (see tip, page 8) (optional)
- 2 cloves garlic, minced
- 1 8.8-ounce pouch cooked brown rice or 2 cups cooked brown rice
- ½ cup chopped tomato
- ¼ cup chopped pitted green olives
- ¼ teaspoon salt
- 2 tablespoons snipped fresh cilantro

① In a skillet heat oil. Add sweet pepper, onion, and, if desired, serrano pepper to skillet. Cook over medium heat for 3 to 5 minutes or until vegetables are crisp-tender, stirring occasionally. Add garlic; cook for 1 minute more.

② Add cooked rice, tomato, green olives, and salt; cook and stir for 2 minutes or until heated through. Stir in cilantro.

PER SERVING 106 calories; 3 g total fat (0 g sat. fat); 0 mg cholesterol; 122 mg sodium; 17 g carbohydrate; 1 g fiber; 2 g protein

Barley-Vegetable Pilaf

MAKES 4 servings **PREP** 15 minutes **COOK** 11 minutes

- 1¾ cups lower-sodium vegetable broth
- ¾ cup quick-cooking barley
- ½ cup small broccoli florets
- ½ cup ½-inch pieces zucchini
- ½ cup chopped red sweet pepper
- 2 tablespoons snipped fresh chives
- 1 teaspoon finely shredded lemon peel
- 2 tablespoons finely shredded Parmesan cheese (optional)

① In a saucepan heat broth to boiling. Stir in barley; return to boiling. Reduce heat. Simmer, covered, 8 minutes. Add broccoli, zucchini, and sweet pepper. Return to boiling and cook, covered, for 3 minutes or until barley and vegetables are tender. Remove from heat; stir in chives and lemon peel. If desired, sprinkle with cheese.

PER SERVING 141 calories; 1 g total fat (0 g sat. fat); 0 mg cholesterol; 251 mg sodium; 29 g carbohydrate; 7 g fiber; 5 g protein

Goat Cheese and Onion Scones

MAKES 12 scones **PREP** 20 minutes **BAKE** 15 minutes **OVEN** at 400°F

- 2 cups flour
- 2 tablespoons finely chopped green onion
- 2 teaspoons baking powder
- ¼ teaspoon baking soda
- ¼ teaspoon salt
- ¼ teaspoon freshly ground black pepper
- 1 egg, lightly beaten
- 4 ounces semisoft goat cheese (chèvre), crumbled or cut into small cubes
- ½ cup buttermilk or fat-free sour milk*

① Preheat oven to 400°F. In a medium bowl combine flour, green onion, baking powder, baking soda, salt, and pepper. Make a well in the center of flour mixture; set aside.

② In a small bowl stir together the egg, goat cheese, and buttermilk. Add egg mixture all at once to flour mixture. Using a fork, stir just until moistened.

③ Turn dough out onto a lightly floured surface. Knead dough by folding and gently pressing dough for 10 to 12 strokes or until dough is nearly smooth. Divide dough in half. Pat or lightly roll half of the dough into a 5-inch circle. Cut into six wedges. Place wedges 1 inch apart on an ungreased baking sheet. Repeat with remaining dough.

④ Bake for 15 to 18 minutes or until golden. Serve warm.

*Tip: To make ½ cup fat-free sour milk, place 1½ teaspoons lemon juice or vinegar in a glass measuring cup. Add enough fat-free milk to equal ½ cup total liquid; stir. Let mixture stand for 5 minutes before using.

PER SCONE 106 calories; 3 g total fat (2 g sat. fat); 22 mg cholesterol; 193 mg sodium; 15 g carbohydrate; 1 g fiber; 5 g protein

Peachy Corn Bread Muffins

(photo page 242)

MAKES 12 muffins **PREP** 15 minutes **BAKE** 14 minutes
OVEN at 400°F

- 1   cup yellow cornmeal
- ¾   cup all-purpose flour
- ¼   cup sugar
- 2½ teaspoons baking powder
- ½   teaspoon salt
- ½   teaspoon apple pie spice
- ¾   cup milk
- 2   eggs
- ¼   cup butter, melted
- ¾   cup chopped fresh or frozen unsweetened peaches

  Light vegetable oil spread (optional)

① Preheat oven to 400°F. Grease twelve 2½-inch muffin cups; set aside. In a medium bowl stir together cornmeal, flour, sugar, baking powder, salt, and apple pie spice; set aside.

② In a small bowl whisk together milk, eggs, and melted butter. Stir in peaches. Add peach mixture to flour mixture; stir just until combined. Spoon batter into prepared muffin cups, filling cups two-thirds full.

③ Bake for 14 to 15 minutes or until edges are golden brown. Serve warm. If desired, serve with vegetable oil spread.

PER MUFFIN 145 calories; 5 g total fat (3 g sat. fat); 47 mg cholesterol; 219 mg sodium; 21 g carbohydrate; 1 g fiber; 3 g protein

Sun-Dried Tomato Focaccia

MAKES 24 wedges **PREP** 40 minutes **STAND** 20 minutes
RISE 1 hour 20 minutes **BAKE** 25 minutes **OVEN** at 375°F

- 4   cups boiling water
- 2   cups dried tomatoes (not oil-packed) (about 8 ounces), snipped
- 2¼ to 2¾ cups all-purpose flour
- 1   package active dry yeast
- ¾   teaspoon salt
- 2   tablespoons olive oil
- 1   cup whole wheat flour
- 1   tablespoon pine nuts, toasted (see tip, page 15)

     Nonstick cooking spray
- 1   cup chopped onion
- 2   cloves garlic, minced
- 1   tablespoon snipped fresh rosemary

  Pine nuts, toasted (optional)

① In a medium bowl pour the boiling water over dried tomatoes. Let stand for 20 minutes to soften tomatoes. Drain well, reserving liquid (squeeze out as much liquid from tomatoes as possible); set tomatoes aside. Measure 1¼ cups of the liquid (temperature of liquid should be 120°F to 130°F). Discard any remaining liquid.

② In a large mixing bowl combine 1¼ cups of the all-purpose flour, the yeast, and salt. Add the 1¼ cups reserved liquid and 1 tablespoon of the oil. Beat with an electric mixer on low to medium for 30 seconds, scraping sides of bowl constantly. Beat on high for 3 minutes. Stir in half of the tomatoes, the whole wheat flour, and 1 tablespoon pine nuts. Stir in as much of the remaining all-purpose flour as you can.

③ Lightly coat a large bowl and two baking sheets with cooking spray; set aside. Turn dough out onto a lightly floured surface. Knead in enough of the remaining all-purpose flour to make a stiff dough that is smooth and elastic (8 to 10 minutes total). Shape dough into a ball. Place in the prepared bowl, turning once to grease surface. Cover and let rise in a warm place until double in size (about 1 hour).

④ Punch dough down. Divide in half. Shape each portion into a ball. Place on the prepared baking sheets. Cover and let rest for 10 minutes.

⑤ Meanwhile, preheat oven to 375°F. For topping, in a skillet heat the remaining 1 tablespoon oil over medium heat. Add onion and garlic. Cook, covered, for 3 to 5 minutes or until onion is tender, stirring occasionally. Cook, uncovered, about 4 minutes more or just until onion starts to brown, stirring frequently. Remove from heat.

⑥ Using your hands, flatten each ball of dough into a 10-inch circle. Using the handle of a wooden spoon or your fingers, make deep indentations every 2 inches in dough. Top with onion mixture, the remaining tomatoes, and rosemary. Cover and let rise in a warm place until nearly double in size (about 20 minutes).

⑦ Bake on separate racks about 25 minutes or until golden, rotating baking sheets halfway through baking. Transfer focaccia to wire racks; cool. If desired, sprinkle with additional pine nuts. Cut into wedges.

PER WEDGE 89 calories; 2 g total fat (0 g sat. fat); 0 mg cholesterol; 169 mg sodium; 16 g carbohydrate; 2 g fiber; 3 g protein

Sun-Dried Tomato Focaccia

Hearty Mixed Grain Bread

Hearty Mixed Grain Bread

MAKES 2 loaves (24 slices) **PREP** 30 minutes
STAND 30 minutes **RISE** 1¼ hours **BAKE** 30 minutes
OVEN at 375°F

- 1¼ **cups boiling water**
- ½ **cup uncooked seven-grain hot cereal**
- 3 **to 3½ cups all-purpose flour**
- 1 **package active dry yeast**
- ¾ **cup fat-free milk**
- ¼ **cup honey**
- 2 **tablespoons canola oil**
- 1½ **teaspoons salt**
- 1½ **cups whole wheat flour or white whole wheat flour**
- ½ **cup rolled oats**
- ¼ **cup flaxseed meal**
  Fat-free milk
- ¼ **cup rolled oats and/or flaxmeal**

① In a medium bowl combine the boiling water and cereal. Let stand for 20 minutes. In a large mixing bowl combine 2 cups of the all-purpose flour and the yeast; set aside. In a small saucepan heat and stir ¾ cup milk, the honey, oil, and salt over medium heat just until warm (120°F to 130°F). Add milk mixture to flour mixture along with cereal mixture. Beat with an electric mixer on low to medium for 30 seconds, scraping sides of bowl. Beat on high for 3 minutes. Using a wooden spoon, stir in whole wheat flour, ½ cup oats, the flaxseed meal, and as much of the remaining all-purpose flour as you can.

② Turn dough out onto a lightly floured surface. Knead in enough of the remaining all-purpose flour to make a moderately stiff dough that is almost smooth and elastic (6 to 8 minutes total). Shape dough into a ball. Place in a lightly greased bowl, turning once to grease surface of dough. Cover; let rise in a warm place until double in size (45 to 60 minutes).

③ Punch dough down. Turn out onto a lightly floured surface. Divide in half. Cover; let rest for 10 minutes. Lightly grease a large baking sheet; set aside.

④ Shape dough halves into 8-inch-long oval loaves that are about 4 inches wide at the center. Place shaped loaves 4 inches apart on prepared baking sheet. Cover and let rise in a warm place until nearly double in size (about 30 minutes).

⑤ Preheat oven to 375°F. Brush tops of loaves lightly with milk; sprinkle with ¼ cup oats and/or flaxmeal. Bake for 30 to 35 minutes or until bread sounds hollow when lightly tapped, covering loosely with foil, if necessary, the last 10 minutes of baking to prevent overbrowning. Transfer loaves to wire racks and cool completely.

PER SLICE 142 calories; 2 g total fat (0 g sat. fat); 0 mg cholesterol; 151 mg sodium; 26 g carbohydrate; 2 g fiber; 4 g protein

Roasted Garlic-Herb Bread

MAKES 1 loaf (12 slices) **PREP** 20 minutes **ROAST** 25 minutes
BAKE 12 minutes **OVEN** at 425°F

- 2 **heads fresh garlic**
- 2 **tablespoons olive oil**
- 3 **tablespoons snipped fresh parsley**
- 1 **tablespoon snipped fresh basil, oregano, and/or thyme**
- ¼ **teaspoon salt**
- ¼ **teaspoon freshly ground black pepper**
- 1 **10- to 12-ounce loaf whole grain Italian bread**

① Preheat oven to 425°F. Peel away the dry outer layers of skin from heads of garlic, leaving skins and cloves intact. Cut off the pointed top portion (about ¼ inch), leaving bulbs intact while exposing individual cloves. Place each garlic head, cut side up, in a custard cup. Drizzle each with about ¼ teaspoon of the olive oil. Cover with foil and roast for 25 to 35 minutes or until the cloves feel soft when pressed. Set aside just until cool enough to handle.

② Squeeze out the garlic paste from individual cloves into a small bowl. Mash garlic with a fork. Stir in remaining olive oil, the parsley, basil, salt, and pepper.

③ Without cutting through bottom crust, cut bread into 12 slices. Spread garlic mixture on one side only between slices. Wrap loaf in heavy foil. Bake about 12 minutes or until heated through. Serve warm.

PER SLICE 88 calories; 3 g total fat (0 g sat. fat); 0 mg cholesterol; 122 mg sodium; 12 g carbohydrate; 3 g fiber; 4 g protein

Pizza Braids

MAKES 2 loaves (20 slices) **PREP** 35 minutes **STAND** 20 minutes
RISE 1½ hours **BAKE** 30 minutes **OVEN** at 350°F

- 1¼ cups warm water (105°F to 115°F)
- 1 package active dry yeast
- 1 tablespoon sugar
- ¼ cup dried tomatoes (not oil-packed), chopped
- ½ cup chopped green sweet pepper
- ½ cup chopped onion
- 2 tablespoons olive oil
- ¼ cup chopped, drained pepperoncini peppers
- ¼ cup finely shredded Parmesan cheese (1 ounce)
- 1 egg, lightly beaten
- 1¼ cups whole wheat flour
- 2¾ to 3 cups all-purpose flour

① In a bowl stir together the warm water, yeast, and sugar. Let stand about 10 minutes or until yeast is foamy. Stir in tomatoes. In a skillet cook sweet pepper and onion in 1 tablespoon of the oil over medium heat for 5 minutes or until tender. Stir pepper mixture, remaining 1 tablespoon oil, pepperoncini, 2 tablespoons of the cheese, egg, and ½ teaspoon *salt* into yeast mixture. Stir in whole wheat flour and as much of the all-purpose flour as you can.

② Turn dough out onto a lightly floured surface. Knead in enough of the remaining flour to make a moderately stiff dough that is smooth and elastic; shape into a ball. Place in a lightly greased bowl, turning once. Cover; let rise in a warm place until double in size (1 to 1½ hours).

③ Punch dough down. Turn out onto a lightly floured surface. Divide into six portions. Cover; let rest for 10 minutes. Lightly grease a very large baking sheet.

④ Roll each portion of dough into a 12-inch rope. To shape, line up three ropes, 1 inch apart, on the prepared baking sheet. Starting from center, loosely braid by bringing the left rope under the center rope. Bring the right rope under the new center rope. Repeat to the end. On opposite end, braid by bringing the outside ropes alternately over the center rope to center. Press ends together to seal; tuck under loaf. Braid remaining three ropes. Cover and let rise in a warm place until nearly double (about 30 minutes).

⑤ Preheat oven to 350°F. Sprinkle braids with remaining 2 tablespoons cheese; bake for 30 to 40 minutes or until tops are browned and braids sound hollow when lightly tapped. Transfer to a wire rack to cool.

PER SLICE 116 calories; 2 g total fat (0 g sat. fat); 11 mg cholesterol; 127 mg sodium; 20 g carbohydrate; 2 g fiber; 4 g protein

Honey and Browned Butter Brioche

MAKES 2 loaves (24 slices) **PREP** 50 minutes **RISE** 3 hours
CHILL 6 hours **BAKE** 35 minutes **OVEN** at 350°F

- 1 package active dry yeast
- ¼ cup warm water (105°F to 115°F)
- ½ cup butter (no substitutes)
- 2½ cups all-purpose flour
- ½ cup honey
- ¾ teaspoon salt
- 1 cup refrigerated or frozen egg product, thawed, or 4 eggs
- ½ cup fat-free milk
- 1 cup whole wheat flour
- 2 tablespoons refrigerated or frozen egg product, thawed, or 1 egg white, lightly beaten
- 1 tablespoon water

① In a small bowl dissolve yeast in the ¼ cup warm water. Let stand for 5 to 10 minutes to soften. Meanwhile, in a small saucepan heat butter over low heat until melted. Continue heating until butter turns a light golden brown (about 20 minutes).

② Transfer butter to a large mixing bowl. Add 1 cup of the flour, the honey, and salt to butter. Beat with an electric mixer until well combined. Beat in 1 cup eggs, the milk, and yeast mixture. Beat in the remaining all-purpose flour. Using a wooden spoon, stir in the whole wheat flour. Place in a greased bowl. Cover; let rise in a warm place until double in size (about 2 hours). Chill dough for 6 hours.

③ Grease two 9 x 5 x 3-inch loaf pans. With floured hands, divide dough in half. Pat dough into prepared pans. Cover; let rise in a warm place until almost double in size (1 to 1¼ hours).

④ Preheat oven to 350°F. In a small bowl stir together 2 tablespoons egg and 1 tablespoon water. Brush some of the egg mixture over tops of loaves. Bake for 35 to 40 minutes or until bread sounds hollow when lightly tapped, covering with foil the last 10 minutes of baking if necessary to prevent overbrowning. Immediately loosen edges and remove bread from pans. Cool on wire racks.

PER SLICE 128 calories; 4 g total fat (2 g sat. fat); 10 mg cholesterol; 125 mg sodium; 20 g carbohydrate; 1 g fiber; 4 g protein

Honey and Browned Butter Brioche

Butternut-Curry Breadsticks

Butternut-Curry Breadsticks

MAKES 20 breadsticks **PREP** 45 minutes **RISE** 50 minutes
STAND 10 minutes **BAKE** 15 minutes **OVEN** at 375°F

- ⅔ cup water
- ⅔ cup peeled, seeded, and cubed butternut squash
- ½ cup buttermilk
- 1 tablespoon sugar
- 1 tablespoon butter
- 2 teaspoons curry powder
- 1 teaspoon salt
- 2¼ to 2¾ cups all-purpose flour
- 1 package active dry yeast
- ¾ cup whole wheat flour or white whole wheat flour
- ½ cup golden raisins, chopped
- 1 egg white
- 1 tablespoon water
  Sesame seeds and/or finely chopped almonds (optional)

① In a small saucepan bring the water and squash to boiling; reduce heat. Simmer, covered, about 15 minutes or until squash is very tender; do not drain. Mash squash in the water. Measure squash mixture. If necessary, add additional water to equal ¾ cup total.

② Return squash mixture to saucepan. Add buttermilk, sugar, butter, curry powder, and salt. Heat or cool as necessary until warm (120°F to 130°F), stirring constantly.

③ In a large mixing bowl combine 1 cup of the all-purpose flour and the yeast. Add the squash mixture. Beat with an electric mixer on low to medium for 30 seconds, scraping the sides of the bowl constantly. Beat on high for 3 minutes. Using a wooden spoon, stir in whole wheat flour, raisins, and as much of the remaining all-purpose flour as you can.

④ Turn dough out onto a lightly floured surface. Knead in enough of the remaining flour to make a moderately stiff dough (6 to 8 minutes total). Shape dough into a ball. Place in a lightly greased bowl, turning once to grease surface of dough. Cover; let rise in a warm place until double in size (30 to 45 minutes). Lightly grease baking sheets; set aside.

⑤ Punch dough down. Turn out onto a lightly floured surface. Cover; let rest for 10 minutes. Roll dough to a 15 x 8-inch rectangle. Cut crosswise into twenty 8 x ¾-inch pieces. Stretch and roll each piece to form a 15-inch long breadstick. Place ¾ to 1 inch apart on prepared baking sheets.

⑥ Preheat oven to 375°F. Cover and let breadsticks rise for 20 minutes. In a small bowl lightly beat egg white and the water; brush over breadsticks. If desired, sprinkle with sesame seeds and/or almonds. Bake for 15 minutes or until lightly browned. Remove to wire rack. Serve warm or at room temperature.

PER BREADSTICK 93 calories; 1 g total fat (0 g sat. fat); 2 mg cholesterol; 131 mg sodium; 19 g carbohydrate; 1 g fiber; 3 g protein

Butternut squash and curry powder give these breadsticks a gorgeous golden hue.

Grilled Plum and Strawberry Kabobs
with Sweet Mint Pesto, page 302

Sweet Somethings

Pecan-Praline Pumpkin Snack Cake ✪

MAKES 16 servings **PREP** 25 minutes **BAKE** 20 minutes
OVEN at 350°F

- 1¼ cups all-purpose flour
- ½ cup whole wheat pastry flour
- 1½ teaspoons pumpkin pie spice
- 1 teaspoon baking powder
- ¼ teaspoon baking soda
- ¼ teaspoon salt
- ¾ cup canned pumpkin
- ⅔ cup packed brown sugar
- ½ cup refrigerated or frozen egg product, thawed, or 2 eggs, lightly beaten
- ⅓ cup fat-free milk
- ¼ cup canola oil
- 2 tablespoons packed brown sugar
- 2 tablespoons flaxseed meal
- ¼ teaspoon ground cinnamon
- 1 tablespoon tub-style vegetable oil spread
- ½ cup coarsely chopped pecans

① Preheat oven to 350°F. Grease a 9 x 9 x 2-inch baking pan. Set aside.

② In a large bowl combine flours, pumpkin pie spice, baking powder, baking soda, and salt. In a medium bowl whisk together pumpkin, ⅔ cup brown sugar, eggs, milk, and oil. Add pumpkin mixture all at once to flour mixture; stir just until moistened. Spoon batter into prepared pan, spreading evenly.

③ In a small bowl combine 2 tablespoons brown sugar, the flaxseed meal, and cinnamon. Using a fork, cut in vegetable oil spread until mixture comes together. Stir in pecans. Sprinkle over batter in pan.

④ Bake for 20 to 25 minutes or until a toothpick inserted near the center comes out clean (center may dip slightly). Cool completely on a wire rack.

PER SERVING 161 calories; 7 g total fat (1 g sat. fat); 0 mg cholesterol; 104 mg sodium; 23 g carbohydrate; 1 g fiber; 3 g protein

Ginger-Spiced Chocolate Cake ✪

MAKES 16 servings **PREP** 25 minutes **BAKE** 30 minutes
COOL 15 minutes **OVEN** at 350°F

- 2⅓ cups cake flour or 2 cups all-purpose flour*
- ⅔ cup unsweetened cocoa powder
- 1½ teaspoons baking powder
- ½ teaspoon baking soda
- ½ teaspoon ground ginger
- ¼ teaspoon salt
- 1¼ cups buttermilk or sour fat-free milk**
- 1 cup granulated sugar
- ½ cup canola oil or cooking oil
- ½ cup refrigerated or frozen egg product, thawed, or 2 eggs
- 1 tablespoon finely chopped crystallized ginger
- 1 teaspoon vanilla
- 1 teaspoon powdered sugar
- Fresh raspberries (optional)

① Preheat oven to 350°F. Grease and lightly flour a 10-inch fluted tube pan. Set pan aside. In a large bowl combine flour, cocoa powder, baking powder, baking soda, ground ginger, and salt; set aside.

② In a medium bowl whisk together buttermilk, granulated sugar, oil, eggs, crystallized ginger, and vanilla. Add buttermilk mixture to flour mixture. Beat with a wire whisk just until combined.

③ Spoon batter into the prepared pan, spreading evenly. Bake for 30 to 35 minutes or until a toothpick inserted near center of cake comes out clean. Cool in pan on a wire rack for 15 minutes. Remove cake from pan. Cool completely on wire rack. Sprinkle with powdered sugar before serving. If desired, garnish with raspberries.

*Tip: You can substitute whole wheat pastry flour or white whole wheat flour for up to half of the total cake flour or all-purpose flour used.

**Tip: To make 1¼ cups sour fat-free milk, place 4 teaspoons lemon juice or vinegar in a glass measuring cup. Add enough fat-free milk to measure 1¼ cups total liquid; stir. Let stand for 5 minutes before using.

PER SERVING 211 calories; 8 g total fat (1 g sat. fat); 1 mg cholesterol; 133 mg sodium; 32 g carbohydrate; 0 g fiber; 4 g protein

Black Tie Cake

Black Tie Cake ✪

MAKES 12 servings **STAND** 30 minutes **PREP** 25 minutes
BAKE 20 minutes **COOL** 15 minutes **OVEN** at 350°F

3	**egg whites**
¾	**cup fat-free milk**
⅓	**cup unsweetened cocoa powder**
2	**ounces unsweetened chocolate, chopped**
	Nonstick cooking spray
⅔	**cup flour**
½	**cup sugar**
½	**teaspoon baking powder**
¼	**teaspoon baking soda**
⅛	**teaspoon salt**
¼	**cup sugar**
1	**recipe White Chocolate Mousse**
½	**ounce semisweet chocolate, melted**
1	**recipe Chocolate-Covered Strawberries (optional)**

① In a medium mixing bowl allow egg whites to stand at room temperature for 30 minutes. Meanwhile, in a small saucepan combine milk and cocoa powder. Heat over medium heat, whisking constantly, just until mixture comes to boiling. Remove from heat. Whisk in unsweetened chocolate until smooth. Cool to room temperature.

② Preheat oven to 350°F. Lightly coat an 8-inch springform pan with cooking spray; set aside. In a large bowl stir together flour, ½ cup sugar, the baking powder, baking soda, and salt. Stir cooled chocolate mixture into flour mixture until well combined (batter will be thick); set aside.

③ Beat egg whites with an electric mixer on medium until soft peaks form (tips curl). Gradually add ¼ cup sugar, about 1 tablespoon at a time, beating on high until stiff peaks form (tips stand straight). Gently fold one-third of the beaten egg whites into the chocolate mixture. Fold in the remaining beaten egg whites just until combined. Spread batter in prepared baking pan.

④ Bake for 20 to 25 minutes or until top springs back when lightly touched. Cool in pan on wire rack for 15 minutes. Remove side of pan. Cool completely.

⑤ Spread White Chocolate Mousse in an even layer over the cooled cake. Drizzle with melted semisweet chocolate and let stand until set. Chill until ready to serve. If desired, garnish with Chocolate-Covered Strawberries.

White Chocolate Mousse: In a small saucepan combine 2 ounces white baking chocolate (with cocoa butter), chopped; ¼ cup light tub-style cream cheese; and 1 tablespoon fat-free milk. Stir over low heat until melted and smooth. Remove from heat. Stir in ¼ cup thawed light whipped dessert topping until smooth. Transfer to a medium bowl and cool for 5 minutes. Fold in 1¼ cups thawed light whipped dessert topping. Chill in refrigerator for 1 hour before spreading on cake.

PER SERVING 175 calories; 6 g total fat (4 g sat. fat); 4 mg cholesterol; 118 mg sodium; 27 g carbohydrate; 2 g fiber; 4 g protein

Chocolate-Covered Strawberries: Clean 12 small fresh strawberries, leaving the tops on. In a small microwave-safe bowl place 2½ ounces chopped semisweet chocolate. Microwave on medium for 1 minute. Stir. Microwave on medium for 30 to 60 seconds more or until chocolate melts, stirring once or twice. Dip strawberries halfway into the melted chocolate. Use a thin metal spatula to spread chocolate to a thin layer on the strawberries and scrape off any excess chocolate. Place on a waxed-paper lined baking sheet. Let stand until chocolate is set.

At just 175 calories a slice, you can indulge in this cake and still look great in your little black dress.

Black Forest Cake Roll ✪

MAKES 10 servings **PREP** 30 minutes **BAKE** 15 minutes
STAND 30 minutes **COOL** 1 hour **CHILL** 2 hours **OVEN** at 375°F

4	eggs
⅓	cup flour
¼	cup unsweetened cocoa powder
¼	teaspoon baking soda
¼	teaspoon salt
¾	cup granulated sugar
	Unsweetened cocoa powder
1	recipe Cherry Cream Filling
1	tablespoon sugar-free hot fudge ice cream topping, warmed
10	maraschino cherries, drained and patted dry

① Allow eggs to stand at room temperature for 30 minutes. Meanwhile, grease a 15 x 10 x 1-inch baking pan. Line bottom of pan with parchment paper; grease and lightly flour paper. Set pan aside. In a small bowl stir together flour, ¼ cup cocoa powder, the baking soda, and salt; set aside.

② Preheat oven to 375°F. In a large mixing bowl beat eggs with electric mixer on high for 5 minutes. Gradually add granulated sugar; beat until thick and lemon color. Fold in flour mixture. Spread batter evenly into prepared pan.

③ Bake about 15 minutes or until top springs back when lightly touched. Immediately loosen edges of cake from pan and turn cake out onto a towel sprinkled with unsweetened cocoa powder. Slowly peel off parchment paper. Starting from a short side, roll up towel and cake into a spiral. Cool on a wire rack for 1 hour. Meanwhile, prepare Cherry Cream Filling.

④ Unroll cake; remove towel. Spread cake with Cherry Cream Filling to within 1 inch of edges. Roll up cake and filling into a spiral. Trim ends. Cover and chill in the refrigerator for 2 to 24 hours before serving. If desired, just before serving, drizzle whole cake with ice cream topping and garnish with cherries.

Cherry Cream Filling: In a small mixing bowl beat ½ cup tub-style light cream cheese with an electric mixer until smooth. Add ½ cup frozen light whipped dessert topping, thawed; beat on low just until combined. Fold in another ½ cup frozen light whipped dessert topping, thawed. Drain, stem, and pat dry ⅔ cup maraschino cherries. Chop cherries and fold into cream cheese mixture. Makes 1½ cups.

PER SERVING 177 calories; 5 g total fat (3 g sat. fat); 91 mg cholesterol; 180 mg sodium; 30 g carbohydrate; 1 g fiber; 5 g protein

Apple-Spice Cake ✪

MAKES 9 servings **PREP** 25 minutes **BAKE** 35 minutes
OVEN at 350°F

	Nonstick cooking spray
¾	cup all-purpose flour
½	cup white whole wheat flour
¼	cup flaxseed meal
1	teaspoon baking powder
¾	teaspoon ground cinnamon
½	teaspoon baking soda
½	teaspoon ground ginger
¼	teaspoon salt
⅛	teaspoon ground cloves
1	egg, lightly beaten
1	6-ounce carton plain low-fat yogurt
⅓	cup packed brown sugar
¼	cup unsweetened applesauce
3	tablespoons vegetable oil
1	tablespoon molasses
1	large apple (such as Granny Smith, Braeburn, or Gala), cored and finely chopped (1 cup)
⅔	cup frozen light whipped dessert topping, thawed

① Preheat oven to 350°F. Lightly coat an 8 x 8 x 2-inch baking pan with cooking spray; set aside.

② In a large bowl stir together all-purpose flour, white whole wheat flour, flaxseed meal, baking powder, cinnamon, baking soda, ginger, salt, and cloves. In a medium bowl combine egg, yogurt, brown sugar, applesauce, oil, and molasses. Add egg mixture to flour mixture; stir just until combined. Fold in apple. Spread batter evenly in the prepared baking pan.

③ Bake about 35 minutes or until a toothpick inserted near center comes out clean. Cool slightly on a wire rack.

④ To serve, cut cake into nine squares. Serve warm. Top each serving with whipped topping and, if desired, sprinkle lightly with additional ground cinnamon.

PER SERVING 193 calories; 7 g total fat (1 g sat. fat); 25 mg cholesterol; 186 mg sodium; 29 g carbohydrate; 2 g fiber; 4 g protein

Maple-Pear Kuchen

Maple-Pear Kuchen ✪

MAKES 9 servings **PREP** 30 minutes **RISE** 1 hour
BAKE 25 minutes **COOL** 30 minutes **OVEN** at 375°F

1¼	cups all-purpose flour
1	teaspoon active dry yeast
¼	cup milk
3	tablespoons granulated sugar
2	tablespoons butter
¼	teaspoon salt
1	egg
2	medium pears, cored and sliced (2 cups)
2	tablespoons packed brown sugar
1½	teaspoons quick-cooking tapioca, crushed
1½	teaspoons lemon juice
½	teaspoon maple flavoring
1	recipe Crumb Topping

① Grease an 8-inch square baking pan; line with parchment paper. Set aside. In a medium mixing bowl combine ½ cup of the flour and the yeast; set aside.

② In a small saucepan heat and stir milk, granulated sugar, butter, and salt just until warm (120°F to 130°F) and butter is nearly melted. Add milk mixture and egg to flour mixture. Beat with an electric mixer on low to medium for 30 seconds, scraping sides of bowl constantly. Beat on high for 2 minutes. Beat in as much of the remaining flour as you can with the mixer. Using a wooden spoon, stir in any remaining flour (batter will be stiff). Spread batter in the prepared baking pan.

③ In another medium bowl combine pears, brown sugar, tapioca, lemon juice, and maple flavoring. Spoon pear mixture on top of batter. Sprinkle with Crumb Topping. Cover and let rise in a warm place for 1 hour.

④ Preheat oven to 375°F. Bake, uncovered, about 25 minutes or until top is browned and pears are tender. Cool on a wire rack for 30 minutes. Cut into squares. Serve warm.

Crumb Topping: In a small bowl combine ¼ cup all-purpose flour, 2 tablespoons packed brown sugar, and 2 tablespoons finely chopped pecans. Using a pastry blender, cut in 1 tablespoon butter until mixture resembles coarse crumbs.

PER SERVING 197 calories; 6 g total fat (3 g sat. fat); 34 mg cholesterol; 105 mg sodium; 33 g carbohydrate; 2 g fiber; 4 g protein

Peanut Butter Blossom Mini Cakes ✪

MAKES 20 servings **PREP** 30 minutes **BAKE** 8 minutes
COOL 5 minutes **OVEN** at 375°F

	Nonstick cooking spray
½	cup flour
3	tablespoons ground lightly salted peanuts
1	teaspoon baking powder
¼	cup creamy peanut butter
¼	cup sugar
¼	cup refrigerated or frozen egg product, thawed, or 1 egg
½	teaspoon vanilla
¼	cup fat-free milk
1	recipe Chocolate Frosting

① Preheat oven to 375°F. Coat twenty 1¾-inch muffin cups with cooking spray or line with paper bake cups; set aside. In a small bowl combine flour, ground peanuts, and baking powder; set aside.

② In a medium mixing bowl beat peanut butter with an electric mixer on medium for 30 seconds. Add sugar; beat on medium until well combined. Beat in egg and vanilla. Alternately add flour mixture and milk to peanut butter mixture, beating on low after each addition just until combined. Spoon 1 tablespoon batter into each prepared muffin cup.

③ Bake for 8 to 10 minutes or until a toothpick inserted in centers comes out clean. While cakes are still warm, press the back of a measuring teaspoon into tops of cakes to flatten the tops. Cool cakes in muffin cups on wire rack for 5 minutes; remove cakes from cups. Cool completely.

④ Place Chocolate Frosting in a piping bag fitted with a star tip. Pipe one large star on each cake.

Chocolate Frosting: In a medium mixing bowl beat 2 tablespoons tub-style vegetable oil spread and ¼ teaspoon vanilla with an electric mixer on medium for 30 seconds. Beat in 1 tablespoon unsweetened cocoa powder. Gradually beat in ½ to ¾ cup powdered sugar until smooth. If needed, add enough fat-free milk, ½ teaspoon at a time, to reach piping consistency.

PER SERVING 81 calories; 4 g total fat (1 g sat. fat); 0 mg cholesterol; 53 mg sodium; 9 g carbohydrate; 1 g fiber; 2 g protein

Carrot Cake Cupcakes ⊙

MAKES 12 cupcakes **PREP** 25 minutes **BAKE** 20 minutes
OVEN at 350°F

Nonstick cooking spray
1   cup all-purpose flour
1   cup white whole wheat flour
1   cup sugar
2   tablespoons flaxseed meal
2   teaspoons ground cinnamon
1   teaspoon baking powder
1   teaspoon baking soda
⅛   teaspoon salt
2   cups shredded carrots
1   cup unsweetened applesauce
1   egg, lightly beaten
1   teaspoon vanilla extract
1   recipe Cream Cheese Frosting or ½ cup
    purchased cream cheese frosting

① Preheat oven to 350°F. Spray 12 muffin cups with
nonstick cooking spray or line with paper cups. In a large
bowl combine all-purpose flour, white whole wheat flour,
sugar, flaxseed meal, cinnamon, baking powder, baking
soda, and salt.

② In a medium bowl combine carrots, applesauce, egg,
and vanilla. Add to flour mixture and mix just until
combined. Divide batter among twelve muffin cups.

③ Bake for 20 to 24 minutes or until a toothpick inserted
in center comes out clean. Cool completely.

④ Frost with Cream Cheese Frosting.

Cream Cheese Frosting: In a small mixing bowl beat
⅓ cup fat-free cream cheese and ⅓ cup powdered sugar
with an electric mixer on medium until smooth. If
necessary, add 1 teaspoon fat-free milk to reach desired
consistency.

PER CUPCAKE 196 calories; 1 g total fat (0 g sat. fat); 19 mg cholesterol;
245 mg sodium; 43 g carbohydrate; 2 g fiber; 5 g protein

May Basket Cupcakes ⊙

MAKES 12 servings **PREP** 40 minutes **BAKE** 18 minutes
COOL 10 minutes **OVEN** at 350°F

Nonstick cooking spray
1⅔ cups all-purpose flour
1½ teaspoons finely shredded lime peel
1¼ teaspoons baking powder
½   teaspoon baking soda
⅛   teaspoon salt
¼   cup butter, softened
¾   cup sugar
½   cup refrigerated or frozen egg product,
    thawed, or 2 eggs
⅔   cup light sour cream
2   tablespoons fat-free milk
1   cup frozen light whipped dessert topping,
    thawed
1½ cups sliced or coarsely chopped fresh
    strawberries, kiwifruit, pineapple, and/or
    whole fresh raspberries or blueberries

① Preheat oven to 350°F. Line twelve 2½-inch muffin
cups with paper bake cups. Coat paper bake cups with
cooking spray; set aside. In a medium bowl combine flour,
lime peel, baking powder, baking soda, and salt; set aside.

② In a large mixing bowl beat butter with an electric
mixer on medium for 30 seconds. Gradually add sugar,
beating until light and fluffy. Beat in eggs. In a small bowl
combine sour cream and milk. Alternately add flour
mixture and sour cream mixture to egg mixture, beating
on low after each addition just until combined.

③ Spoon batter evenly into prepared muffin cups, filling
each two-thirds to three-fourths full. Bake for 18 to
20 minutes or until a toothpick inserted near the centers
comes out clean. Cool in cups on a wire rack for
5 minutes. Remove cupcakes from pans. Cool completely
on wire rack.

④ Using a small knife, cut a shallow dip in the top of
each cupcake. Save cut-off cake tops for another use, such
as for making fruit parfaits. Top cupcakes with whipped
topping and fruit.

PER SERVING 186 calories; 6 g total fat (4 g sat. fat); 14 mg cholesterol;
157 mg sodium; 30 g carbohydrate; 1 g fiber; 3 g protein

Pear-Gingerbread Cupcakes

Pear-Gingerbread Cupcakes ✪

MAKES 12 cupcakes **PREP** 25 minutes
BAKE 15 minutes **COOL** 10 minutes **OVEN** at 350°F

Nonstick spray for baking

1½	cups all-purpose flour
1	teaspoon baking powder
1	teaspoon ground ginger
1	teaspoon ground cinnamon
½	teaspoon baking soda
¼	teaspoon salt
1	egg, lightly beaten
⅔	cup molasses
¼	cup packed brown sugar
¼	cup canola oil
½	cup boiling water
1	large pear, peeled, cored, and finely chopped (1 cup)
2	tablespoons chopped crystallized ginger

① Preheat oven to 350°F. Lightly coat twelve 2½-inch muffin cups with nonstick spray for baking; set aside.

② In a large bowl stir together flour, baking powder, ground ginger, cinnamon, baking soda, and salt. In a medium bowl combine egg, molasses, brown sugar, and oil. Add egg mixture to flour mixture, stirring until combined. Stir in the boiling water until combined. Stir in chopped pear. Spoon batter evenly into the prepared muffin cups.

③ Bake for 15 to 18 minutes or until a toothpick inserted into centers comes out clean. Sprinkle with crystallized ginger; press lightly into cupcakes.

④ Cool in muffin cups for 10 minutes. Remove from muffin cups; cool completely on a wire rack.

PER CUPCAKE 189 calories; 5 g total fat (0 g sat. fat); 18 mg cholesterol; 147 mg sodium; 34 g carbohydrate; 1 g fiber; 2 g protein

Crystallized ginger adds spicy-sweet flavor to these gingerbread cupcakes. Look for it in the baking aisle of your supermarket.

Berry Tart with Lemon Cookie Crust ✪

MAKES 8 servings **PREP** 30 minutes **BAKE** 12 minutes
OVEN at 375°F

¼	cup butter, softened
¼	cup granulated sugar
1	teaspoon finely shredded lemon peel
½	teaspoon baking powder
½	teaspoon vanilla
⅛	teaspoon salt
2	tablespoons refrigerated or frozen egg product, thawed, or 1 egg white, lightly beaten
1¼	cups flour
¾	cup tub-style fat-free cream cheese, softened
2	tablespoons powdered sugar
1	teaspoon finely shredded lemon peel
½	cup thick plain nonfat Greek yogurt
2	cups fresh blueberries, blackberries, and/or raspberries

Honey (optional)

Fresh mint sprigs

Lemon peel curls (optional)

① Preheat oven to 375°F. For crust, in a medium mixing bowl beat butter with an electric mixer on medium for 30 seconds. Add granulated sugar, 1 teaspoon lemon peel, the baking powder, vanilla, and salt; beat until combined. Add egg; beat until combined. Beat in as much of the flour as you can with the mixer. Using a wooden spoon, stir in any remaining flour (or knead gently until combined).

② Press dough onto the bottom and up the sides of a 9-inch round tart pan with removable bottom. Line crust with a double thickness of foil. Bake crust for 6 minutes. Remove the foil and bake for 6 to 7 minutes more or until crust is lightly browned. Cool crust on a wire rack.

③ Meanwhile, for lemon cream, in a small bowl stir together cream cheese, powdered sugar, and 1 teaspoon lemon peel. Fold in yogurt. Spread on the cooled crust. Top with berries. If desired, drizzle lightly with honey and garnish with fresh mint and/or lemon peel curls. Remove sides of pan and cut into wedges to serve.

PER SERVING 206 calories; 6 g total fat (4 g sat. fat); 18 mg cholesterol; 272 mg sodium; 30 g carbohydrate; 2 g fiber; 8 g protein

Fruit Tarts ✪ ③⓪

MAKES 6 tarts **START TO FINISH** 20 minutes

- 1   cup fresh strawberries
- ½   of an 8-ounce package reduced-fat cream cheese (Neufchâtel), softened
- 1   tablespoon honey
- 1   4-ounce package (6) purchased graham cracker crumb tart shells
- 1½   cups assorted fresh berries or other chopped fruit (blueberries, kiwi, strawberries, and/or raspberries)

① Mash or puree strawberries until saucelike. In a medium bowl stir cream cheese until smooth; gradually blend in mashed berries. Stir in honey. Divide mixture among the tart shells. Top with fresh fruit.

Make Ahead: Cream cheese filling can be made up to 4 hours ahead and stored, covered, in refrigerator.

PER TART 207 calories; 9 g total fat (3 g sat. fat); 14 mg cholesterol; 189 mg sodium; 27 g carbohydrate; 2 g fiber; 3 g protein

Mini Raspberry-Chocolate Tarts ✪ ③⓪

MAKES 5 servings **START TO FINISH** 15 minutes

- 1   1.9-ounce package baked miniature phyllo dough shells (15 shells)
- 3   ounces milk chocolate or dark chocolate, melted
- 15   fresh raspberries
- 2   tablespoons slivered almonds, toasted if desired

① Place phyllo dough shells on a serving platter. Spoon melted chocolate into shells. Top chocolate in each shell with a raspberry and some of the almonds.

PER SERVING 175 calories; 9 g total fat (4 g sat. fat); 4 mg cholesterol; 43 mg sodium; 19 g carbohydrate; 2 g fiber; 3 g protein

Spoon the melted chocolate into the pastry shells right before serving so they stay crisp.

Pear-Cranberry Deep-Dish Pie ✪

MAKES 10 servings **PREP** 40 minutes **BAKE** 55 minutes **COOL** 30 minutes **OVEN** at 375°F

- ⅓   cup sugar
- 2   tablespoons all-purpose flour
- ¼   teaspoon ground nutmeg
- ¼   teaspoon ground ginger
- 6   medium pears, cored and sliced (2 to 2½ pounds total)
- 1   cup fresh or thawed frozen cranberries
- 1   recipe Pastry
- 1   tablespoon fat-free milk

① Preheat oven to 375°F. For filling, in a very large bowl stir together sugar, flour, nutmeg, and ginger. Add pear slices and cranberries; toss gently to coat. Transfer to a 2-quart round baking dish or casserole.

② On a lightly floured surface, flatten Pastry dough. Using a rolling pin, roll dough from center to edge into a circle that is about 1 inch wider than the top of the baking dish or casserole. Using small cookie cutters, cut a few shapes from center of the pastry. Set aside shapes. Transfer the dough circle to the top of the fruit mixture. Trim edge as needed to fit the baking dish or casserole; if desired, crimp edge. Brush top of pastry and dough cutouts with milk. Place dough cutouts on top of the pastry, leaving openings to vent steam.

③ Place baking dish or casserole on a foil-lined baking sheet. Bake for 55 to 60 minutes or until filling is very bubbly. Cool pie about 30 minutes on a wire rack. Serve warm or cool completely.

Pastry: In a medium bowl stir together ¾ cup cake flour, ¼ cup whole wheat flour, and ¼ teaspoon salt. Using a pastry blender cut in ¼ cup chilled tub-style vegetable oil spread until pieces are pea size. Sprinkle 1 tablespoon cold water over part of the flour mixture; toss gently with a fork. Push moistened dough to side of bowl. Repeat with additional cold water, 1 tablespoon at a time (3 to 4 tablespoons total), until all the flour mixture is moistened. Shape into a ball.

PER SERVING 169 calories; 4 g total fat (1 g sat. fat); 0 mg cholesterol; 96 mg sodium; 34 g carbohydrate; 4 g fiber; 2 g protein

Pear-Cranberry Deep-Dish Pie

Vanilla Meringue Tarts

Vanilla Meringue Tarts ✪

MAKES 10 servings **PREP** 40 minutes **BAKE** 1 hour 15 minutes
CHILL 2 hours **OVEN** at 250°F

- 1   recipe Meringue Shells
- ⅓   cup granulated sugar
- 2   tablespoons cornstarch
- 2¼   cups low-fat (1%) milk
- ¼   cup refrigerated or frozen egg product, thawed
- 1   tablespoon 60% to 70% tub-style vegetable oil spread
- 1½   teaspoons vanilla
- 1   cup fresh whole or sliced berries, sliced banana, sliced kiwifruit, sliced kumquats, and/or sliced oranges

① Prepare Meringue Shells. Meanwhile, for filling, in a medium saucepan combine sugar and cornstarch. Gradually stir in milk. Cook and stir over medium heat until thickened and bubbly; reduce heat. Cook and stir for 2 minutes more. Remove from heat. Gradually stir about 1 cup of the hot filling into egg. Add egg mixture to milk mixture in saucepan. Bring to a gentle boil; reduce heat. Cook and stir for 2 minutes. Remove from heat. Stir in vegetable oil spread and vanilla. Place saucepan in a very large bowl half-filled with ice water. Stir filling constantly for 2 minutes to cool quickly. Transfer filling to a medium bowl. Cover surface of filling with plastic wrap. Chill for 2 to 24 hours.

② Spoon filling into Meringue Shells. Serve at once or cover and chill for up to 30 minutes before serving. Top servings with fruit.

Meringue Shells: Preheat oven to 250°F. Cover one or two large baking sheets with parchment paper. Draw ten 2½-inch circles on the paper. Set aside. In a medium mixing bowl combine 2 egg whites, ½ teaspoon vanilla, ¼ teaspoon cream of tartar, and ⅛ teaspoon salt. Beat with an electric mixer on medium until soft peaks form (tips curl). Gradually add ½ cup sugar, about 1 tablespoon at a time, beating on high until stiff peaks form (tips stand straight). Spoon meringue into a pastry bag fitted with an open star tip. Pipe mixture in spirals on the circles, piping sides of each up to a height of 1¼ inches. Bake about 1¼ hours or until meringues appear dry and are firm when lightly touched. Cool on paper on wire rack. Peel from paper; transfer to a serving platter.

PER SERVING 117 calories; 2 g total fat (1 g sat. fat); 3 mg cholesterol; 85 mg sodium; 23 g carbohydrate; 1 g fiber; 3 g protein

Cherry-Berry Pie ✪

MAKES 10 servings **PREP** 25 minutes **STAND** 45 minutes
BAKE 1½ hours **OVEN** at 375°F

- ⅓   cup granulated sugar
- 3   tablespoons cornstarch
- 1   12-ounce package frozen unsweetened pitted dark sweet cherries
- 1   12-ounce package frozen unsweetened raspberries
- ¼   teaspoon almond extract (optional)
- 1   recipe Oil Pastry
- 1   tablespoon powdered sugar
- ⅔   cup frozen light whipped dessert topping, thawed
-    Lemon peel curls (optional)

① For filling, in a large bowl stir together the granulated sugar and cornstarch. Add cherries, raspberries, and almond extract, if using. Gently toss until berries are coated. Let mixture stand for 45 minutes or until fruit is partially thawed but still icy.

② Preheat oven to 375°F. Prepare Oil Pastry. On a lightly floured surface, roll pastry to a 12-inch circle. Transfer pastry to a 9-inch pie plate. Trim pastry to ½ inch beyond rim of pie plate. Fold under extra pastry even with the edge of the pie plate. Crimp edge as desired.

③ Stir fruit mixture; transfer to the pastry-lined pie plate. To prevent overbrowning, cover top of pie loosely with foil. Bake for 70 minutes. Remove foil. Bake pie for 20 to 25 minutes more or until filling is bubbly across surface and pastry is golden. Cool on a wire rack.

④ To serve, sprinkle lightly with powdered sugar. Top with dessert topping. If desired, garnish with lemon curls.

Oil Pastry: In a bowl stir together 1⅓ cups flour and ¼ teaspoon salt. Add ¼ cup canola oil and 3 tablespoons fat-free milk all at once to flour mixture. Stir lightly with a fork until combined. If necessary, stir in 1 tablespoon additional fat-free milk to moisten (pastry will appear crumbly). Form pastry into a ball.

PER SERVING 196 calories; 6 g total fat (1 g sat. fat); 0 mg cholesterol; 61 mg sodium; 33 g carbohydrate; 3 g fiber; 3 g protein

Triple-Berry Crisp ✪

MAKES 12 servings **PREP** 25 minutes **BAKE** 50 minutes
OVEN at 350°F

3	12-ounce packages (8 cups) frozen mixed berries (raspberries, blueberries and/or blackberries)
¼	cup sugar
2	tablespoons cornstarch
½	cup all-purpose flour
¼	cup packed brown sugar
2	tablespoons butter
1½	cups regular rolled oats
⅓	cup chopped walnuts

① Preheat oven to 350°F. Thaw berries. Drain and reserve ½ cup of the juices; discard remaining juices. In a large bowl combine berries, sugar, reserved juices, and cornstarch. Mix well and transfer to a 2-quart rectangular baking dish.

② For topping, in a medium bowl combine flour and brown sugar. Using a pastry blender, cut in butter until pieces are pea size. Stir in oats and nuts. Sprinkle over berry mixture.

③ Bake for 50 to 55 minutes or until filling is bubbly and topping is golden brown. Serve warm.

PER SERVING 214 calories; 5 g total fat (2 g sat. fat); 5 mg cholesterol; 16 mg sodium; 38 g carbohydrate; 5 g fiber; 5 g protein

White whole wheat flour is relatively new to the market. It has all the fiber and nutrition of whole wheat flour yet bakes as light in texture as all-purpose flour. Use it in place of all-purpose flour in most recipes—including the topping for this berry crisp.

Peach-Blueberry Ginger-Oat Crisp ✪

MAKES 8 servings **PREP** 25 minutes **BAKE** 35 minutes
COOL 30 minutes **OVEN** at 375°F

4	cups sliced fresh peaches or frozen unsweetened peach slices, thawed and undrained
3	tablespoons packed brown sugar
2	tablespoons flour
½	teaspoon ground ginger
1	cup fresh or frozen unsweetened blueberries, thawed
¼	cup water
8	gingersnaps
⅔	cup quick-cooking rolled oats
¼	cup chopped pecans (optional)
2	tablespoons butter, melted
1	cup frozen light whipped dessert topping, thawed (optional)

① Preheat oven to 375°F. In a large bowl toss together peach slices, brown sugar, flour, and ginger. Add blueberries and the water; toss to combine. Spoon fruit mixture into a 2-quart square baking dish. Bake, uncovered, for 20 minutes.

② Meanwhile, place gingersnaps in a heavy plastic bag. Seal bag. Using the flat side of a meat mallet or a rolling pin, crush cookies to ¼- to ½-inch pieces. Transfer cookies to a medium bowl. Stir in rolled oats and, if desired, chopped pecans. Stir in butter until well mixed. Sprinkle over partially baked fruit mixture.

③ Bake for 15 to 20 minutes more or until fruit is bubbly and topping is lightly browned. Cool on a wire rack for 30 minutes. Serve warm. If desired, top with whipped topping.

PER SERVING 153 calories; 4 g total fat (2 g sat. fat); 8 mg cholesterol; 68 mg sodium; 29 g carbohydrate; 3 g fiber; 2 g protein

Peach-Blueberry Ginger-Oat Crisp

Caramel-Pear Bread Pudding

Caramel-Pear Bread Pudding ✪

MAKES 12 servings **PREP** 25 minutes **BAKE** 50 minutes
STAND 30 minutes **OVEN** at 350°F

Nonstick cooking spray

8 slices whole grain white bread or whole grain wheat bread, cut into ½-inch pieces and dried*

2 tablespoons tub-style vegetable oil spread, melted

2 large red-skinned pears

¼ dried cranberries (optional)

2 cups fat-free milk

¾ cup refrigerated or frozen egg product, thawed, or 3 eggs, lightly beaten

⅔ cup sugar-free caramel ice cream topping

½ teaspoon ground cinnamon

½ cup coarsely chopped pecans, toasted (see tip, page 15) (optional)

① Preheat oven to 350°F. Lightly coat a 2-quart rectangular or square baking dish with cooking spray; set aside. In a large bowl toss together dried bread and melted vegetable oil spread until coated. Core and chop one of the pears and add to the bread mixture along with the cranberries, if using. Gently toss to combine. Transfer to prepared baking dish.

② In a medium bowl whisk together milk, eggs, ⅓ cup of the caramel topping, and the cinnamon. Slowly pour milk mixture evenly over bread mixture in baking dish. Using the back of a large spoon, gently press down bread mixture.

③ Bake, uncovered, for 50 to 60 minutes or until a knife inserted near center comes out clean. Let stand on a wire rack for 30 minutes.

④ To serve, cut pudding into 12 portions and place on serving plates. Quarter and core the remaining pear. Cut into very thin slices and place a few slices on top of each portion of pudding. If desired, sprinkle with pecans. Drizzle each serving with some of the remaining ⅓ cup caramel topping. Serve pudding warm.

*Tip: To dry bread cubes, preheat oven to 300°F. Place bread cubes in an ungreased 15 x 10 x 1-inch baking pan. Bake for 10 to 12 minutes or until bread cubes are dry and crisp, stirring once or twice. You should have about 5 cups dried bread cubes.

PER SERVING 147 calories; 2 g total fat (1 g sat. fat); 2 mg cholesterol; 169 mg sodium; 28 g carbohydrate; 2 g fiber; 5 g protein

Ice Cream Finger Sandwiches ✪

MAKES 12 sandwiches **PREP** 25 minutes **FREEZE** 30 minutes

1 cup low-fat or light strawberry ice cream or no-sugar-added reduced-fat cherry vanilla ice cream

12 ladyfingers, split

3 ounces bittersweet, semisweet, or milk chocolate, melted

½ cup flaked coconut, toasted

① Line a large baking sheet with waxed paper; set aside. Spoon ice cream into a small chilled bowl; stir just until ice cream is slightly softened. Working quickly,* spread ice cream on the cut sides of half of the ladyfinger halves. Top with the remaining ladyfinger halves, cut sides down. Gently press together.

② Dip one end of each sandwich in melted chocolate, using a thin metal spatula or butter knife to spread chocolate over the ice cream. Sprinkle with coconut. Place on prepared baking sheet. Freeze for 30 minutes before serving.

*Tip: To prevent the ice cream from getting too soft during assembly, prepare half of the sandwiches at a time.

PER SANDWICH 118 calories; 6 g total fat (4 g sat. fat); 26 mg cholesterol; 37 mg sodium; 15 g carbohydrate; 1 g fiber; 2 g protein

Ice Cream Finger Sandwiches

Pear Johnnycakes ✪

MAKES 5 servings **PREP** 20 minutes **STAND** 15 minutes
COOK 2 minutes per batch **OVEN** at 250°F

- 1 cup stone-ground yellow or white cornmeal
- ½ cup whole wheat flour
- 1 tablespoon sugar
- ½ teaspoon salt
- ¾ cup boiling water
- ½ cup finely chopped ripe pear
- ½ cup fat-free milk
- 1 tablespoon canola oil
- ½ teaspoon baking powder
- ¾ cup sliced pear
- ½ cup frozen sugar-free whipped dessert topping, thawed
  Grated fresh nutmeg (optional)

① In a medium bowl stir together cornmeal, flour, sugar, and salt. Gradually stir in the boiling water (mixture will be thick). Let stand for 15 minutes. Stir in chopped pear, milk, oil, and baking powder.

② Preheat oven to 250°F. Preheat a lightly greased nonstick griddle over medium-high heat. For each johnnycake, pour ¼ cup of the batter onto hot griddle. Cook for 2 to 3 minutes or until golden, turning once (turn carefully to avoid breaking). If cakes brown too quickly, reduce heat to medium. Keep warm in oven while cooking remaining johnnycakes. Grease griddle as needed to prevent sticking.

③ Arrange sliced pear on each serving of johnnycakes. Top with whipped topping and, if desired, sprinkle with grated nutmeg.

PER SERVING 211 calories; 5 g total fat (1 g sat. fat); 0 mg cholesterol; 290 mg sodium; 40 g carbohydrate; 5 g fiber; 5 g protein

Grilled Plum and Strawberry Kabobs with Sweet Mint Pesto ③⓪

MAKES 4 servings **PREP** 20 minutes **GRILL** 3 minutes

- ⅔ cup lightly packed fresh mint leaves
- ¼ cup lightly packed fresh basil
- 3 tablespoons pine nuts, toasted
- ½ teaspoon finely shredded orange peel
- 3 tablespoons orange juice
  Dash salt
- 4 plums, pitted and each cut into wedges
- 8 large strawberries
  Nonstick cooking spray

① For sweet mint pesto, in a blender or small food processor combine mint, basil, pine nuts, orange peel, orange juice, and salt. Cover and blend or process until smooth, stopping and scraping side as needed. Set aside.

② Thread plum wedges and strawberries on eight 6-inch-long skewers.* Lightly coat fruit with nonstick cooking spray. For a charcoal grill, grill kabobs on the rack of an uncovered grill directly over medium coals for 3 to 4 minutes or until heated through and grill marks are visible, turning occasionally to brown evenly. (For a gas grill, preheat grill. Reduce heat to medium. Place kabobs on grill rack over heat. Cover and grill as above.)

③ Serve kabobs with sweet mint pesto.

*Tip: If using wooden skewers, soak skewers in enough water to cover for at least 1 hour before grilling.

PER SERVING 85 calories; 4 g total fat (1 g sat. fat); 0 mg cholesterol; 36 mg sodium; 12 g carbohydrate; 1 g fiber; 3 g protein

In summer, barely adorned fresh fruit makes a lovely light dessert.

Grilled Plum and Strawberry Kabobs
with Sweet Mint Pesto

Baked Stuffed Apples

Baked Stuffed Apples

MAKES 6 servings **PREP** 20 minutes **BAKE** 25 minutes
OVEN at 350°F

- ¼ cup sugar
- ¼ cup chopped walnuts, toasted (see tip, page 15)
- ¼ cup dried cranberries, chopped
- 6 medium tart apples (such as Jonathan, Granny Smith, and/or honeycrisp)
- 2 tablespoons tub-style light vegetable oil spread, melted
- ¼ teaspoon ground nutmeg

  Frozen sugar-free whipped dessert topping, thawed, and/or dried cranberries (optional)

① Preheat oven to 350°F. For filling, in a small bowl toss together sugar, walnuts, and ¼ cup dried cranberries; set aside.

② Cut off about ½ inch from the bottom of each apple so it will stand upright. Using an apple corer, core apples. Place apples in an ungreased 2-quart rectangular baking dish. In a small bowl combine melted vegetable oil spread and nutmeg; brush over apples. Spoon filling evenly into centers of apples.

③ Bake, uncovered, for 25 to 40 minutes or just until apples are tender. Serve warm. If desired, top with whipped topping and/or additional dried cranberries.

PER SERVING 192 calories; 5 g total fat (1 g sat. fat); 0 mg cholesterol; 30 mg sodium; 38 g carbohydrate; 5 g fiber; 1 g protein

You can't beat preground nutmeg for convenience, but there is nothing quite like the intense flavor and aroma of freshly ground nutmeg. Find whole nutmeg in the spice aisle and simply grate it on a microplane. Store whole nutmeg in a tightly sealed container in a cool, dry place. It will last indefinitely.

Brown Sugar Peaches

MAKES 8 servings **PREP** 10 minutes **COOK** 10 minutes

- 4 peaches, halved and pitted
- ¼ cup packed brown sugar
- 1½ teaspoons cornstarch
- 2 tablespoons water
- 3 tablespoons half-and-half
- 1 tablespoon light-color corn syrup
- 1 tablespoon butter
- ¼ teaspoon vanilla
- 2 tablespoons coarse, raw sugar or packed brown sugar (optional)

  Light vanilla frozen yogurt (optional)

① Fill a large Dutch oven with water to a depth of 1 inch. Bring water to boiling. Place a steamer basket in the Dutch oven. Steam peaches in steamer basket, covered, for 5 minutes or until tender. Remove peaches from steamer basket and place in a large colander to drain.

② Meanwhile, for caramel sauce, in a small heavy saucepan combine brown sugar and cornstarch. Stir in the water. Stir in half-and-half and corn syrup. Cook and stir until thickened and bubbly (mixture will appear curdled before it thickens). Cook and stir for 2 minutes more. Remove saucepan from heat; stir in butter and vanilla.

③ Drizzle peaches with caramel sauce and, if desired, sprinkled with coarse raw sugar. If desired, top with a scoop of frozen yogurt.

PER SERVING 85 calories; 2 g total fat (1 g sat. fat); 6 mg cholesterol; 16 mg sodium; 17 g carbohydrate; 1 g fiber; 1 g protein

Brown Sugar Peaches

Cherry-Pistachio Cannoli ③⓪

MAKES 12 servings **START TO FINISH** 10 minutes

1	cup light ricotta cheese
½	cup chopped dried cherries
¼	cup chopped roasted pistachio nuts or chopped almonds, toasted
2	tablespoons honey
¼	teaspoon ground ginger
1	4.8-ounce package (12) mini cannoli shells
1	ounce white baking chocolate, melted

① For filling, in a medium bowl combine ricotta cheese, cherries, nuts, honey, and ginger.

② Spoon filling into a pastry bag fitted with a large open tip. (Or spoon into a resealable plastic bag; snip off a corner of the bag.) Pipe filling into cannoli shells.

③ Drizzle filled cannoli with white chocolate. Let stand until chocolate is set.

PER SERVING 130 calories; 6 g total fat (3 g sat. fat); 10 mg cholesterol; 60 mg sodium; 17 g carbohydrate; 1 g fiber; 4 g protein

Blackberry-Banana Lemon Trifles ✪ ③⓪

MAKES 2 servings **START TO FINISH** 10 minutes

2	3.75-ounce containers lemon or vanilla* sugar-free reduced-calorie ready-to-eat pudding
1	small banana, sliced
½	cup fresh blackberries, blueberries, raspberries, or sliced strawberries
1	100-calorie pack shortbread cookies, coarsely broken

① Evenly divide one of the containers of pudding between two 8-ounce straight-sided glasses. Top pudding in glasses with half of the banana slices, half the blackberries, and half the cookies. Repeat with the remaining pudding, banana, berries, and cookies.

*Tip: If using vanilla pudding, stir ¼ teaspoon finely shredded lemon peel into each container of pudding.

PER SERVING 165 calories; 3 g total fat (2 g sat. fat); 0 mg cholesterol; 236 mg sodium; 35 g carbohydrate; 3 g fiber; 2 g protein

Tiramisu Shots

MAKES 12 servings **PREP** 25 minutes **CHILL** 30 minutes

1	ounce dark or bittersweet chocolate, chopped
1	12.3-ounce package firm silken tofu
¼	cup brewed espresso, cooled
¼	cup sugar
1	teaspoon lemon juice
⅛	teaspoon salt
24	1-inch pieces purchased angel food cake (about half of a 7-inch cake)
2	tablespoons brewed espresso, cooled, or coffee-flavor liqueur
	Unsweetened cocoa powder
12	chocolate-covered espresso beans

① Place chocolate in a food processor. Cover and process until finely chopped. Add tofu, ¼ cup espresso, sugar, lemon juice, and salt. Cover and process until nearly smooth.

② Place 2 cakes pieces in each of 12 shot glasses or demitasse cups, pressing lightly. Drizzle each with about ½ teaspoon espresso or liqueur. Spoon about 1 tablespoon of the tofu mixture on each cake piece in the glasses. Top each with a remaining cake piece. Spoon remaining tofu mixture on each.

③ Place glasses on a tray. Cover with plastic wrap. Chill for 30 minutes or up to 24 hours.

④ To serve, lightly sift cocoa powder over tiramisu and top each with an espresso bean.

PER SERVING 75 calories; 2 g total fat (0 g sat. fat); 0 mg cholesterol; 106 mg sodium; 12 g carbohydrate; 0 g fiber; 3 g protein

A smart way to save calories on dessert is simply to eat less of it. Mini desserts, such as Cherry-Pistachio Cannoli or Tiramisu Shots, provide a satisfying bite of something sweet without overindulgence.

Dark Chocolate-Orange Pudding

Dark Chocolate-Orange Pudding

MAKES 5 servings **PREP** 30 minutes **CHILL** 2 hours

⅓	cup sugar
2	tablespoons cornstarch
2	tablespoons unsweetened cocoa powder
2¼	cups fat-free milk
¼	cup refrigerated or frozen egg product, thawed, or 1 egg, lightly beaten
2	ounces dark chocolate, finely chopped
1	tablespoon tub-style 60% to 70% vegetable oil spread
1	teaspoon vanilla
1	teaspoon finely shredded orange peel
	Kumquat, orange, or clementine slices (optional)
⅓	cup frozen light whipped dessert topping, thawed (optional)

① In a medium saucepan combine sugar, cornstarch, and cocoa powder. Gradually stir in milk. Cook and stir over medium heat until thickened and bubbly; reduce heat. Cook and stir for 2 minutes more. Remove from heat. Gradually stir about ¼ cup of the hot milk mixture into egg. Gradually stir in another ¼ cup of the milk mixture into egg. Add egg mixture and chocolate to the remaining milk mixture in saucepan. Bring to a gentle boil, whisking constantly; reduce heat. Cook and whisk for 2 minutes more. Remove from heat.

② Whisk in vegetable oil spread, vanilla, and orange peel. Place saucepan in a very large bowl half-filled with ice water. Whisk pudding constantly for 2 minutes to cool quickly. Transfer pudding to a medium bowl. Cover surface of pudding with plastic wrap. Chill in the refrigerator for 2 to 24 hours.

③ Spoon pudding into dessert dishes. If desired, garnish with kumquat slices and/or whipped dessert topping.

PER SERVING 196 calories; 6 g total fat (3 g sat. fat); 2 mg cholesterol; 102 mg sodium; 30 g carbohydrate; 1 g fiber; 6 g protein

Coffee Shop Custard

MAKES 4 servings **PREP** 20 minutes **STAND** 5 minutes **CHILL** 4 hours 15 minutes

1	envelope unflavored gelatin
2	cups fat-free milk
3	egg yolks
⅓	cup sugar
1½	teaspoons vanilla
1½	teaspoons instant espresso coffee powder
	Chopped coffee beans (optional)

① In a small bowl sprinkle gelatin over ¼ cup of the milk. Let stand for 5 minutes. Meanwhile, in a medium saucepan whisk together egg yolks and sugar. Gradually whisk in remaining 1¾ cups milk. Cook and stir over medium heat just until boiling. Remove from heat. Gradually whisk about ½ cup of the hot milk mixture into the gelatin mixture. Whisk gelatin mixture into remaining milk mixture in saucepan. Place saucepan in a large bowl of ice water. Stir in vanilla. Stir for a few minutes to cool the custard. Remove ½ cup of the custard to a small bowl; stir in espresso powder until dissolved. Cover and set aside.

② Pour the remaining custard into four 6-ounce dishes, custard cups, or glasses. Cover loosely and chill for 15 to 20 minutes. Drizzle the espresso mixture over the custard in dishes. Using a thin metal spatula, lightly swirl espresso mixture into top of the custard.* Cover dishes loosely and chill for at least 4 hours or until set. If desired, top with coffee beans.

*Tip: If custard is too firm to swirl, drizzle mixture over custard and spread to cover.

PER SERVING 177 calories; 3 g total fat (1 g sat. fat); 160 mg cholesterol; 72 mg sodium; 24 g carbohydrate; 0 g fiber; 12 g protein

Desserts that contain citrus—such as Dark Chocolate-Orange Pudding—are best made during the winter, when citrus fruits are at their peak. Juicy oranges, grapefruit, and clementines are at their best December through February.

Banana Cream Pie Squares ✪

MAKES 9 servings **PREP** 15 minutes **BAKE** 5 minutes
CHILL 4 hours **OVEN** at 375°F

- 24   reduced-fat vanilla wafers
- 3   tablespoons tub-style vegetable oil spread with 40% to 50% fat
- 1½   cups fat-free milk
- 1   4-serving size package fat-free, sugar-free vanilla or banana cream instant pudding mix
- ½   of an 8-ounce container frozen light whipped dessert topping, thawed
- 4   large bananas, sliced
- 2   teaspoons lemon juice
    Frozen light whipped dessert topping, thawed and/or toasted sliced almonds (optional)

① Preheat oven to 375°F. In a food processor process vanilla wafers until finely crushed. Add vegetable oil spread. Cover and process until mixture begins to cling together. Transfer to a 2-quart square baking dish and press to cover the bottom of the dish. Bake for 5 minutes or until lightly browned. Cool completely.

② In a medium bowl combine milk and pudding mix. Whisk for 1 to 2 minutes or until pudding is thickened. Fold in half a container dessert topping until combined.

③ In a medium bowl toss the sliced bananas with lemon juice to coat. Layer half the banana slices on the cooled crust. Top with half the pudding. Repeat with remaining bananas and pudding. Cover and chill for 4 to 24 hours.

④ To serve, cut into 9 squares. If desired, garnish with additional dessert topping and/or sliced almonds.

PER SERVING 179 calories; 5 g total fat (2 g sat. fat); 6 mg cholesterol; 231 mg sodium; 31 g carbohydrate; 2 g fiber; 3 g protein

Tossing the sliced bananas with just a little bit of lemon juice prevents them from oxidizing—or turning brown—when they're exposed to air. The same trick works for apples and pears.

Layered Brownies ✪

MAKES 24 brownies **PREP** 30 minutes **BAKE** 25 minutes
OVEN at 350°F

- ⅔   cup packed brown sugar
- ⅔   cup vegetable oil spread
- ¼   teaspoon baking soda
- ¾   cup refrigerated or frozen egg product, thawed, or 3 eggs, lightly beaten
- 2   cups flour
- 1½   cups quick-cooking rolled oats
- ¼   cup granulated sugar
- ¼   cup canola oil
- 3   tablespoons unsweetened cocoa powder
- ½   teaspoon baking powder
- 2   tablespoons miniature semisweet chocolate pieces
- 2   tablespoons chopped walnuts
- 2   tablespoons quick-cooking rolled oats

① Preheat oven to 350°F. Line a 9 x 9 x 2-inch baking pan with foil, extending foil up over the edges of the pan. Lightly grease the foil. Set aside.

② For crust, in a large mixing bowl combine brown sugar, vegetable oil spread, and baking soda; beat with an electric mixer on medium until well mixed, scraping sides of bowl occasionally. Beat in ¼ cup of the egg product or 1 egg. Beat in 1½ cups of the flour. Stir in the 1½ cups oats.

③ Set aside ½ cup of the oat mixture. Spread the remaining oat mixture into the bottom of the prepared pan. Bake about 12 minutes or just until crust is set.

④ Meanwhile, in a medium bowl whisk together the remaining ½ cup egg product or 2 eggs, the granulated sugar, and oil. Stir in the remaining ½ cup flour, the cocoa powder, and baking powder. Stir in semisweet chocolate pieces. Pour evenly over partially baked crust. If necessary, gently spread with a metal spatula. Stir nuts and the 2 tablespoons oats into the reserved oat mixture (mixture may be a little soft). Crumble over the top of the mixture in the baking pan.

⑤ Bake for 13 to 15 minutes or until the top is puffed and set. Cool completely in pan on a wire rack. Using the edges of the foil, lift the uncut brownies out of the pan; cut into 24 bars. To store, layer brownies between waxed paper in an airtight container. Cover; seal. Store in the refrigerator up to 5 days or freeze up to 3 months.

PER BROWNIE 163 calories; 8 g total fat (2 g sat. fat); 0 mg cholesterol; 75 mg sodium; 21 g carbohydrate; 1 g fiber; 3 g protein

Pumpkin Bars

Pumpkin Bars ✪

MAKES 25 bars **PREP** 25 minutes **BAKE** 12 minutes
COOL 10 minutes **OVEN** at 350°F

- ½ cup 60% to 70% tub-style vegetable oil spread, softened
- ½ cup packed brown sugar
- ½ teaspoon baking soda
- ½ teaspoon pumpkin pie spice
- ⅓ cup canned pumpkin
- ¼ cup refrigerated or frozen egg product, thawed, or 1 egg
- 1½ cups all-purpose flour
- ½ of an 8-ounce package reduced-fat cream cheese (Neufchâtel), softened
- 1 cup frozen light whipped dessert topping, thawed
   Freshly grated nutmeg (optional)

① Preheat oven to 350°F. Grease and lightly flour a 9 x 9 x 2-inch baking pan. Set aside.

② In a large mixing bowl combine vegetable oil spread, brown sugar, baking soda, and pumpkin pie spice; beat with an electric mixer on medium until well mixed. Beat in pumpkin and egg. Beat in as much of the flour as you can with the mixer. Using a wooden spoon, stir in any remaining flour.

③ Spread batter into prepared pan. Bake for 12 to 15 minutes or until a wooden toothpick inserted near the center comes out clean. Cool in pan on a wire rack for 10 minutes. Remove from pan; cool completely on a wire rack.

④ Meanwhile, in a medium mixing bowl beat cream cheese with an electric mixer on medium until smooth. Beat in half the dessert topping. Fold in remaining dessert topping. Spread on cooled pumpkin layer. If desired, sprinkle with nutmeg. Cut into bars.

PER BAR 90 calories; 4 g total fat (2 g sat. fat); 3 mg cholesterol; 75 mg sodium; 11 g carbohydrate; 0 g fiber; 1 g protein

Pumpkin Cookies with Cream Cheese Frosting: Prepare batter and cream cheese topping as directed above. Preheat oven to 350°F. Drop batter by rounded teaspoonfuls 1 inch apart on ungreased cookie sheets. Bake for 8 to 10 minutes or until tops are set. Transfer to wire racks; cool completely. Spread cooled cookies with cream cheese frosting. If desired, sprinkle with freshly grated nutmeg. Makes about 25 cookies.

Apple-Spice Bars ✪

MAKES 16 servings **PREP** 25 minutes **BAKE** 50 minutes
OVEN at 350°F

- 1½ cups all-purpose flour
- ½ cup quick cooking oats
- ⅓ cup granulated sugar
- ½ teaspoon baking powder
- ¼ teaspoon salt
- ½ cup 60% or more vegetable oil spread
- ¼ cup refrigerated or frozen egg product or 1 egg, lightly beaten
- 5 medium cooking apples, peeled if desired, cored and chopped (5 cups)
- ½ cup dried cherries
- 2 tablespoons lemon juice
- 3 tablespoons packed brown sugar
- 2 tablespoons all-purpose flour
- 1 teaspoon ground cinnamon
- ½ teaspoon ground ginger
- ¼ teaspoon ground cloves

① Preheat oven to 350°F. In a large bowl combine 1½ cups flour, the oats, granulated sugar, baking powder, and salt. Cut in vegetable oil spread until mixture resembles coarse crumbs. Stir in egg product. For crust, press half the mixture into a 9 x 9 x 2-inch baking pan. Set aside remaining flour mixture for topping.

② In a large bowl combine apples, dried cherries, and lemon juice. Add brown sugar, 2 tablespoons flour, the cinnamon, ginger, and cloves; toss to combine. Layer apple mixture evenly over the crust. Sprinkle with remaining flour mixture.

③ Bake about 50 minutes or until topping is lightly browned and apples are tender. Cool slightly; serve warm. Cut into bars to serve.

PER SERVING 167 calories; 4 g total fat (1 g sat. fat); 0 mg cholesterol; 100 mg sodium; 30 g carbohydrate; 2 g fiber; 2 g protein

No-Bake Apricot-Almond Balls

MAKES 18 balls **PREP** 20 minutes **STAND** 15 minutes
CHILL 15 minutes

- ⅓ cup creamy peanut butter
- ¼ cup 68% vegetable oil spread
- 2 tablespoons honey
- ¼ teaspoon almond extract
- 2 cups rice and wheat cereal flakes, crushed slightly
- ⅓ cup finely snipped dried apricots
- 2 tablespoons finely chopped toasted almonds (see tip, page 15)
- ¼ teaspoon ground ginger
- 2 ounces bittersweet or semisweet chocolate, chopped
- ¼ teaspoon shortening

① In a medium saucepan combine peanut butter, vegetable oil spread, honey, and almond extract. Cook over low heat just until melted and nearly smooth, whisking constantly. Stir in cereal, apricots, almonds, and ginger until well mixed. Using slightly wet hands or a 1-ounce scoop, shape mixture into balls. Let stand on a waxed paper-lined baking sheet about 15 minutes or until firm.

② In a small saucepan combine chocolate and shortening; stir over low heat until melted. Drizzle balls with melted chocolate. Chill about 15 minutes or until chocolate is set. Store in the refrigerator.

PER BALL 93 calories; 6 g total fat (2 g sat. fat); 0 mg cholesterol; 65 mg sodium; 9 g carbohydrate; 1 g fiber; 2 g protein

Pumpkin Tassies ✪

MAKES 12 tassies **PREP** 30 minutes **BAKE** 37 minutes
COOL 10 minutes **OVEN** at 325°F

- ½ of a 3-ounce package cream cheese, softened
- 2 tablespoons butter, softened
- ½ cup all-purpose flour
- 1 egg yolk
- ¼ cup packed brown sugar
- ¼ cup canned pumpkin
- 2 teaspoons fat-free milk
- 2 teaspoons canola oil
- 1 teaspoon vanilla
- ⅛ teaspoon ground nutmeg
- ¼ cup coarsely chopped mixed nuts

① Preheat oven to 325°F. For pastry shells, in a medium mixing bowl combine cream cheese and butter. Beat with an electric mixer on medium until smooth. Stir in flour until combined. Shape dough into 12 balls (about 1 inch in diameter). Press dough evenly onto the bottoms and up the sides of 12 ungreased 1¾-inch muffin cups. Bake for 12 minutes.

② Meanwhile, for filling, in a small bowl combine egg yolk, brown sugar, pumpkin, milk, oil, vanilla, and nutmeg. Spoon filling evenly into warm pastry shells. Sprinkle with nuts.

③ Bake about 25 minutes or until filling is set. Cool in muffin cups for 10 minutes. Carefully remove tassies from muffin cups; cool completely on a wire rack.

PER TASSIE 97 calories; 6 g total fat (2 g sat. fat); 26 mg cholesterol; 28 mg sodium; 10 g carbohydrate; 1 g fiber; 2 g protein

Just a nibble—like these bite-size pumpkin tarts—can satisfy your craving for something sweet.

Chocolate Whoopie Pies

Chocolate Whoopie Pies ✪

MAKES about 30 whoopie pies **PREP** 40 minutes
BAKE 5 minutes per batch **OVEN** at 375°F

- 2   cups flour
- 2   tablespoons unsweetened cocoa powder
- ½   teaspoon baking soda
- ⅛   teaspoon salt
- ½   cup vegetable oil spread
- ⅔   cup packed brown sugar
- ¼   cup refrigerated or frozen egg product, thawed, or 1 egg
- 1   teaspoon vanilla
- ½   cup buttermilk or fat-free sour milk*
- 1   recipe Filling
- 2   teaspoons powdered sugar (optional)

① Preheat oven to 375°F. Line cookie sheets with parchment paper; set aside. In a medium bowl stir together flour, cocoa powder, baking soda, and salt; set aside.

② In large mixing bowl combine vegetable oil spread and brown sugar; beat with an electric mixer on medium until light and fluffy. Beat in egg and vanilla. Alternately add flour mixture and buttermilk to egg mixture, beating on low after each addition just until combined.

③ Using a rounded measuring teaspoon (about 2 level teaspoons), spoon batter onto prepared cookie sheets, leaving 1 inch between rounds. Bake for 5 to 7 minutes or until tops are set. Cool cookies 1 minute on cookie sheets. Transfer cookies to wire racks; cool completely.

④ Spread Filling on the flat sides of half the cookies. Top with the remaining cookies, flat sides down. If desired, sprinkle tops with powdered sugar. Store, covered, in the refrigerator.

Filling: In a small bowl stir together ¼ cup frozen light whipped dessert topping, thawed, and ¼ cup light sour cream. Fold in ¾ cup frozen light whipped dessert topping, thawed. If desired, tint with several drops of blue or green food coloring.

*Tip: To make ½ cup sour milk, pour 1½ teaspoons lemon juice or vinegar into a 1-cup glass measure. Add enough fat-free milk to equal ½ cup; stir. Let stand for 5 minutes before using. (For ⅔ cup sour milk, use 2 teaspoons lemon juice or vinegar and enough fat-free milk to equal ⅔ cup total liquid.)

PER WHOOPIE PIE 82 calories; 3 g total fat (1 g sat. fat); 1 mg cholesterol; 65 mg sodium; 12 g carbohydrate; 0 g fiber; 1 g protein

Rosemary-Orange Shortbread

MAKES 18 cookies **PREP** 25 minutes **BAKE** 12 minutes
OVEN at 375°F

- 1¼   cups flour
- 3   tablespoons sugar
- 2   teaspoons finely snipped fresh rosemary
- 1   teaspoon finely shredded orange peel
- ¼   cup chilled butter, cut up
- ¼   cup chilled tub-style vegetable oil spread
- 1   ounce white baking chocolate, melted

① Preheat oven to 375°F. In a large bowl whisk together flour, sugar, rosemary, and orange peel. Using a pastry blender, cut in butter and vegetable oil spread until mixture resembles fine crumbs and starts to cling together. Using your hands, knead the dough for several minutes until smooth; form into a ball.

② Shape into a 9-inch square, using a rolling pin to flatten to approximately ⅛-inch thickness. Cut square into nine equal squares. Cut each square diagonally in half to form two triangles. Separate and transfer to a cookie sheet.

③ Bake about 12 minutes or until bottoms of triangles are starting to brown. Transfer cookies to a wire rack and cool completely. Drizzle tops with white chocolate and let stand until set.

PER COOKIE 90 calories; 5 g total fat (2 g sat. fat); 7 mg cholesterol; 37 mg sodium; 10 g carbohydrate; 0 g fiber; 1 g protein

Cocoa powder comes two ways—natural and Dutch-process. Dutch-process cocoa has been treated with alkali to neutralize some of its acid. It has a reddish-brown color and mild chocolate flavor. Natural cocoa powder is more bitter and lends a more intense chocolate taste to baked goods. You can use either type in Chocolate Whoopie Pies.

Peppermint Checkerboard Cookies ✪

MAKES about 60 cookies **PREP** 40 minutes **CHILL** 2 hours
BAKE 7 minutes **OVEN** at 350°F

- ½ cup tub-style vegetable oil spread
- ½ cup sugar
- 1 teaspoon baking powder
- ¼ teaspoon salt
- 2 ounces white baking chocolate, melted and cooled slightly
- ¼ cup canola oil
- ¼ cup refrigerated or frozen egg product, thawed, or 1 egg
- 2½ cups flour
- ½ teaspoon peppermint extract
  Red paste food coloring

① In a large mixing bowl beat vegetable oil spread, sugar, baking powder, and salt with an electric mixer on medium to high until well combined, scraping sides of bowl occasionally. Beat in melted white chocolate, oil, and egg. Beat in as much of the flour as you can with the mixer. Using a wooden spoon, stir in any remaining flour.

② Divide dough in half. Stir peppermint extract into one portion of dough and tint dough with red food coloring.

③ Shape each portion of dough into a rectangular log, 7 inches long and 1½ inches wide. Wrap each log in plastic wrap or waxed paper. Chill logs about 2 hours or until dough is firm enough to slice.

④ Cut each log lengthwise into four strips. Stack four strips of dough together, alternating colors, to create a checkerboard. Trim edges as needed to straighten sides and ends. If necessary, wrap each log in plastic wrap and chill about 30 minutes or until firm enough to slice.

⑤ Preheat oven to 350°F. Cut logs crosswise into ¼-inch-thick slices. Place slices 1 inch apart on ungreased cookie sheets.

⑥ Bake for 7 to 9 minutes or just until edges are firm. Cool on cookie sheet for 1 minute. Transfer cookies to a wire rack and let cool.

PER COOKIE 51 calories; 3 g total fat (1 g sat. fat); 0 mg cholesterol; 29 mg sodium; 6 g carbohydrate; 0 g fiber; 1 g protein

Lemon Meringue Sandwich Cookies ✪

MAKES about 34 sandwich cookies **STAND** 30 minutes
PREP 20 minutes **BAKE** 10 minutes **OVEN** at 300°F

- 2 egg whites
- ¼ teaspoon lemon extract
- ¼ teaspoon cream of tartar
- ⅛ teaspoon salt
- ½ cup sugar
- 1 tablespoon cornstarch
- 1 tablespoon finely shredded lemon peel
- 1 recipe Yellow Cream Filling

① In a medium mixing bowl allow egg whites to stand at room temperature for 30 minutes. Preheat oven to 300°F. Line two large cookie sheets with parchment paper; set aside.

② Add lemon extract, cream of tartar, and salt to egg whites. Beat with an electric mixer on medium to high until soft peaks form (tips curl). In a small bowl combine sugar and cornstarch. Gradually add the sugar mixture to the egg white mixture, about 1 tablespoon at a time, beating on high until stiff peaks form (tips stand straight). Fold in lemon peel.

③ Transfer meringue to a disposable piping bag fitted with a large round tip. Pipe 1½-inch circles between ¼ and ½ inch thick onto the prepared cookie sheets, leaving 1 inch between circles.

④ Place cookie sheets on separate oven racks; bake for 10 minutes. Turn off oven; let cookies dry in oven with door closed for 1 hour. Carefully lift meringues off parchment paper. Transfer to wire racks; let stand just until meringues cool.

⑤ Just before serving, place Yellow Cream Filling in a piping bag fitted with a large round tip or in a resealable plastic bag with a corner snipped off. Pipe 1 teaspoon filling onto the flat side of half the cooled meringues. Top with remaining meringues, flat sides down, to make sandwich cookies.

Yellow Cream Filling: In a medium mixing bowl beat ½ cup softened light tub-style cream cheese with an electric mixer on medium until smooth. Beat in ¼ cup light sour cream and 2 tablespoons powdered sugar until smooth. Add 4 drops yellow food coloring or more until desired shade is reached.

PER SANDWICH COOKIE 48 calories; 1 g total fat (1 g sat. fat); 5 mg cholesterol; 61 mg sodium; 8 g carbohydrate; 0 g fiber; 1 g protein

Lemon Meringue Sandwich Cookies

Almond Cream Cutouts

Almond Cream Cutouts ✪

MAKES about 48 cookies **PREP** 45 minutes **CHILL** 1 hour
BAKE 6 minutes **OVEN** at 400°F

½	cup butter, softened
¼	cup reduced-fat cream cheese (Neufchâtel), softened
1	8-ounce can almond paste
1	teaspoon baking powder
¼	teaspoon salt
¼	cup refrigerated or frozen egg product, thawed, or 1 egg
2½	cups flour
	Decorating (optional)

① In a large mixing bowl beat butter and cream cheese with an electric mixer on medium until smooth. Add almond paste, baking powder, and salt; beat until well combined. Beat in egg. Beat in as much of the flour as you can with the mixer. Using a wooden spoon, stir in any remaining flour. Divide dough in half. Cover and chill for 1 to 2 hours or until easy to handle.

② Preheat oven to 400°F. On a lightly floured surface roll dough, half at a time, to ⅛-inch thickness. Using a 2½-inch cookie cutter, cut in desired shapes. Place cutouts 1 inch apart on ungreased cookie sheets. Reroll scraps as necessary. If desired, decorate unbaked cookies with sugar sprinkles or brush on egg white "paint" before baking.

③ Bake for 6 to 8 minutes or until edges are firm and just starting to brown. Transfer cookies to a wire rack and let cool. If desired, decorate plain cooled baked cookies with piped chocolate.

Glazed Cookies: To decorate cookies with glaze, combine ½ cup powdered sugar, ½ teaspoon cornstarch, 1 drop of lemon or almond extract, and enough milk to make a thin glaze. Brush over cooled cookies and sprinkle with finely shredded lemon peel.

Painted Cookies: In a small mixing bowl beat 1 egg white with food coloring until well combined. Use a new or a clean paintbrush that is used only for food to lightly brush colored egg white on unbaked cookies. Bake as directed. Color will be more intense after baking.

PER COOKIE 66 calories; 4 g total fat (2 g sat. fat); 6 mg cholesterol; 40 mg sodium; 7 g carbohydrate; 0 g fiber; 1 g protein

Fruited Oatmeal Cookies

MAKES about 48 cookies **PREP** 25 minutes
BAKE 9 minutes per batch **OVEN** at 375°F

2	cups rolled oats
	Nonstick cooking spray
½	cup butter, softened
1½	cups packed brown sugar
¾	teaspoon baking soda
¼	teaspoon salt
¼	teaspoon ground allspice
1	6-ounce carton plain low-fat yogurt
½	cup refrigerated or frozen egg product or 2 eggs, lightly beaten
1	teaspoon vanilla
2¼	cups all-purpose flour
¼	cup snipped dried apricots
¼	cup currants
¼	cup chopped walnuts, toasted (see tip, page 15)

① Preheat oven to 375°F. Spread oats in a shallow baking pan. Bake about 10 minutes or until toasted, stirring once; set aside. Lightly coat cookie sheet with cooking spray or line with parchment paper; set aside.

② In a large mixing bowl beat butter with an electric mixer on medium to high for 30 seconds. Add brown sugar, baking soda, salt, and allspice; beat until combined. Beat in yogurt, egg product, and vanilla. Beat in as much of the flour as you can with the mixer. Using a wooden spoon, stir in oats, apricots, currants, walnuts, and any remaining flour. Drop dough by rounded teaspoons 2 inches apart on prepared cookie sheet. Bake 9 to 11 minutes or until edges and bottoms are browned. Transfer cookies to a wire rack; cool.

PER SERVING 101 calories; 3 g total fat (1 g sat. fat); 5 mg cholesterol; 55 mg sodium; 17 g carbohydrate; 1 g fiber; 2 g protein

Index

Note: Page references in **bold** type indicate photographs.

In-a-Pinch Substitutions

It can happen to the best of us: Halfway through a recipe,
you find you're completely out of a key ingredient. Here's what to do:

Recipe Calls For:	You May Substitute:
1 square unsweetened chocolate	3 Tbsp. unsweetened cocoa powder + 1 Tbsp. butter/margarine
1 cup cake flour	1 cup less 2 Tbsp. all-purpose flour
2 Tbsp. flour (for thickening)	1 Tbsp. cornstarch
1 tsp. baking powder	¼ tsp. baking soda + ½ tsp. cream of tartar + ¼ tsp. cornstarch
1 cup corn syrup	1 cup sugar + ¼ cup additional liquid used in recipe
1 cup milk	½ cup evaporated milk + ½ cup water
1 cup buttermilk or sour milk	1 Tbsp. vinegar or lemon juice + enough milk to make 1 cup
1 cup sour cream (for baking)	1 cup plain yogurt
1 cup firmly packed brown sugar	1 cup sugar + 2 Tbsp. molasses
1 tsp. lemon juice	¼ tsp. vinegar (not balsamic)
¼ cup chopped onion	1 Tbsp. instant minced
1 clove garlic	¼ tsp. garlic powder
2 cups tomato sauce	¾ cup tomato paste + 1 cup water
1 Tbsp. prepared mustard	1 tsp. dry mustard + 1 Tbsp. water

How to Figure What You Need

Making a shopping list based on a recipe can be tricky if you don't know
how many tomatoes yields 3 cups chopped. Our handy translations:

When the Recipe Calls For:	You Need:
4 cups shredded cabbage	1 small cabbage
1 cup grated raw carrot	1 large carrot
2½ cups sliced carrots	1 lb. raw carrots
4 cups cooked cut fresh green beans	1 lb. beans
1 cup chopped onion	1 large onion
4 cups sliced raw potatoes	4 medium-size potatoes
1 cup chopped sweet pepper	1 large pepper
1 cup chopped tomato	1 large tomato
2 cups canned tomatoes	16-oz. can
4 cups sliced apples	4 medium-size apples
1 cup mashed banana	3 medium-size bananas
1 tsp. grated lemon rind	1 medium-size lemon
2 Tbsp. lemon juice	1 medium-size lemon
4 tsp. grated orange rind	1 medium-size orange
1 cup orange juice	3 medium-size oranges
4 cups sliced peaches	8 medium-size peaches
2 cups sliced strawberries	1 pint
1 cup soft bread crumbs	2 slices fresh bread
1 cup bread cubes	2 slices fresh bread
2 cups shredded Swiss or cheddar cheese	8 oz. cheese
1 cup egg whites	6 or 7 large eggs
1 egg white	2 tsp. egg white powder + 2 Tbsp. water
4 cups chopped walnuts or pecans	1 lb. shelled